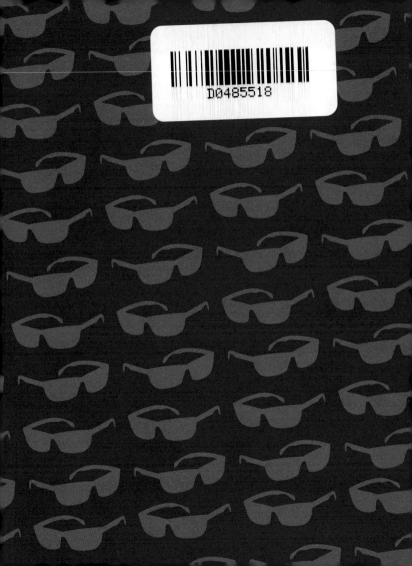

101CULT
MOVIES
YOU MUST SEE BEFORE YOU DIE

101CULT
MOVIES
YOU MUST SEE BEFORE YOU DIE

GENERAL EDITOR
STEVEN JAY SCHNEIDER

A Quint**essence** Book

First edition for the United States and Canada
published in 2010 by Barron's Educational Series, Inc.

ISBN-13: 978-0-7641-6349-4
ISBN-10: 0-7641-6349-3
QSS.CULM

Library of Congress Number: 2010929326

All inquiries should be addressed to:
Barron's Educational Series, Inc.
250 Wireless Boulevard
Hauppauge, NY 11788
www.barronseduc.com

This book was designed and produced by:
Quint**essence**
226 City Road
London EC1V 2TT
www.1001beforeyoudie.com

Project Editor	Helena Baser
Editor	James Harrison
Designer	Nick Withers
Editorial Director	Jane Laing
Publisher	Tristan de Lancey

Color reproduction in Singapore by Pica Digital Pte Ltd.
Printed in China by 1010 Printing International Ltd.
9 8 7 6 5 4 3 2 1

CONTENTS

INTRODUCTION Steven Jay Schneider, General Editor

Cult movies encompass some of the most obscure, eccentric, controversial, and downright weird films ever made. Despite often struggling to find success at the box office, cult movies (or "cult classics") tend to attract a small, yet obsessively devoted, fan base. The appeal of such movies can be attributed to both their subject matter and to the mentality of their audience. There is a certain sense of exclusivity in being a fan of something of which few others are either aware or able to appreciate. Often restricted to a very limited (at best) theatrical release, cult movies have regularly found renewed success once released on home video and DVD as a result of intense, word-of-mouth publicity among film watchers. Consequently, such movies usually remain popular among their fans for significantly longer than even the most successful blockbusters. Cult movies are often the creation of eccentric filmmakers, such as David Lynch (*Blue Velvet*), Ed Wood (*Plan 9 from Outer Space*), and John Waters (*Pink Flamingos*), who use innovative techniques and styles of storytelling to explore controversial topics not traditionally embraced by mainstream audiences. Moreover, most cult movies are independently financed and made on modest budgets with a specific audience in mind. This often results in production values that are below par (to put it mildly). Yet, while the majority of movies that achieve cult status begin as box-office failures, some commercially successful studio films, for example *The Blues Brothers*, have managed to earn cult status because of their sustained popularity. Here's to cult cinema—in all its weird, wild, transgressive, and ribald glory!

Steven J. Schneider

Hollywood, U.S.A.

UN CHIEN ANDALOU 1928 (FRANCE)

Director Luis Buñuel **Producer** Luis Buñuel, Salvador Dalí **Screenplay** Luis Buñuel, Salvador Dalí **Cinematography** Albert Duverger, Jimmy Berliet **Art Direction** Pierre Schild **Music** Silent movie; Luis Buñuel (1960 sound version) **Cast** Simone Mareuil, Pierre Batchef, Luis Buñuel, Salvador Dalí

Both Luis Buñuel and Salvador Dalí were unknown and impoverished Spanish artists when they made *Un Chien Andalou*. The most iconic and parodied of all surrealist films, *Un Chien Andalou* presents a series of seemingly unconnected images and symbols. The montage of imagery is both bizarre and rapid: an oddly attired cyclist rides through the street and falls for seemingly no reason; a man drags two grand pianos filled with two rotting donkeys, two attendant bishops, and a tablet of the Ten Commandments; and ants scurry out of a wound in a man's palm.

Among these juxtapositions, perhaps the most iconic is the eye-slicing scene, an image that has ensured an enduring legacy for film as both surreal and shocking. In it a man (played by Buñuel himself) sharpens a razor, tests it, looks out from a balcony, and then proceeds to slice through the eyeball of a seated young girl. The speed of the editing means that images are presented and opposed to other images before one has time to contemplate their meaning. The use of the apparently random intertitles, "Once upon a time" and shortly after, "Eight years later," render any attempt to establish time and space

◄
Buñuel's films aimed to shock and satirize. They certainly provoked right-wing attacks in Paris cinemas.

impossible and the film's protagonists, Simone Mareuil and Pierre Batchef, take part in a series of increasingly surreal scenes that appear to suggest no logical narrative. Indeed, the film has no story in any conventional sense. Recounting the plot, *Un Chien Andalou* is a purely futile exercise (and entirely beside the point). The repetition of some of the imagery merely adds to the willfully manic sense of fun and a feeling that both Buñuel

"OPEN YOUR EYES, TRULY OPEN THEM TO THE WORLD, FOR YOU LOOK BUT YOU DO NOT SEE." MAN

and Dalí were attempting to be both provocative and have a darn good laugh at our expense at the same time. *Un Chien Andalou* is an experience as much as a film.

Popular legend has it that when he first screened the film, Buñuel hid behind the screen, his pockets filled with stones for fear of being attacked by the audience. Whatever the truth, *Un Chien Andalou* has become the reference point for those wishing to ape (or pay homage to) the surrealist film style worldwide. Crucially, for a film that was made more than eighty years ago it has lost none of its potency and remains a brilliantly bizarre and shocking work. While some critics have suggested that the film foreshadows some of the themes that would infuse much of Buñuel's later work—a sense of both anticlerical and antibourgeois sentiment—in the end, in true surrealist fashion the film defies easy, or indeed perhaps any, explanation. **RH**

► Buñuel's hand about to slice Simone Mareuil's eye with a razor. This is famously juxtaposed with an image of clouds slicing across the moon, then cutting back to fluid oozing out of the wound.

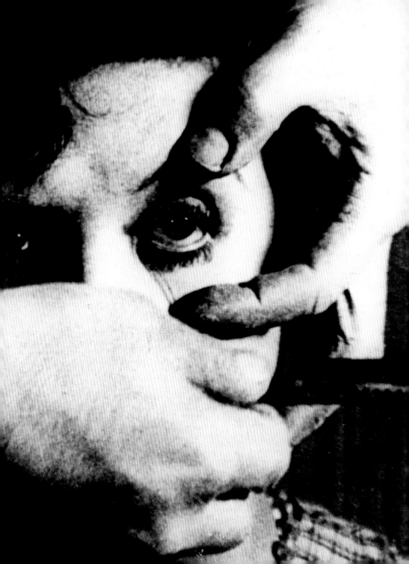

REEFER MADNESS 1936 (U.S.)

Director Louis Gasnier **Producer** Dwain Esper **Screenplay** Lawrence Meade, Arthur Hoerl, Paul Franklin **Cinematography** Jack Greenhalgh **Music** Abe Meyer
Cast Dorothy Short, Kenneth Craig, Lillian Miles, Dave O'Brien, Thelma White, Warren McCollum, Carleton Young, Josef Forte

High school principal Dr. Carroll (Josef Forte) addresses parents at a school P.T.A. meeting. Slamming his fist down on the desk, he bellows out a *grave* warning: America must take steps to wipe out "the real public enemy number one—the deadly danger of . . . marijuana!"

Let us take a few moments here to set the scene: It is 1936, and marihuana (they spelled it with an "h" in those days) was not yet illegal. Largely used by ethnic groups, jazz musicians, and almost all of Hollywood, there was a growing fear that it was spreading to more respectable corners of American society. Some decided to take action, so it came to pass that a church group set about funding a film that would educate parents of the dire consequences of an illicit puff. They would call it *Tell Your Children*.

Back to the story. The ranting Dr. Carroll illustrates his argument with the salutary tale of a couple of his students. Mary (Dorothy Short) is kind, studies hard, and plays tennis; Bill (Kenneth Craig) cares for his kid brother, respects his parents, and is so polite that he calls Mary a "swell girl." But that all changes when Bill is coerced along to a party, where he

◀

Today *Reefer Madness* is uttered in the same breath as *Plan 9 From Outer Space* (1959), and is considered to be among the most absurd of the "so-bad-they're-good" cult movies.

experiences the evil weed. We quickly learn that casual marijuana use will make us give up school; try to have sex with anything that moves; laugh maniacally while running people down in the street; listen to jazz; dance like a crazed lunatic; play the piano too fast like a crazed lunatic; shoot your friends; and not remember any of this the following day. Why, then, did the makers of what was intended to appeal to the minds of

"JUST A YOUNG BOY . . . UNDER THE INFLUENCE OF DRUGS . . . WHO KILLED HIS ENTIRE FAMILY WITH AN AXE." DR. CARROLL

caring responsible parents instead end up aiming at body parts further south? In fact, if there's one word that describes this film, it would be "sleazy." We are treated to frame after frame of doped-up femme fatale, Mae, removing her stockings; orgiastic scenes and intimate dancing at marijuana parties; youngsters disappearing together into bedrooms . . . even wholesome little Mary seems to be wearing a suspiciously tight jumper. This is hot stuff for 1936.

There was one final indignity to come. Shortly after completion, the film was bought by notorious producer Dwain Esper, who cut in a few more salacious inserts, renamed it *Reefer Madness,* and played it on the exploitation circuit. Within a few years it was forgotten—that is until 1971, when it was discovered in the Library of Congress archives. Reprinted, it became a midnight movie sensation among campus stoners. **TB**

▶

Reefer Madness was originally black and white, though a colorized version was released in 2004 by 20th Century Fox.

Veronica Lake's on the take

JOEL McCREA ★ VERONICA LAKE

SULLIVAN'S TRAVELS

A Paramount Picture with
ROBERT WARWICK · WILLIAM DEMAREST · MARGARET HAYES
PORTER HALL · FRANKLIN PANGBORN · ERIC BLORE
Written and Directed by PRESTON STURGES

SULLIVAN'S TRAVELS 1941 (U.S.)

Director Preston Sturges **Producer** Preston Sturges **Screenplay** Preston Sturges
Cinematography John Seitz **Music** Charles Bradshaw, Leo Shukin
Cast Joel McCrea, Veronica Lake, Robert Warwick, William Demarest,
Franklin Pangborn, Porter Hall, Byron Foulger, Margaret Hayes

Sullivan's Travels is the story of John Sullivan (Joel McCrea), a
Hollywood director of dumb comedies. He tells his boss,
Lebrand (Robert Warwick), that he wants to do a film about
everyday people called "O Brother, Where Art Thou?" Lebrand
suggests he do another comedy instead but Sullivan decides
to become a tramp and travel the country, learning about the
lives of "real" people. Along the way he meets a wannabe
actress, The Girl (Veronica Lake), but misunderstandings ensue,
so Sullivan and The Girl go on the run. They live on the road, eat
in soup kitchens, and sleep in shelters. When Sullivan longs for
home because life on the road is hard, he hands out $5 bills to
the homeless people he feels have appropriately educated
him. One man takes exception and assaults Sullivan, then the
thief is killed while wearing Sullivan's shoes and the world is led
to believe that the real Sullivan is dead.

   Unable to prove who he is and enjoy the privilege of his
former life, Sullivan gets into a fight and is sentenced to hard
labor in a prison camp. He learns firsthand what it is to be poor
in America. When his chain gang is taken to a black church to
watch a movie (Disney's *Playful Pluto* cartoon), Sullivan

◀

Veronica Lake's
visage dominates
this poster of the
sharp satirical tale
of a Hollywood
comedy director in
search of a realistic
subject that will
establish him as
a serious artist.

recognizes the fact that the real value of his dumb comedies is in the form of escapism since so much of ordinary life is difficult.

To prove he's actually Sullivan rather than a common criminal, he confesses to being his own killer. Newspapers run headlines with his picture and he's eventually freed from prison to resume his former life, this time with The Girl at his side and a new attitude about the work he'd formerly scorned.

"I LIKED YOU BETTER AS A BUM." THE GIRL
"I CAN'T HELP WHAT KIND OF PEOPLE YOU LIKE." JOHN L. SULLIVAN

This Preston Sturges vehicle is really a movie in two parts. One half is a lighthearted satire of Hollywood; the second part is a sobering examination of racial hierarchies, class-based segregation, and pain. The 1930s turn in Hollywood toward socially relevant movies (part of the response to sound and to the Great Depression) missed the point of what movies, generally, and Sturges's movies, in particular, do well, which is to entertain. The extended sequence when Sullivan's chain gang goes to the movies is particularly extraordinary. Sturges puts black people on-screen, not merely as maids or baggage handlers, but as human beings recognizable in a slice of America that's both connected to, and separated from, the kind of images then dominant on movie screens. For its outstanding embodiment of smart writing and cinematic art, *Sullivan's Travels* was included in the U.S. National Film Registry in 1990. **GC-Q**

▶
Joel McCrea living the life of the down and out in this biting and black-humored movie.

OUT OF THE PAST 1947 (U.S.)

Director Jacques Tourneur **Producer** Warren Duff, Robert Sparks **Screenplay** Daniel Mainwaring **Cinematography** Nicholas Musuraca **Music** Roy Webb **Cast** Robert Mitchum, Jane Greer, Kirk Douglas, Virginia Huston, Dickie Moore, Rhonda Fleming, Richard Webb, Steve Brodie, Ken Niles

Film noir masterpiece *Out of the Past* is arguably one of the best films of director Jacques Tourneur's lengthy and impressive oeuvre. Tourner, son of noted French filmmaker Maurice Tourneur, helmed other cult classics including *Cat People* (1942) and *I Walked with a Zombie* (1943). His 1947 film *Out of the Past*, however, is a stunning and influential work that continues to please both critics and audiences alike.

Enigmatic Jeff Bailey (Robert Mitchum) has a mundane life, running a Connecticut gas station and dating pretty, sincere town resident, Ann Miller (Virginia Huston). His life is disrupted one day when a man from his past passes through town. Bailey flashes back to a series of events from his former life as a New York City private investigator. Bailey had been hired by the wealthy Whit Sterling (Kirk Douglas) to track down his ex-girlfriend, Kathie Moffat (Jane Greer), and recover a large sum of money she reportedly stole from Sterling. Bailey's discovery of Kathie in Alcapulco should end the story; instead, it marks the beginning of a tale rife with sex, murder, and treachery. *Out of the Past* remains popular with viewers not only for its finely crafted narrative care of Daniel Mainwaring (*Invasion of the Body*

◄

Also known as *Build My Gallows High*, many consider this the definitive flashback movie, with Robert Mitchum as the fated hero on a hallucinatory rewind of his life.

Snatchers; 1978), mesmerizing music from Nick Musuraca, and stunning visuals, but for the outstanding performances of its lead actors. Douglas is slick and menacing as Sterling, and Greer's Kathie is sly and sensual. Child star Dickie Moore is a standout as The Kid, Bailey's staunchly loyal young assistant. However, it is Mitchum's performance as the tough but easily manipulated Bailey that most resonates with the film's viewers.

"ALL WOMEN ARE WONDERS, BECAUSE THEY REDUCE ALL MEN TO THE OBVIOUS." *LEONARD EELS*

Out of the Past is considered by film critics to be one of the best examples of the film noir style. It holds a place in the National Film Registry and was remade by Taylor Hackford as *Against All Odds* (1984). The remake does not have quite the cultural cache as the original film, but it is a solid example of neo-noir that features two of the actors from *Out of the Past*: star Jane Greer and supporting actor Paul Valentine. The visual and atmospheric accomplishments of *Out of the Past* have inspired many subsequent directors, notably David Cronenberg, whose 2005 film *A History of Violence* owes a significant debt to Tourneur's noir classic. Recently, Martin Scorsese reportedly screened *Out of the Past* (along with Tourneur's *Cat People* from 1942 and *I Walked with a Zombie* from 1943) to cast and crew as they prepared to shoot Scorsese's 2010 movie *Shutter Island*. **AK**

▶

B movie meets superbly crafted pulp in this noir thriller, as Jane Greer makes Robert Mitchum confront his past.

SUNSET BOULEVARD 1950 (U.S.)

Director Billy Wilder **Producer** Charles Brackett **Screenplay** Billy Wilder, Charles Brackett, D. M. Marshman, Jr. **Cinematography** John Seitz **Music** Franz Wexman
Cast Gloria Swanson, Erich von Stroheim, William Holden, Nancy Olson, Cecil B. DeMille, Buster Keaton, Fred Clark, Jack Webb, Lloyd Gough

A hack screenwriter (William Holden) toils through his drab, daily life, composed of compromises and disappointments. In spite of his many deals with the devil he still finds himself well short of any real promise of mammon and is thus bankrupt, financially and creatively. By circumstance (a broken-down car) he finds himself domiciled at the faded and unlikely mansion of one of the silent film era's greatest stars, Norma Desmond (Gloria Swanson), on the now anachronistic Sunset Boulevard. A ghost of his former self, he consigns his creativity to crafting (or recrafting) his patron's own vision of herself and the best of that world left behind–the innocent days of film before "words, words, words" corrupted the ripe Eden of early Hollywood.

From its earliest frames, *Sunset Boulevard* proclaims a different genre altogether from the melodrama with which we are presented. Is it noir? The street name, splayed across the gutter; the pan over credits of the street surface itself . . . the grit is explicit. Wilder seems conscious from the start that what he is making is not what it seems: he is situating his movie well beyond the genre which "contains" it. So, what is this Grand Guignol that Wilder is making? An indictment,

◄

More than a beautifully art directed noir melodrama, *Sunset Boulevard* is an acidic exposé of all that is rotten in Tinseltown.

surely, of the complicity of the star-maker machinery that made Wilder and his leading actors the celebrities they were.

Sadly, *Sunset Boulevard* is often written off as a camp movie, which is ridiculous, and it's entirely possible that it has always been somewhat too close for comfort, thus consigned to the fringes of cinema history. Many otherwise admirable cinephiles simply cannot seem to access its arch subversion of

"YOU'RE NORMA DESMOND. YOU USED TO BE IN SILENT PICTURES. YOU USED TO BE BIG." *JOE GILLIS*

the obscene machine that created it, and that created sad heroine Norma Desmond, cast off when she was no longer needed.

Surely a disproportionate number of films deemed "cult" or "midnight" feature some kind of celebrity self-reference, some kind of fallen figure or messianic type either before or ahead of their times. The "cult" in cult film could as much refer to the cult status of its heroes and heroines as to the group of initiates who propagate the myth of the film's brilliance to other would-be initiates who then populate that film's "cult." But Norma Desmond has her own cult, and perhaps the cult status of *Sunset Boulevard* is as much about cinephiles who can appreciate the plight of this odd creature in a world that she has been cast out from. We are all castaways, *Sunset Boulevard* says, on an abandoned ship, crewed by the rats. It looks gorgeous, but it's not a pretty picture. **GS**

► A forgotten silent movie star (Gloria Swanson) makes her grand entrance for the paparazzi as a bemused William Holden looks on. "I am big, it's the pictures that got small."

THE NIGHT OF THE HUNTER

1955 (U.S.)

Director Charles Laughton **Producer** Paul Gregory **Screenplay** Charles Laughton, James Agee (based upon the novel by Davis Grubb) **Cinematography** Stanley Cortez **Music** Walter Schumann **Cast** Robert Mitchum, Shelley Winters, Lillian Gish, Billy Chapin, Sally Jane Bruce

L-O-V-E and H-A-T-E. Few overwrought teenagers who etch these icons across opposing rows of knuckles know their origin: none other than the fists of Robert Mitchum as sociopath Harry Powell in *The Night of the Hunter*.

Powell (Mitchum) is a religious zealot and serial killer, who is in prison for a motor offense. Upon his release, he tracks down the family of his since-executed cell-mate and wheedles his way into their lives. Swiftly, he destroys his new wife (played with exquisite empathy by Shelley Winters) and aims his sights on his original target, the children (Billy Chapin and Sally Jane Bruce), acting on his only clue as to the whereabouts of the takings from his dead cell-mate's final theft: "And a little child shall lead them," quoted from scripture in his sleep.

Already apprehensive of their clearly unstable and dissembling stepfather, the children, now under direct attack, flee down the river their house abuts. Eventually, they find their way into a home for lost children run by Rachel Cooper (screen legend Lillian Gish). Powell promptly tracks them down to Cooper, who stands firm against his lies: a sincerely God-fearing

◄

Charles Laughton has rendered Grubbs's tale of good versus evil most piquantly. Its mythic status as Laughton's only film behind the lens is more grist for reflection.

woman, Cooper believes in evil, and believes she has seen it in Powell. After a spectacularly haunting night sequence—Cooper, a rifle on her knees on the veranda, and Powell, lurking nearby in the bushes, singing Christian hymns together through the night—the villain is at last apprehended and brought to justice. Famously, Cooper gets the last line in direct address: "Children are man at his strongest. They abide." These are strong

"THOSE FINGERS . . . IS ALWAYS A-WARRING AND A-TUGGING, ONE AGIN T'OTHER. NOW WATCH 'EM!" HARRY POWELL

sentiments for the postwar period complicated by McCarthy, the Rosenberg executions, the Military-Industrial complex, the terror of communism, and rock 'n' roll.

The Night of the Hunter is no easy noir or genre cinema whose content can be taken at face value as a vehicle for style. It is the first film in a new genre that never materialized. Shot on black and white in strikingly composed shots, Laughton borrows an expressive language from the cinema of Murnau, crafting an almost two-dimensional visual plane. Nonetheless, the style lulls us: Laughton's lushness in treating the moonlit descent of his innocents down the faceless river of America, stalked by the altogether too familiar boogeyman of Mitchum's Powell cloaked in reeds, the shores themselves a menace to the flow of innocence along its progress, invokes the real terrors to be found in America after the Second World War. **GS**

► **Mitchum at his most scary as the psycho killer preacher—an embodiment of absolute evil.**

REBEL WITHOUT A CAUSE 1955 (U.S.)

Director Nicholas Ray **Producer** David Weisbert **Screenplay** Stewart Stern, Irving Shulman **Cinematography** Ernest Haller **Music** Leonard Rosenman
Cast James Dean, Natalie Wood, Sal Mineo, Corey Allen, Ann Doran, Dennis Hopper, Edward Platt, Steffi Sidney

There are plenty of B-movie "juvenile delinquent" moments in *Rebel*—knife fights, shootings, gang culture, and early death—but at heart the movie is alienation. Jim (James Dean) is the new boy in town. He desperately wants to fit in, but the cool kids first reject him, then turn on him.

Dean's Jim is tormented and bewildered, often writhing as if physically torn by the sheer agony of growing up. As a matter of honor, he is forced to take part in a "chickie race" toward a sheer cliff edge. "Why do we do this?" Jim asks his challenger, gang leader Buzz (Corey Allen). "Got to do something," Buzz shrugs, before plunging to his death. Jim's smothering, bickering parents alternately blame him and try to cajole him into not admitting responsibility to the police. Jim finds their attitudes impossible to accept: for Jim, as for Holden Caulfield in *The Catcher in the Rye* (published only five years earlier), this is a conflict between what is "phoney" and what is "sincere." His father, with a puzzled but dismissive look, tells Jim he'll look back at this time and not be able to see why it all mattered so much. Jim takes refuge in an abandoned mansion with Buzz's girlfriend, Judy (Natalie Wood) and the lonely outsider Plato (Sal

◄

The eternal teen struggle to understand and be understood by their parents forms one of the themes of this beautifully composed B-shocker and sociological drama.

Mineo). Here for the first time they can relax and be themselves. But the rest of the gang is on their tail, and in the confrontation that follows, Plato shoots one of the gang members. Plato runs off to hide in the nearby planetarium, followed by Jim and Judy. With the building surrounded by the police, Jim manages to calm Plato down and take the bullets from his gun. All through the movie's twenty-four-hour time frame, there are moments

"I DIDN'T CHICKEN. YOU SAW WHERE I JUMPED. WHAT DID I HAVE TO DO, KILL MYSELF?" JIM STARK

like this when redemption is possible, when things might go right, but instead the scales tip further toward tragedy. So, as Plato emerges to give himself up, he becomes fearful and brandishes the gun and the police react as police do.

Rebel without a Cause may not seem radical compared to modern portraits of teen angst. But the fundamental truths it bears about the struggle of teens to fit in with their peers and to form their adult selves remain timeless. The material may teeter on a knife-edge between being a sociological document or a B-movie shocker, but director Nicholas Ray has transformed it into a thing of beauty, full of memorable images. These include Jim's red jacket against the darkness and his father wearing his mother's frilly apron, and beautifully composed scenes, such as the dancelike fights and the two cars racing toward the cliff edge between ranks of headlights. **CW**

►
James Dean in his finest film, both iconically and actorly, and much imitated since.

THE BLOB 1958 (U.S.)

Director Irvin S. Yeaworth, Jr. **Producer** Jack H. Harris **Screenplay** Theodore Simonson, Kay Linaker (as Kate Phillips) **Cinematography** Thomas Spalding **Music** Ralph Carmichael **Cast** Steve McQueen, Aneta Corsaut, Earl Rowe, Olin Howland, Steven Chase, John Benson, George Karas

Nuclear paranoia makes for good nightmare. A survey of Cold War invasion movies such as *The War of the Worlds* (1953) and serious political thrillers such as *Dr. Strangelove* (1964) ably demonstrate this preoccupation with atomic annihilation. The same nightmare exists when silicone is injected with red vegetable dye to form the "body" of a viscous, carnivorous, space-born monster.

Conceived as a disposable genre piece under the auspices of Paramount Pictures, albeit using expensive color film stock and the widescreen format, Irvin Yeaworth's *The Blob* stays in memory because it really does center on a blob that consumes every person with whom it makes contact. Luckily one of those people is the painfully young Steve McQueen (billed as "Steven") playing Steve, a small-town guy who, with his friend Jane (Aneta Corsaut), seeks out a meteor crash. An Old Man (Olin Howland) beats them to the crash site and becomes the nascent blob's first victim. To save the Old Man's life, Steve and Jane visit the local doctor, and from there the blob eats and eats and grows larger. Overwhelmed, Steve and Jane seek out the disbelieving police and are taken home, presumed to be horny teenagers or else miscreants temporarily out from under

◄

Steve McQueen's debut becomes a traffic sign into an age when monstrosity lay "out there" and could still be defeated by a well-timed dose of American ingenuity.

the control of mom and dad. But Steve and Jane know there's something rotten in town. They sneak out to a midnight movie to warn their friend but the blob pursues them. Cornered, they discover that the blob is repulsed by the cold when it pulls back from the refrigerator in which they've taken refuge.

An air-raid alarm leads to an impromptu community meeting in the Colonial Theater (the location shoot was in Valley Forge

"HOW DO YOU GET PEOPLE TO PROTECT THEMSELVES FROM SOMETHING THEY DON'T BELIEVE IN?" STEVE ANDREWS

Studios), where the blob threatens everyone as it seeps through the projection booth, forcing the crowd to retreat to a local diner. Screaming won't kill the blob and neither will electricity. Then Steve remembers the cold and shoots the thing-that-will-not-die with a fire extinguisher. Voilà! The Blob can't stand it, and so the townsfolk freeze it with compressed air in time for an army plane to drop the icicle into the frozen north, presumably to save us all from lining the "gut" of a Jello mold.

Modern viewers will admire the stripped-down plot that puts teenagers in jeopardy and avoids personalizing the monster. In the 1970s, horror movies would revisit this depersonalization to extraordinary effect, but the strange charge of Jack H. Harris's *The Blob* is the exaggeration it presents of slack-jawed wonder and hysterical naivety that is emblematic of the 1950s, specifically, and the past, generally. **GC-Q**

► **Olin Howland as the Old Man chancing upon the crater where the Blob awaits its first meal.**

PLAN 9 FROM OUTER SPACE 1959 (U.S.)

Director Ed Wood **Producer** Ed Wood **Screenplay** Ed Wood
Cinematography William C. Thompson **Music** Gordon Zahler
Cast Gregory Walcott, Mona McKinnon, Duke Moore, Tom Keene,
Carl Anthony, Paul Marco, Tor Johnson, Dudley Manlove, Joanna Lee, Lyle Talbot

The worst film ever, beyond competition, *Plan 9* (originally
Grave Robbers From Outer Space) is a testament to filmmaking in
its purest, most naïve form. As the last film of legendary horror
actor Bela Lugosi, it also carries historical significance. Actually,
Lugosi, whose health had deteriorated due to substance
addictions, died in 1956 during the shooting of another Wood
film, *Tomb of the Vampire*, which remained unfinished. Wood
later used the footage for *Plan 9* and hired another actor—who
did not even look like Lugosi and wore a cape to hide his face—
to fill in for the deceased star. The anecdote, simultaneously
embarrassing and endearing, explains much of the cult appeal
of this "so bad it's good" cult movie.

◄

**Numerous TV
series, *The X-Files*
most notably
among them, paid
homage to this
film, further
solidifying its
status as the
undisputed worst
movie ever.**

   The story itself is nonsensical. An introduction warns viewers
that what they are about to witness is based on "future events."
Flying saucers are noticed above a cemetery, and as a result
zombies rise from their graves (the rising of the undead by aliens
is the so-called *Plan 9*). Among the zombies is Vampira (TV's first
horror show). A team of detectives (led by Tor Johnson, who is
killed and turns into a zombie) and eventually the army are

called in to combat the zombies and aliens, who retreat to their spaceship. It comes to a standoff on the ship, in which the humans prevail and the aliens perish. With cardboard sets that threaten to tumble at any time, ludicrous continuity errors, poor acting, and inexplicable occurrences and twists, it should be no wonder that *Plan 9* was an unmitigated disaster—though teen audiences of the time reported being "roused" by the film.

"I'LL BET MY BADGE THAT WE HAVEN'T SEEN THE LAST OF THOSE WEIRDIES."

LT. JOHN HARPER

After being forgotten, *Plan 9* was dug up from its grave by the Medved brothers, critics who championed it as the worst film ever in their Golden Turkey Awards of 1980. This gave the film a new life, and sci-fi and horror festivals from around the world included the film in their late night and midnight retrospectives—where it became a riot. It led to a video release, a DVD release, a book, and a documentary.

During the 1990s, the reputation of *Plan 9* intensified. Tim Burton's excellent black and white tribute *Ed Wood*, with Johnny Depp, immortalized the director as a tragic angora-fetishist and a romantic chasing dreams, rather than an inept figure of ridicule. Tellingly, the (fictional) meeting between Wood and Orson Welles in *Ed Wood* suggests the two have a lot in common. This reappraisal made *Plan 9* somewhat of a totemic icon with aspiring filmmakers. **EM**

▶
Vampira (Maila Nurmi) had her own U.S. TV show that ran for five episodes in 1954.

MORE THAN 50 OF AMERICA'S TOP JAZZ MUSICIANS, INSTRUMENTALISTS
and VOCALISTS STAR IN — THE BRILLIANT

JAZZ ON A SUMMER'S DAY

Music of COUNT BASIE
DUKE ELLINGTON
HOAGY CARMICHAEL

FILMED AT THE WORLD FAMOUS NEWPORT
JAZZ FESTIVAL — PRESENTS SOME OF THE
MOST REMARKABLE SCENES AND SOUNDS OF
JAZZ IN THE MAKING EVER BROUGHT TO THE SCREEN

JAZZ ON A SUMMER'S DAY 1960 (U.S.)

Director Bert Stern, Aram Avakian **Producer** Harvey Kahn **Screenplay** Albert D'Annibale, Arnold Perl **Cinematography** Bert Stern **Music** George Avakian
Cast Louis Armstrong, Dinah Washington, Chuck Berry, Thelonious Monk, Max Roach, Jim Hall, Art Farmer, Sonny Stitt, Eric Dolphy, Bob Brookmeyer

After the mania for *Le Jazz-Hot* came *Le Jazz-Cool*—bebop, the postwar product of the tune-out intelligentsia, a form playful in a different way, speaking far more of its time than the brassy jazz of the past. From the opening frames of *Jazz On A Summer's Day*, this somewhat esoteric sound bubbles through its process (the Jimmy Giuffre Trio playing "Train and the River"), and it is the first of many rare performances we are soon to hear. Director and cinematographer Bert Stern's camera shows not the stage but the expressive dance of reflections on water, the names of the stellar roster of performers we're about to see lighting up the screen. The experience, we know already, is indeed going to be rare.

The film takes place over one day at the Newport Jazz Festival in 1958. We begin with the sea, switch to the stage, sojourn the afternoon at a beery house party, and settle into the evening with private rehearsals before returning for headlining sets. Throughout all of this visually dense material, *Jazz On A Summer's Day* benefits greatly from the commercial savvy of its maker who, experienced in fashion and advertising, is an early example of a taste-conscious craftsman whose

◄

Audiences swoon at the intricate configurations of the music they're hearing around their heat and substance-addled heads: this is where *Jazz On A Summer's Day* really lives.

vision provides the audience with what it was not yet aware that it wanted. We see an America changing. There is innocence. There is class. The weather is wonderful, and the town life is charming. There is real promise here; *and* art. The camera soars over a test sailing race, happening simultaneously, which appears as a major motif in the film: blue water, white sails, the summer sun dappling the waves; the sea as respite

"WHAT DO THEY SAY, 'THE JOINT IS REALLY JUMPING?' I THINK THAT'S KINDA PASSÉ." *DONNA MARTIN (NEWS REPORTER)*

from the gathering storm in this enclave, an isolated coastal point, an affluent outlet on the American continent. The crowd is undoubtedly quite educated: the announcer's introduction to Thelonious Monk, for example, includes a description of his method of striking two notes side by side in the absence of a key for the quarter tone. A woman in matching red hat and sweater with a black and white gingham blouse stretches her arms breezily, listening on.

The whole thing is like peering into the Kennedy mystique, the agony being that the innocence of this age (if ever it was, in fact, innocent) died with him shortly after. Imagine these days, when a popular form such as jazz descended from gospel and folk song from the black South, flirts with the precision and delicacy of the European classical tradition, taking in influences from the Far East all the while. **GS**

▶
Anita O'Day in this sympathetic documentary that distills from a jazz festival the final period of near perfection in American life that was Kennedy's Camelot.

DIRK BOGARDE
SARAH MILES
WENDY CRAIG

The
SERVANT

introducing
JAMES FOX

ELSTREE DISTRIBUTORS LIMITED present A SPRINGBOK Production

Directed by JOSEPH LOSEY   Produced by JOSEPH LOSEY & NORMAN PRIGGEN   Screenplay by HAROLD PINTER   Original Score by JOHN DANKWORTH   ASSOCIATED BRITISH · PATHE

THE SERVANT 1963 (U.K.)

Director Joseph Losey **Producer** Joseph Losey, Norman Priggen
Screenplay Robin Maugham, Harold Pinter **Cinematography** Douglas
Slocombe **Music** Johnny Dankworth **Cast** Dirk Bogarde, James Fox, Sarah Miles,
Wendy Craig, Catherine Lacey, Richard Vernon, Patrick Magee, Harold Pinter

Based on a 1948 novel by Robert Maugham and penned by
Harold Pinter (who walks on in the film), Joseph Losey's *The
Servant* stands as one of the sharpest, most acerbic comments
on the British class system ever committed to film. It was also
one of three collaborations between Losey and Pinter (the
others being *Accident* in 1967 and *The Go-Between* in 1970), all of
which were critical explorations of contemporary Britain. *The
Servant* remains as much a social allegory of class relations as a
straightforward film narrative.

  Tony (James Fox) is a rich young Londoner, freshly arrived
back from a stay in Africa. After hiring butler Hugo Barrett (Dirk
Bogarde), it appears that his life is perfectly in order: he has a
nice home and his girlfriend, Susan (Wendy Craig), is both
attractive and wealthy. However, while Tony and Barrett
develop a professional relationship that borders on friendship,
Susan becomes suspicious of the working-class Barrett's true
motives. When he says he needs more help running the
household and introduces his "sister" Vera (Sarah Miles, who is
really his fiancée) to his master, she proceeds to seduce him,
causing an irreparable rift between Tony and Susan.

◄

**Part class critique,
part psychological
melodrama,
The Servant
exudes a strangely
disquieting, tightly
claustrophobic,
and yet entirely
compelling view of
a changing Britain.**

By the end of the film there has been a radical role reversal. Tony, whose vices Barrett encourages, falls into a never-ending cycle of drunkenness and develops a stupefying caninelike obedience to Barrett who has, in effect, now become his master. As the film closes, it is clear that Barrett, along with girlfriend Vera, have taken over both Tony's life and his home. It is tempting to view the movie as a kind of "victory" of clever

"I PLAYED YOU FALSE, I ADMIT THAT. BUT SHE WAS TO BLAME. IT WAS HER FAULT. SHE DONE US BOTH." HUGO BARRETT

working-class northerner Barrett over stupid aristocrat Tony and stuck-up aristocrat Susan—and therefore purely as an extended film critique of the British class system. But *The Servant* is much more than that. The film also serves as an exploration of the dynamics of the abuse of personal influence, stressing the Machiavellianism inherent in the abuse of power and trust. Some movie watchers have also seen an underlying homoerotic tone to the film.

Speculation over what might be the real nature of the relationship between Tony and Barrett, despite the presence of various girlfriends and lovers, is something that has intensified since details of Bogarde's own homosexuality has been revealed. His performance as the coy and intensely devious Barrett and Miles' seductive femme fatale Vera are central to the success of the film. **RH**

► **James Fox's benign, identity-losing Tony presages his later turn as Chas in Nicholas Roeg's** *Performance* **(1970).**

"SHOCK CORRIDOR" OPENS THE DOOR TO SIGHTS YOU'VE NEVER SEEN BEFORE!

SHOCK CORRIDOR

STARRING PETER BRECK · CONSTANCE TOWERS · co-starring GENE EVANS · JAMES BEST · HARI RHODES

WRITTEN PRODUCED DIRECTED BY SAMUEL FULLER · A LEON FROMKESS · SAM FIRKS PRODUCTION · AN ALLIED ARTISTS RELEASE

SHOCK CORRIDOR 1963 (U.S.)

Director Samuel Fuller **Producer** Samuel Fuller **Screenplay** Samuel Fuller
Cinematography Stanley Cortez **Music** Paul Dunlap **Cast** Peter Breck,
Constance Towers, Gene Evans, James Best, Hari Rhodes, Paul Dubov, Larry Tucker,
Chuck Roberson, Neyle Morrow, John Matthews

Fuller's hard-hitting allegorical film, shot in black and white,
owes much to his experiences both as a war veteran and as a
crime reporter. The plot of *Shock Corridor* is simple. An egotistical
reporter, Johnny Barrett (Peter Breck), goes undercover at a
mental asylum to solve a recent murder, hoping that this will
win him the Pulitzer Prize. In order to do this, he pretends that
he suffers from incestuous desires toward his sister, who is in
fact his stripper girlfriend, Cathy (Constance Towers). However,
the solution of the crime comes at the cost of his sanity.

Like the later *One Flew Over the Cuckoo's Nest* (1975), *Shock
Corridor* shows that sanity is but a thin veneer behind which
lies madness. Personal madness doubles for societal madness:
the hysteria of American anticommunism; the existence of
the atomic bomb; racism and xenophobia; and sexual deviancy
and depravity are embodied by the men that Johnny
encounters in the asylum. The most important of these are the
three witnesses to the murder. Firstly there is Stuart (James
Best), who served during the Korean War and thinks that he is
General Ewell Brown "Jeb" Stuart, leader of the confederate
forces during the American Civil War. Then there is Dr. Boden

◀

**The inmates are
used by Fuller
to critique 1960s
American ideology
and society. By
doing so, Fuller
implies that
America itself is
an insane asylum.**

(Gene Evans), a Nobel Prize-winning physicist who has reverted to an infantile state and spends his time drawing and playing games of hide-and-seek. Finally, and most ironically, there is Trent (Hari Rhodes), a young black man who was the first African-American to be admitted to an all-white Southern University, and has so assimilated the views and ideology of his peers that he believes himself to be a grand wizard

"RIGHT ABOUT NOW IS WHEN HE'S SUPPOSED TO ASK ME IF I HEAR VOICES." JOHNNY "DO YOU HEAR VOICES?" DR. CRISTO

of the Klu Klux Klan and spends his time inciting violence against other black inmates and spouting overtly racist rants.

Through his encounters with madness, Johnny becomes increasingly deranged, believing that his stripper girlfriend, Cathy, *is* actually his sister, adding the suggestion of incest to the potpourri of mental disorders that Fuller zooms in on. The stunning black-and-white cinematography by Stanley Cortez and surreal dream sequences add to the psychological impact of the film. The fact that Johnny fulfills his dream but ends up as "an insane mute with a Pulitzer Prize" (Dr. Menkin) provides a powerful political statement against state lunacy. On its release, *Shock Corridor* was deemed by some to be a hysterical melodrama with little inherent artistic value. But in 1996 the film was deemed "culturally, historically, or aesthetically significant" and was placed on the National Film Registry. **CB**

▶

Reporter Johnny Barrett (Peter Breck) slips from self-imposed simulated madness into real lunacy in this gripping drama.

BANDE

ANNA
KARINA
SAMI
FREY
CLAUDE
BRASSEUR

dans un film de
**JEAN-LUC
GODARD**

à PART

D'après le roman
"Pigeon vole" de Dolores Hitchens
publié aux Éditions Gallimard - Série noire
Directeur de la photographie
RAOUL COUTARD
Musique de MICHEL LEGRAND
Une co-production
ANOUCHKA FILMS - ORSAY FILMS
Distribution par COLUMBIA

BANDE À PART 1964 (FRANCE)

Director Jean-Luc Godard **Producer** Jean-Luc Godard **Screenplay** Jean-Luc Godard (from the story by Delores Hitchens) **Cinematography** Raoul Coutard **Music** Michel Legrand **Cast** Anna Karina, Sami Frey, Claude Brasseur, Danièle Girard, Louisa Colpeyn

Critic turned filmmaker, Jean-Luc Godard was one of the founding members of the French *Nouvelle Vague* ("New Wave"). Characterized by existential themes, miniscule budgets, "make-do" locations, and actors with little (or no) experience, the most basic tenet of the New Wave was the "auteur theory" ("La politique des auteurs")—the notion of the director as lone visionary, whose personal signature is etched into every frame of the film. This, however, was no posturing intellectual diversion: that Godard's compadres included François Truffaut, Éric Rohmer, Claude Chabrol, Alain Resnais, Agnès Varda, and Jacques Demy is testament to the importance of the New Wave and its influence on European cinema over the ensuing decades.

Godard's films featured unprecedented methods of expression, such as lengthy tracking shots and jump cuts. He would pointedly challenge the conventions of traditional Hollywood cinema and, as the 1960s progressed, his work took on an increasingly political edge, often citing Marxist philosophy and denouncing cinema history almost in its entirety as "bourgeois" and thus without merit. The most radical director of the New Wave, his films were experimental and seen as too

◄

In spite of Godard's "difficult" reputation, this is an accessible film. Indeed, New York's *Village Voice* **called it "a Godard film for people who don't much care for Godard."**

"difficult" for mainstream viewers. After the critical success in 1963 of *Les Mépris (Contempt)*—a film that took in Greek mythology, Danté's Inferno, and the conflicts between artistic integrity and commercialism—Godard chose an obscure American gangster novel, *Fool's Gold* by Dolores Hitchens, as the basis for his next project. In its way, *Bande à Part* is a good old-fashioned love triangle. Two young men fall in love with

> " . . . ODILE'S, FRANZ'S AND ARTHUR'S FEELINGS . . . IT'S ALL PRETTY CLEAR. SO . . . LET THE IMAGES SPEAK." *LE NARRATEUR*

the beautiful Odile and try to convince her to take part in a robbery at the home of her wealthy guardian. This slender premise enables Godard to go off on all manner of tangents as the would-be crooks hang out in cafés, dance, take part in pretend shoot-outs, recite newspaper stories to each other, and generally— rather charming— keep reality at bay.

Bande à Part is remembered for moments like the "Madison" scene, where Odile and Arthur dance in a café to the jukebox (a groovy little Stax-style instrumental by Michel Legrand); Franz joins them as they line up to perform a neat little routine. It would remain definitively cool until John Travolta and Uma Thurman took to the floor thirty years later in Quentin Tarantino's *Pulp Fiction*. (And if anyone doubted that *this* was anything less than a homage to a beloved film, they need only look at the name of Tarantino's production company—A Band Apart!) **TB**

► *Bande à Part* **is a deliciously spontaneous piece of filmmaking enhanced by the obvious chemistry between the three central figures.**

"A WONDERFULLY COCK-EYED HALLUCINATION!" —N.Y. TIMES

IMPACT FILMS PRESENTS

ROBERT DOWNEY'S
CHAFED
ELBOWS

AND

KENNETH ANGER'S
SCORPIO
RISING

Color

SCORPIO RISING 1964 (U.S.)

Director Kenneth Anger **Producer** Kenneth Anger **Screenplay** Kenneth Anger
Cinematography Kenneth Anger **Music** Jack Brooks, David Raksin **Cast** Ernie Allo,
Bruce Byron, Frank Carifi, Steve Crandell, Johnny Dodds, Bill Dorfman, Nelson Leigh,
John Palone, Barry Rubin, Johnny Spaienza

Scorpio Rising is the brainchild of cultist and occultist Kenneth
Anger, follower of Aleister Crowley's philosophy of Magick. It is
also largely about cult rituals in and around New York in the early
1960s. The film is a recipe for controversy, but Anger had already
caused a stir with previous films, such as the gay manifesto
Fireworks (1947) and the meditation on Crowley, *Inauguration of
the Pleasure Dome* (1954). He was also known for his tell-all book
of scandals, *Hollywood Babylon*, in which he painted the film
industry as a seedy, sectarian, and paranoid community
obsessed with its star-cult status. *Hollywood Babylon* was only
available clandestinely in English in the early 1960s, but it
secured Anger's position as a radical conjurer among directors.

Like most of Anger's films, *Scorpio Rising* does not tell a
straightforward story. It is a mix of impressions propelled by a
soundtrack and rhythmic editing. Basically, the film throws
together various moral panics of the time: deviant youth
gangs, neo-Nazis, Hell's Angels, rockers, comic books,
controversial movies (especially *Rebel Without a Cause* in 1955
and *The Wild One* in 1953), and rock 'n' roll music. The film starts
with slow scenes to leisurely paced lyrical songs (such as "Blue

◄

**Martin Scorsese,
David Lynch, and
Guy Maddin have
counted** *Scorpio
Rising* **as a key
influence. Thanks
to a painstakingly
restored DVD
release, everyone
can now see why
this is one film that
truly casts spells as
Anger would like
all films to.**

Velvet") that feature a few Hell's Angels (one of them called Scorpio) dressing up, posing in fetishist and homoerotic poses, chroming and fixing their motorcycles, and showing their prized possessions: skull rings, chains, a Nazi flag, leather jackets, and pinup pictures of James Dean and Marlon Brando. The editing gradually speeds up, "from toy to terror" as Anger described it, until it reaches a frenetic whirlwind of collaged

"THERE ARE ONLY A FEW FLASHES OF NUDITY, GENITALIA . . . IF YOU BLINK, YOU WON'T EVEN SEE THEM." KENNETH ANGER

images of Walpurgis Night hazing rituals, sped-up amateur motorcycling crashes, blurry flashes of youths on bikes posturing outside a diner, and a montage that links Jesus to the Nazis, to the tunes of some of the wildest rock 'n' roll of the time—fittingly, the last tune is The Surfaris's "Wipe Out."

Not surprisingly, controversy accompanied *Scorpio Rising* on its theatrical release. A court ruling decided the film was not pornographic but it had difficulty finding distribution. It caused upheaval at some festivals (especially the Knokke-le-Zoute festival that also saw *Flaming Creatures* (1963) being banned). Eventually it found an audience with other American experimental cinema of the time in the urban grind and art house circuit in New York. Near the end of the 1960s, it became a totemic film for the gay community, and it also helped pave the way for the midnight movies of the 1970s. **EM**

► **A movie that blended Hell's Angels, devils, Jesus, and the Nazis was going to have to go underground.**

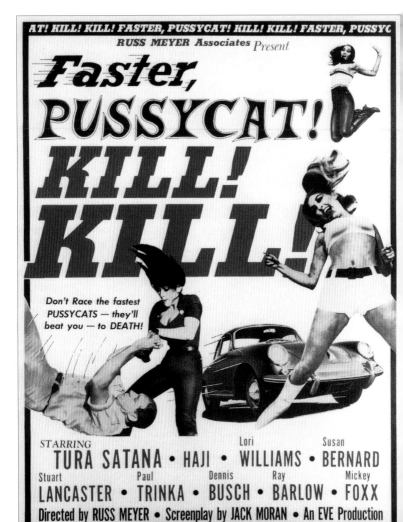

FASTER, PUSSYCAT—KILL! KILL!

1965 (U.S.)

Director Russ Meyer **Producer** Russ Meyer, Eve Meyer, George Costello, Fred Owens **Screenplay** Jack Moran, Russ Meyer **Cinematography** Walter Schenk **Music** Richard Brummer **Cast** Tura Satana, Haji, Lori Williams, Ray Barlow, Sue Bernard, Michael Finn, Dennis Busch, Stuart Lancaster, Paul Trinks

---

The ways of the world are passing strange. Russ Meyer, who could hardly get arrested at one time, is now one of the undisputed kings of cult movies. Although he was derided in his life as strictly a tits 'n' bums merchant, the sheer bravado and panache of his movies, the over-the-top intensity of the acting styles (with every line in CAPITAL LETTERS), and the relentless excitement of every moment in a film such as *Faster, Pussycat—Kill! Kill!* are all seen as harbingers of today's semi sex-crazed action blockbusters. But things now aren't as much fun as they used to be in the (relatively) innocent 1960s.

As usual in a Meyer movie, the plot is stripped to the bone and the pace rises inexorably toward a Grand Guignol climax. Three impossibly pneumatic young strippers (Tura Satana, Haji, and Lori Williams) in sports cars seeking thrills on the highway encounter a young couple in the desert. After dispatching the boyfriend (Ray Barlow), they take the girl (Sue Bernard) hostage and plan to do in a crippled old man (Stuart Lancaster) living with his two sons (Dennis Busch and Paul Trinks) in the desert, reputedly hiding a tidy sum of cash. They become houseguests

◄

Russ Meyer named the movie as he did because he claims that a movie has everything when it contains speed (faster), sex (pussycat), and violence (kill exclamation, times two).

of the old man and the girls idle around, trying recklessly to seduce the sons in an attempt to locate the money, little realizing that the old man (a forerunner of the folks in *The Texas Chain Saw Massacre* of 1974) has a few sinister intentions of his own. It is this additional twist of horror to the sex, fast cars, and gorgeous girls that has also proved enormously influential on the inexorable rise of the teen slasher pics.

"YOU GIRLS A BUNCH OF NUDISTS, OR ARE YOU JUST SHORT OF CLOTHES?"

THE OLD MAN

Within its own extensive limitations, the acting is perfectly fine, sustaining that intensity referred to throughout. But the main draw is the tight jeans, large breasts, and décolletage of Satana and Haji (black-haired in black) and Williams (blonde in white). Their hostage, Bernard, no slouch herself in normal company, looks puny in comparison. So do the men—Meyer not having much interest in them—although Stuart Lancaster hams it up with great relish as the crippled patriarch.

Of course, it seems quite tame nowadays when set against, say, some of Hollywood's sex and silicone adult movie excesses. Nevertheless, the film did not receive a U.K. certificate until 1980. Apparently, Tura Satana, the lead actress, legally owns her likeness and image. So, whenever Meyer wanted to change the artwork or rerelease the project, he had to get her permission and sometimes pay her all over again. **MH**

► **Cleavage and cleaving as Satana meters out no mercy in search of easy money. Meyer's other 1960s movies include *Mondo Topless* (1966), *Finders, Keepers, Lovers, Weepers!*, and *Vixen!* (both 1968).**

GRAN PREMIO INTERNAZIONALE AL FESTIVAL DI CANNES 1967

METRO GOLDWYN MAYER presenta una produzione di **CARLO PONTI**

Un film di
**MICHELANGELO
ANTONIONI**

VANESSA REDGRAVE

BLOW-UP

DAVID HEMMINGS · SARAH MILES   METROCOLOR

BLOW-UP 1966 (U.K. • ITALY)

Director Michelangelo Antonioni **Producer** Carlo Ponti, Pierre Rouve
Screenplay Michelangelo Antonioni, Tonino Guerra, Edward Bond
Cinematography Carlo Di Palma **Music** Herbie Hancock, The Yardbirds
Cast David Hemmings, Vanessa Redgrave, Sarah Miles, Veruschka von Lehndorff

Italian director Michelangelo Antonioni's first film in English, *Blow-Up* is a movie of firsts. Regarded as a seminal work of the 1960s, it liberalized attitudes toward the depiction of nudity and sexuality in film. Made by M.G.M., it was the first British movie to depict full-frontal female nudity, and in the United States the studio created a subsidiary, Premiere Productions, to distribute the film as a way of bypassing Production Code censorship. Not that *Blow-Up* is all about sex, rather Antonioni's attempt to portray the cool of London's swinging sixties demands the inclusion of sex, drugs, and rock 'n' roll to be effective. The film is about ways of seeing, and it is apt that it challenges the notion of censorship and what can be viewed by adults.

Blow-Up tells the story of a successful fashion photographer, Thomas (David Hemmings), loosely based on contemporary photographers David Bailey and Terence Donovan. Nihilistic and misogynistic, Thomas is the ultimate unlikable antihero. Shooting supermodels like Veruschka von Lehndorff for his job satisfies his lust, whereas ignoring the attentions of women like Patricia (Sarah Miles) satisfies his ego. But Thomas suffers from a cynical ennui about his successful lifestyle and has pretensions

◄

An Italian poster for the movie created by one of the masters of Italian film posters, Ercole Brini, this has become an iconic image of postwar Italian cinema.

to be seen as an artist, photographing London's poor in an effort to publish a monograph. His boredom means he abandons a fashion shoot to walk the streets of London. He takes a shot of a couple in a park, one of whom, Jane (Vanessa Redgrave), is alarmed and asks him for the roll of film. Curious as to what it contains, Thomas enlarges the shot and thinks he has captured an image of a murderer and his victim.

"SOME PEOPLE ARE BULLFIGHTERS, SOME PEOPLE ARE POLITICIANS. I'M A PHOTOGRAPHER." THOMAS

What seems like a murder thriller is so much more, as the audience is left to decide what Thomas really saw. They are also asked to question what is really going on in society. Antonioni's exquisite images of beautiful people suggest a cultural malaise in Britain that perhaps only an outsider can portray. On top of this his cast features actors Hemming, Redgrave, and Miles in the bloom of youth and a cameo appearance by The Yardbirds, including Jeff Beck and Jimmy Page. Aided by Carlo Di Palma's freewheeling cinematography and an unflinching script he cowrote with Edward Bond and Tonino Guerra, Antonioni makes a film that is beautiful to look at and resonates with all that was thought to be avant-garde at the time. It is a statement on style over substance, engaging yet disconnected, enigmatic and erotic, as it lifts the lid on turbulent human emotions experienced beneath the swinging sixties' sheen. **CK**

► The image of the photographer mid-shoot sums up the voyeuristic nature of the film.

CHELSEA GIRLS 1966 (U.S.)

Director Andy Warhol, Paul Morrissey **Producer** Andy Warhol **Screenplay** Andy Warhol, Ronald Tavel **Cinematography** Andy Warhol, Paul Morrissey **Music** The Velvet Underground **Cast** Nico, Brigid Berlin, Ondine, Ingrid Superstar, Gerard Malanga, Randy Borscheidt, Patrick Fleming, Marie Menken

Too often Warhol is remembered for soup tins and mechanical reproduction, but where Warhol really shines, and where Warhol really exposes his own actual, authentic interest in art-making, is in his cinema. And *Chelsea Girls* is easily his magnum opus. Notoriously, its genesis was on a napkin, which he divided into two frames, and the cult status of *Chelsea Girls* is aided by its cumbersome and unconventional projection needs: twin 16 mm projectors with opposing soundtracks. The impossibility of exact synchronization (and the film's unwieldy length, roughly three and a half hours of film) rarefies the film's art house appeal considerably, adding an air of improvisation and performance to any presentation of the work.

On the screen, two stories unfold simultaneously on the same basic themes: New York. Late 1960s. Disaffection. Sex. The new cool. The subtext is occasionally explicit: Vietnam. Social unrest. A sinking disbelief in the promise of America. We do not perceive much more of a "plot" than the everydayness of what streams before us. Occasional flickers of conventional narrative do not reward; they are merely feints. Andrea Picard, writing in *Cinemascope*, references the violence in Warhol, "the riots,

◄

This is a movie that allows us to mooch on the "scene" that we can never be a part of, but in the moment it was, of course, too real. We can detect a real sense of refuge in the Chelsea Hotel, in the Warhol superstars, and in the Factory itself.

Vietnam, the blood, the anger—splattered all over . . . and the ensemble's narcissistic angst," a startling observation on this thoroughly upsetting work.

Watching *Chelsea Girls* is like watching live art, and is evocative of both the best and worst of a scene that created itself self-consciously from moment to moment. Warhol favored the long, long take; he languished where his

"EVERY TIME I SEE MARILYN MONROE I GET A QUIVER . . . WHEN I'M STARTING TO SWEAT, I'M FEELING BETTER." *GERARD MALANGA*

contemporaries settled with lingering. Their products gestured toward their goals; Warhol's proclaimed them, proudly, in an insistent, American voice. The perverse is always present. Having engendered a scene, he seems to pleasure himself in reconfiguring his superstars for effect as if to say: I can reproduce the living, too. But they created him as much as he them, and thus the queer paradox of Warhol's odd, infuriatingly pertinent and revelatory art.

▶

Just as a soup tin is an original creation that can be reproduced endlessly, so too are the people who populated Warhol's world, such as the strangely strange but oddly normal Ondine.

The power of *Chelsea Girls* rests in accumulation. As image builds upon image, Warhol constructs something both personal and remote, made more so on both counts by considering how he seems to have viewed almost everyone in his orbit as an object both individual and of his own creation. He does seem to admire them all, nonetheless. And The Velvet Underground's music is a historic footnote. **GS**

INGMAR BERGMANS
PERSONA

BIBI ANDERSSON · LIV ULLMANN

PERSONA 1966 (SWEDEN)

Director Ingmar Bergman **Producer** Ingmar Bergman **Screenplay** Ingmar Bergman, Kerstin Berg **Cinematography** Sven Nykvist **Music** Lars Johan Werle **Editing** Ulla Ryghe **Cast** Bibi Andersson, Liv Ullmann, Margaretha Krook, Gunnar Björnstrand, Jörgen Lindström

Not many well-respected feature films present an adult male erection. Ingmar Bergman's *Persona* (1966), as shot by his longtime cinematographer Sven Nykvist, is one of them. The penis in question is only a brief insert shot, so don't blink at the wrong moment or you'll miss it. But the fact remains: Bergman's boner belongs to us all and becomes a kind of negative fetish object, speaking to both the controls expressed by a male-dominated image-making process and to the prerogatives of men to express the stories of women.

So then, *Persona* is the story of two women, Sister Alma (Bibi Andersson) and Elisabeth Vogler (Liv Ullmann), who find themselves uniquely entwined in psychoanalytically rich ways. Elisabeth is a successful actress but she's gone mute and requires some yet-to-be realized talking therapy to "cure" her of her silence, which is where Alma steps in to provide round-the-clock care that will bring out the voice of her charge.

Much of what really excites film theorists depends upon Bergman's self-conscious address, his high modernist sensibility. The movie opens with a montage about making movies and the ideological potency of image-making, including a crucifixion

◄

Bergman's later oeuvre explored women and their personal relationships in a totally experimental fashion as with *Persona*, and later *Cries and Whispers* (1972).

to exclaim the appropriate effect of cinema. Then the story begins to take shape with Alma as she's assigned care of Elisabeth. The pair has been lent a seaside cottage and it is here that they truly confront one another in their isolation, along with TV images of self-immolating Buddhist monks straight from Vietnam. In the absence of Elisabeth's speech, Alma fills the time talking about herself. She talks and she talks and she talks,

> *"IF SHE WON'T SPEAK OR MOVE BECAUSE SHE DECIDES NOT TO . . . IT SHOWS SHE IS MENTALLY VERY STRONG." SISTER ALMA*

eventually confessing to infidelities and to having had an abortion. Naturally, Alma, the presumably "healthy" woman, seems to come partly unhinged. Then Bergman offers a second modernist turn and breaks up the story with scratched and torn film to remind us that we're watching a constructed story, a movie.

Tension between the women escalates until violence looms. Mr. Vogler (Gunnar Björnstrand) visits. Sexual entanglements ensue. Biographies become intermingled. There's an iconic shot of Alma and Elisabeth, each woman's image dissolving into one another, which has been repeated innumerable times in film scholarship and mimicked in other films. Transference occurs as Alma retells the story of Elisabeth's life, mastering the details both require in order to manage the ungovernable aspects of their histories. Then we get another modernist bit of self-reflexivity as Bergman's crew appears on-screen. **GC-Q**

▶
Liv Ullmann, one of Bergman's muses, in a classic of gloomy navel-gazing that was mercilessly lampooned by Woody Allen in *Love and Death* (1975).

JANE FONDA BARBARELLA

See
Barbarella
do
her
thing!

JOHN PHILLIP LAW · MARCEL MARCEAU · DAVID HEMMINGS
UGO TOGNAZZI

BARBARELLA 1968 (U.S.)

Director Roger Vadim **Producer** Dino de Laurentiis **Screenplay** Terry Southern, Roger Vadim **Cinematography** Claude Renoir **Music** Michel Magne, James Campbell (uncredited) **Cast** Jane Fonda, David Hemmings, Anita Pallenberg, John Phillip Law, Milo O'Shea, Marcel Marceau, Ugo Tognacci, Claude Dauphin

---

Barbarella: Queen of the Galaxy (its U.S. promotional title) stems from a hugely successful 1960s comic strip, and, fired by the relative success of *Modesty Blaise* (1966), de Laurentiis was prepared to bankroll it. The original author, Jean-Claude Forest, based the character of Barbarella on Brigitte Bardot—ironically, the first wife of chosen director Roger Vadim. Vadim must have had the best taste and the most exciting life of anyone outside Warren Beatty: discovered and married Bardot; next up, Danish beauty Annette Stroyberg; early 1960s quick affair and child with Catherine Deneuve; married Jane Fonda in 1965 for eight years; even quicker marriage and child to heiress Catherine Schneider; and final marriage to Marie-Christine Barrault— and they all attended his funeral in 2000.

However, as resident wife, Fonda wasn't a shoo-in for casting as Barbarella, Vasim's preferred modus operandi. Raquel Welch, 1960s sex symbol, turned down the title role. When Italian sex goddess Virna Lisi was ordered to play the part, she terminated her contract with United Artists and returned to Italy. So many screenwriters listed in the credits should give ample warning to experienced filmgoers about where the problems lay. The

◄
The film's bad scientist inspired the band name of 1980s pop stars Duran Duran.

amazing thing is that, given such obvious gestation problems, the script is actually as coherent as it is. And often extremely witty (thanks to Terry Southern in the main). But then again, most people don't come to a comic strip brought to life for the screenplay; the production design and camera work is the draw, as is Barbarella shedding her already pretty sexy costumes (by Jacques Fonteray and Paco Rabanne) at regular intervals.

"MY FANCY, FUZZY FREAK: WHAT DO YOU THINK OF, WHEN YOU MAKE LOVE TO BARBARELLA?" GREAT TYRANT

The film's opening titles offer an in-flight antigravity striptease before Barbarella, a forty-first-century supergirl, lands on far planet Lythion tasked with finding evil Durand Durand (Milo O'Shea) in the city of Sogo, where they invent a new sin every hour. She soon comes across the Excessive Machine, a genuine sex organ on which an accomplished artist of the keyboard, in this case, Durand Durand himself, can drive a victim to death by pleasure—satirized by Woody Allen in *Sleeper* (1973) as the Orgasmatron. She meets the lesbian Great Tyrant (Anita Pallenberg) who, in her dream chamber, can make her fantasies take form, and ladies smoking a giant hookah that, via hapless victims in its glass globe, dispenses Essence of Man. The design of the film by Jean-Claude Forest as shot by Claude Renoir and the palatial sets by Mario Garbuglia are magical, delivering the visual thrills worthy of its cult reputation. **MH**

▶
Barbarella (Jane Fonda) falls in love with Pygar (John Phillip Law), a blind angel, and together they look simply stunning on-screen. The costumes and set design provide the rest.

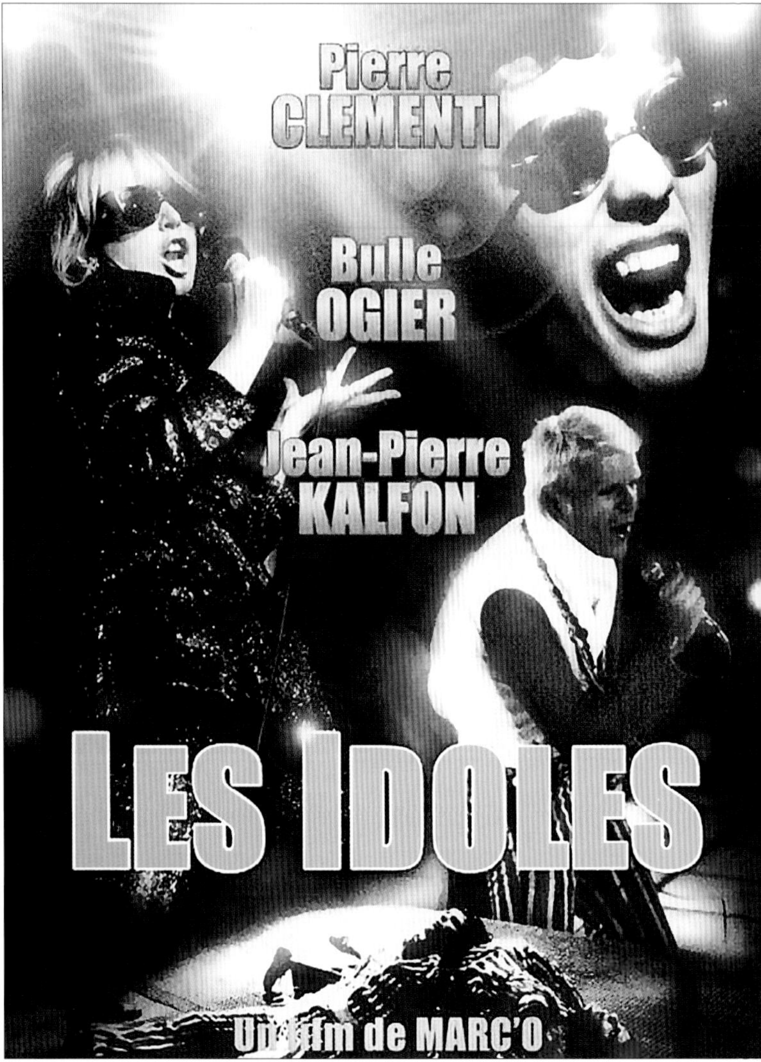

Pierre
CLEMENTI

Bulle
OGIER

Jean-Pierre
KALFON

LES IDOLES

Un film de MARC'O

LES IDOLES 1968 (FRANCE)

Director Marc-Gilbert Guillaumin (as Marc'O) **Producer** Henri Zaphiratos
Screenplay Marc'O **Cinematography** Jean Badal **Music** Patrick Greussay,
Stéphane Vilar **Cast** Bulle Ogier, Pierre Clémenti, Jean-Pierre Kalfon, Bernadette
Lafont, Valérie Lagrange, Michèle Moretti, Jöel Barbouth

The only film of French theater artist Marc'O, *Les Idoles* has never
been much more than a curiosity; far too cool and knowing for
great success, its prominence on the cult circuit is assured by
other cineastes and scholars of cinema, bestowing upon it a
quiet renown. Today, in the world of *The X Factor* and *American
Idol*, it seems quite prescient.

The conceit: three 1960s yé-yé (French girl pop) idols
performing (French stars Bulle Ogier, Pierre Clémenti, and
Jean-Pierre Kalfon), manufactured for superstardom, arrive at a
press conference staged to revive their careers. All three have
been fashioned for maximum returns to their various keeper—
labels, agents, theater operators—and have had their fill. The
creations take over and attempt to take the whole contraption
down. Their end, though, can never be final, as their downfall is
spectacle and those handlers they've hoped to drag down
with them are now merely, momentarily, part of the act.

The shadow of Marshall McLuhan looms large. The presence
of broadcast media in the film is huge, and one of the most
satisfying aspects of *Les Idoles* is the inclusion of the audience
of spectators. Yes, this is the world of Beatlemania, but mainly

◄
**Not released in the
United States until
2008, this avant-
garde stage event
and musical was
made into a film
in 1968 and made
possible by the
French Nouvelle
vague movement.**

of its French echo, which took a few years in coming, hence some of the quaintness of *Les Idoles*. But this very quaintness makes it less exotic than actually shocking. Thus *Les Idoles*, forgotten by all but its initiates, exists as a document of a time and place, and also might very well be the first substantial satire on the creation of pop stars as mechanisms of conformity and mass control.

"IT'S THE FOURTEENTH OF JULY—YÉ-YÉ —NATIONAL—THE CELEBRATION."

GIGI LA FOLLE

Those who know the film insist upon its advanced acknowledgment of the process of celebrity creation. Implicit in all of this is the reaction that this creation causes in a public primed by the same media used to promote them. The trickle down is obvious, and Marc'O relishes the succinctness of his conceit, focusing on crafting an engrossing piece of filmed theater, not at all humorless despite its political ramifications. It is thus a closed circuit, wherein people are both products and consumers of products. The position that the machine can be shut down only by self-destruction witnesses the unique cultural ferment of Paris pre-May 1968. It also prefigures, more presciently, the craze for televised talent shows and their ready-made stars or "idols." It is a vital and entertaining assault on everyone involved in the process, with some amusing swipes at the vacuity of cultural tourism so in vogue at the time. **GS**

► *Les Idoles* is unique in suggesting that the individual has the power to rewrite the state history for the collective good, and this is likely what has kept it obscure all these years.

THIS YEAR IT'S easy RIDER

PANDO COMPANY in association with RAYBERT PRODUCTIONS presents

easy RIDER starring PETER FONDA · DENNIS HOPPER · JACK NIC...

Written by · Directed by · Produced by · Associate Producer · Executive Producer
PETER FON... · DENNIS HOPPER · PETER FONDA · WILLIAM HAYWARD · BERT SCHNEIDER
DENNIS HO...
TERRY SOU... ...ESTRICTED — Persons under 16 not admitted unless accompanied by parent or adult guardian... · Released by COLUMBIA PICTURES

EASY RIDER 1969 (U.S.)

Director Dennis Hopper **Producer** Peter Fonda **Screenplay** Peter Fonda, Dennis Hopper, Terry Southern **Cinematography** Laszlo Kovacs **Music** The Byrds, Steppenwolf, Bob Dylan, The Band, Jimi Hendrix, Roger McGuinn **Cast** Peter Fonda, Dennis Hopper, Jack Nicholson, Karen Black, Antonia Mendoza, Phil Spector

Now here's a real cult classic for its subject matter, rather than for any obscurity. It's a simple road movie : Billy (Dennis Hopper) and Captain America (Peter Fonda) chug across the South from California to New Orleans and have adventures. They were drunk and stoned most of the time. That's it. Famously, Hopper and Fonda never wrote a full script, making most of it up as they went along (much cooler, and a near Oscar alert). However, they took care to hire writer du jour Terry Southern, hot from *Barbarella* (1968). They didn't hire a crew but picked up hippies at communes across the country, using friends and passersby to hold the cameras.

Hopper and Fonda were inspired by the Italian film *Il Sorpasso* (*The Easy Life*, 1962, hence the movie's title), about two guys making a trip through Italy in an open car. *Il Sorpasso* was a pioneer in using pop songs as part of the soundtrack, and *Easy Rider* was virtually the first English language movie to do the same (excepting The Beatles' films and other special cases).

The film also catapulted Jack Nicholson, deservedly, to stardom, although Rip Torn was originally cast in his role of George Hanson. According to Torn, Hopper pulled a knife on

◀

From the opening strains of Steppenwolf's "The Pusher," this was the first film to push a multiartist "sourced," contemporary popular music soundtrack.

him during a preproduction meeting. Hopper claimed it was Torn who flourished the knife. Torn later sued Hopper for defamation—and won. Bruce Dern was also originally mooted for the role but declined. Hopper, meanwhile, was going through a very bad time during production, screaming at everyone in a state of drug-induced paranoia. Crew members secretly recorded his tirades and sent tapes to the production

"THIS USED TO BE A HELLUVA COUNTRY. I CAN'T UNDERSTAND WHAT'S GONE WRONG WITH IT." GEORGE HANSON

company to explain why so many were quitting. Hopper had the original cut around three hours, but upon reviewing it with surviving key members of his staff the length was cut by half.

Easy Rider presaged the souring of the American hippie dream. Among the many memorable scenes is Fonda's tripping soliloquy in a New Orleans cemetery (St. Louis No.1 Catholic Cemetery in which no other film crews—documentaries apart—have been allowed in subsequently). Hopper asked Fonda to talk to the statue as if to his mother, who committed suicide when he was ten years old. Fonda didn't want to, as he'd never confronted his feelings about his mother, but Hopper insisted: Fonda calls the statue "Mother," saying he both loves and hates her. This scene persuaded Dylan to allow the use of his song "It's Alright Ma" in one of the final scenes. Fonda told Dylan, "I need to hear those words"—with lyrics referencing suicide. **MH**

▶
Peter Fonda's bike was seriously chopped and he was an accomplished biker. Hopper, however, was not a natural or "easy" rider.

This time...
they've
really
gone

Beyond
the Valley
of the
Dolls

A Russ Meyer Production

The world
is full of them,
the super-octane
girls who are
old at twenty

If they get to be twenty.

From 20th Century-Fox Starring DOLLY READ / CYNTHIA MYERS / MARCIA MC BROOM / JOHN LA ZAR / MICHAEL BLODGETT / DAVID GURIAN

Co-starring EDY WILLIAMS / Produced and Directed by RUSS MEYER / Screenplay by ROGER EBERT / Story by ROGER EBERT and RUSS MEYER

PANAVISION® Color by DE LUXE® Hear THE SANDPIPERS and THE STRAWBERRY ALARM CLOCK on the original soundtrack album from 20th Century-Fox records

This is not a sequel—
there has **never** been
anything like it

 NO ONE UNDER 17 ADMITTED
(Age limit may vary in certain areas)

BEYOND THE VALLEY
OF THE DOLLS 1970 (U.S.)

Director Russ Meyer **Producer** Russ Meyer, Eve Meyer, Red Hershon
Screenplay Roger Ebert **Cinematography** Fred J. Koenekamp
Music Stu Phillips **Cast** Dolly Read, Cynthia Myers, Marcia McBroom, John Lazar,
Michael Blodgett, David Gurian, Edy Williams, Erica Gavin, Phyllis Davis

Meyer once said he considers this film to be his "most important."
It was certainly his biggest earner. Budgeted at a modest
$900,000 (now worth more than five times that), the film grossed
ten times this amount in the U.S. market, qualifying it as a hit for
the beleaguered 20th Century Fox. Though tame by modern
standards, *Beyond The Valley of the Dolls* was slapped with an X
rating, generating much negative publicity about a major
studio allowing a "pornographer" (called "King Leer" by the
mainstream press) to make a Hollywood film under its aegis.

According to Ebert, the film's scriptwriter, Meyer was unaware
that the film would get an X rating. He claims Meyer would have
added more nudity and sex to the film if he had known. The
actress Grace Kelly, who was a member of Fox's board of directors,
was outraged and lobbied to have the studio's contract with
Meyer terminated. But after *Seven Minutes* (1971), his next Fox
film, flopped at the box office (possibly due to its low nudity
and titillation ratio), the studio terminated its relationship with
Meyer. He never made another film for a major studio.

◄

How the all-girl
rock band ends up
was not in the
original script.
Ebert and Meyer
came up with the
idea on the day of
shooting, based on
the recent Manson
Family murders.
And perhaps
Meyer's career was
cursed thereafter.

This movie, as you might guess, was originally intended as a sequel to *Valley of the Dolls* (1967), the Jacqueline Susann blockbuster that turned into good box office. Susann submitted a screenplay for a sequel, but when Fox found it unsatisfactory, the studio's contract gave it the right to produce a separate version. Susann was reportedly so offended by the results, she threatened to sue the studio.

"I WANT IT, I NEED IT, I LOVE IT WHEN A BEAUTIFUL WOMAN LICKS BETWEEN MY TOES." HARRIS ALLSWORTH

Refining his previous formula of girls, speed, and violence to an updated sex, drugs, and rock 'n' roll ethos, the director hit paydirt. It worked—the girls are beauties and most of the movie is great fun to watch. Meyer's other trademark was recycling actors and costumes wherever possible. Two women wear costumes in the film inspired by *Batman* (1966). The Robin costume worn by Casey (Cynthia Myers) was actually one of the costumes worn by Burt Ward on the *Batman* TV series. During a bedroom scene, Kelly (Dolly Read) wears the same flimsy red nightgown worn by heroines in two earlier Meyer pictures—*Vixen!* and *Finders, Keepers, Lovers, Weepers!* (both 1968). The outfit that Kelly borrows from her Aunt Susan to wear to the party at the beginning of the film is the one-piece pants suit worn by Sharon Tate in *Valley of the Dolls*. **MH**

► The character of Ronnie "Z-Man" Barzell (John Lazar) was based loosely on legendary record producer Phil Spector. Neither Ebert nor Meyer had met Spector, but acquaintants told them they'd caught the oddball well.

UNA ESCLUSIVA P.D.A.

EL TOPO

DI **ALEXANDRO JODOROWSKY**

TECHNICOLOR   PRODOTTO DA **ALLEN KLEIN** PER LA **ABKCO FILMS**

EL TOPO 1970 (MEXICO)

Director Alejandro Jodorowsky **Producer** Mick Gochanour, Robin Klein, Juan Lopez Moctezuma, Moshe Rosemberg, Saul Rosemberg **Screenplay** Alejandro Jodorowsky **Cinematography** Rafeal Corkidi **Music** Alejandro Jodorowsky, Nacho Méndez **Cast** Alejandro Jodorowsky, Brontis Jodorowsky, José Legarreta, Alf Junco

A hybrid between a spaghetti Western-on-acid and a surrealist nightmare, *El Topo* is the film that started the heydays of the midnight movie in New York in 1970. There had been midnight screenings in urban theaters in Manhattan before, but *El Topo* set the tone for the underground and countercultural atmosphere of ritual rewatching for which midnight movies became known—an atmosphere that brought the upheaval of the late 1960s from the streets into the theaters.

The film tells the story of a traveling gunfighter-messiah, El Topo (the mole, played by Alejandro Jodorowsky), across four parts, named Genesis, Prophecies, Psalms, and Apocalypse. During the first two stages, El Topo travels through the desert with his seven-year-old naked son, avenges the slaughtered people of a village, leaves his son in the custody of monks, duels four gun masters, and is shot by his two women companions. In the latter two stages, he is resurrected by a band of deformed outcasts imprisoned in a cave and frees himself. But when he liberates the others, they are massacred by the gun-crazy citizens of a nearby town. He encounters his son again, who is a priest now and resents him. Shattered, El Topo goes on a killing spree. His

◀

Violent and bloody, "The Mole" is a religious allegory dressed in a spaghetti Western poncho. A DVD box release of Jodorowsky's work has broadened the film's appeal.

son, now dressed in his father's black outfit from the beginning of the story, drives off into the distance with El Topo's new baby and dwarf companion. Throughout, the story abounds with sudden blasts of violence, references to 1960s politics (especially Vietnam), biblical martyrdom and self-sacrifice, heavy surrealist symbolism (from whipping to shoe fetishes to graves made of bees and rabbits), and disabled outsiders of all strike and flavor.

"YOU ARE SEVEN YEARS OLD. YOU ARE A MAN. BURY YOUR FIRST TOY AND YOUR MOTHER'S PICTURE." EL TOPO

El Topo was Jodorowsky's debut feature, but he had already had a successful career as a theater actor and playwright. With Fernando Arrabal and Roland Topor he started the Panic Movement in 1962, in which he explored how terror, violence, and humor could be combined. He also wrote surrealist comic books. All these influences feed into *El Topo*. They make it one of the most enigmatic and mind-boggling films of all time, in which, perhaps, too much meaning is tucked away. Initially without distributor, *El Topo* was picked up for a run of New York midnight screenings that, without publicity, ran for six months straight. Thanks to the support of John Lennon and former Beatles manager Allen Klein, *El Topo* was distributed across the world, where it became a cult classic. It has been in and out of circulation since, but as an icon of the countercultural era it still draws faithful crowds. **EM**

► El Topo, the director Alejandro Jodorowsky, with his real (and naked) seven-year-old son Brontis Jodorowsky.

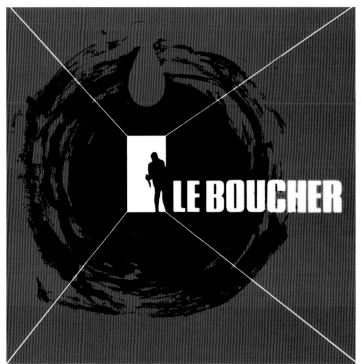

LE BOUCHER

LE BOUCHER

UN FILM DE
CLAUDE
CHABROL

SCENARIO ET DIALOGUE DE
CLAUDE CHABROL

LE BOUCHER 1970 (FRANCE)

Director Claude Chabrol **Producer** André Génovès, Fred Surin
Screenplay Claude Chabrol **Cinematography** Jean Rabier
Music Pierre Jansen **Cast** Stéphane Audran, Jean Yanne, Antonio Passalia,
Pascal Ferone, Mario Beccara, William Guérault, Roger Rudel

Although this movie is rightfully a cult classic, there's no doubt that Claude Chabrol, not unlike Luis Buñuel, was a very great director in anyone's language. The essential difference is that Chabrol is a realist, and Buñuel is primarily a surrealist, although both follow ruthless logic in their separate ways.

Chabrol has also often been compared to Alfred Hitchcock, but he's even more interested in how individuals respond to the inconstancies of life, and extends especial sympathy to his leading characters, a trait not always connected with the dazzling English director. *Le Boucher* is a prototypical example of Chabrol's art, showing his unrivaled ability to find the extraordinary in scenes of everyday life.

Although the title refers to the butcher, the film is really a masterful character study of a headmistress, a good woman gradually coming under intense pressure, played with wonderful precision by the supremely talented and beautiful Stéphane Audran (at the time Chabrol's wife; they divorced in 1980). The plot is spare and deceptively simple. In the small village of Tremolat, couched beautifully on the Dordogne near Bergerac in southwestern France, the lonely headmistress,

◀

Chabrol harks back to his first film *Le Beau Serge* (1958) in the protagonist's search for redemption in provincial France.

Helene befriends the local butcher, Popaul (Jean Yanne), at the wedding of her assistant teacher, Leon Hamel (Mario Beccara). They become good friends, but in spite of Popaul's evident interest in her, they do not become lovers—Helene has been badly burned by a disastrous end to her last relationship.

On Popaul's birthday, Helene gives him a lighter. During an excursion with her class to one of the prehistoric caves in the

"I'VE SEEN A CORPSE OR TWO—THEIR HEADS IN THE WIND, CUT IN HALF, MOUTH OPEN." POPAUL

nearby woods, she sees blood dripping from a hand on the cliffs above. She climbs up and finds the latest victim of a serial killer stabbed to death. She realizes that the dead woman is Leon's young wife and recognizes Popaul's lighter at the crime scene—but hides the evidence from the police.

When Popaul visits later, Helene is not unnaturally in a state of uneasiness. She discovers to her intense relief that he still has the lighter and instantly relaxes. Yet when he begins painting her house, one of her pupils signposts a discovery that throws the identity of the killer back into the melting pot.

After this long slow burner of a buildup, Chabrol fires up the tension for the denouement, once again demonstrating his ability to marry the relentless demands of the thriller genre with the cool introspection of the chamber piece, and sympathetic yet unflinching portraits of fascinating women. **MH**

▶
Jean Yanne as Popaul le boucher seeking possible redemption through the love of a straightlaced teacher (Stéphane Audran).

VIETATO ai minori di 18 anni

ESOTiKA EROTiKA PSiCOTiKA

un film di **RADLEY METZGER**

con **SILVANA VENTURELLI** · **ERIKA REMBERG** · **PAOLO TURCO** · **KARL OTTO ALBERTY**

musiche di **STELVIO CIPRIANI** · dialoghi di **ALBERTO CAVALLONE** · **TECHNICOLOR**

THE LICKERISH QUARTET
1970 (ITALY • U.S. • GERMANY)

Director Radley Metzger **Producer** Radley Metzger, Peter Carsten, Enrico Sabbatini **Screenplay** Michael DeForrest (story by Radley Metzger) **Cinematography** Hans Jura **Music** Stelvio Cipriani **Cast** Silvana Venturelli, Frank Wolff, Erika Remberg, Paolo Turco

For many filmgoers of a certain age, a first encounter with *The Lickerish Quartet* might have come courtesy of some soft porn played at midnight on a local cable station. Innocent teenagers would have been shocked by seeing actual sex on TV, and then curiosity aroused by the tone and color and extensive dialogue might have set in. More than anything, a few may have recognized that here was brilliant cinema. And they would be right.

The movie is complex and somewhat mysterious. A presumably fabulously wealthy couple watch a porn movie at their castle, with the woman's adult son from a previous partnership in attendance. The son, moody and in no small way a sullen brat, puts an end to it and, for his entertainment, they head into town. There they watch an odd daredevil spectacle in which they think they recognize the actress from the said movie. They invite her back to their castle and she stays the night, over which the son, mother, and stepfather enlist her in their own private fantasies through which she moves dispassionately. Preoccupied, she asks regularly, "Where is the gun?"

◄

Known as *Esotika Erotika Psicotika* in Italy, this is much more than a blue movie: this is late night screening for cineasts and academics rather than for the dodgy raincoat brigade.

The Lickerish Quartet is a surprisingly dense film; the layers are nuanced. Its action is packed with novel scenes, cleverly considered, which allow the audience plenty of thrills other than the flesh. Only sometimes is the acting a struggle, which is to be expected. Although there are plenty of actors willing to do plenty of things on camera without hesitation, actual sex acts and full male nudity tend to separate the herd.

"THE LICKERISH QUARTET *IS AN OUTRAGEOUSLY KINKY MASTERPIECE. GO [SEE IT]."* ANDY WARHOL

The Lickerish Quartet is gorgeously constructed. Metzger seems genuinely interested in exposing the mysteries of sexual desire, not merely for physical impact (that is the shock value inherent in the very possibility of depicting material that goes this far). If it weren't for several telling titillations (examples of moments when we are made suddenly aware that we are watching erotica first, film second), we might even forget that it's a piece of erotica that we're watching at all, so sincerely connected to the narrative are the scenes of actual lovemaking. Or is it lustmaking? Metzger seems to focus very much on the illogic of sexual compulsion, and from this psychological brew he activates mystery to generate intrigue. The design is big and the camera catches all of it; it is extremely deft styling preoccupied with depicting a complex psychological landscape. **GS**

► **Even the lenses lend a quality that seems at once wet-clear and opaque, misted, the product of fantasy, sexual and otherwise.**

Vice. And Versa.

Mick Jagger.   And Mick Jagger.

James Fox.   And James Fox.

See them all in a film about fantasy. And reality. Vice. And versa.

performance.

Hear Mick Jagger sing his own song "Memo From Turner."

James Fox/Mick Jagger/Anita Pallenberg/Michele Breton

Written by Donald Cammell /Directed by Donald Cammell & Nicolas Roeg/Produced by Sanford Lieberson in Technicolor
A Goodtimes Enterprises Production from Warner Bros. THIS FILM IS RATED (X) NO ONE UNDER 17 ADMITTED
Hear Mick Jagger sing "Memo From Turner" in the original sound track album on Warner Bros. Records and tapes.

PERFORMANCE 1970 (U.K.)

Director Donald Cammell, Nicolas Roeg   **Producer** Sanford Lieberson
Screenplay Donald Cammell   **Cinematography** Nicolas Roeg
Music Jack Nitzsche   **Cast** James Fox, Mick Jagger, Anita Pallenberg,
Michèle Breton, Stanley Meadows, Johnny Shannon

Legend and myth surround this decadent exploration of fantasy and reality starring a packed-with-cool Mick Jagger in his first on-screen acting role. According to one source, the preview of *Performance* to Warner Bros. executives—who had been expecting something akin to The Beatles' *A Hard Day's Night* (1964)—sparked such outrage with its explicit scenes of sex and drug taking that the company's chief executive Ken Hyman had to be persuaded not to bury the film's negatives in the ground. Despite the spade being put to one side, it still took another two years for a heavily edited version to reach the public, only to be marginalized by accusations of depravity and sadism from appalled critics.

With each passing year, a greater degree of appreciation arrives for Cammell and Roeg's seminal piece of work—its influence felt most closely in the likes of Guy Ritchie's *Lock, Stock and Two Smoking Barrels* (1998) and Tarantino's *Pulp Fiction* (1994). The first half hour is straight gangster flick, ensconced in London's criminal underworld with James Fox as Chas, an enforcer for a protection racket who takes to his job with calculated fury. At that time Fox was the bright young star of

◀

A groundbreaking moment in British cinema, the movie mixed innovative cut-up techniques, and had an experimental soundtrack with one of the first ever Moog synthesizers and *Memo for Turner*, a precursor of MTV-style music videos.

British cinema, renowned for playing upper-class characters. He seemed an unlikely choice to perform the role of a violent, psychopathic cockney, but further legend would have us believe he immersed himself among real criminals to perfect his violent persona. Whatever the truth may be, it worked.

After ignoring orders from his boss, Johnny Flowers (Johnny Shannon), Chas has to lay low while waiting to escape abroad,

"THE ONLY PERFORMANCE . . . THAT MAKES IT ALL THE WAY, IS THE ONE THAT ACHIEVES MADNESS." TURNER

renting a basement room in a house belonging to Turner (Mick Jagger), a fading rock star trying to rediscover his mojo. Things start to take a turn for the weird as Turner indulges in a ménage à trois with Pherber (Anita Pallenberg) and Lucy (Michèle Breton) while devouring lots of class A drugs, dragging a clearly spooked Chas into their bohemian world by tricking him into feasting on a magic mushroom. The story goes that Jagger and Pallenberg really did slip Fox a tab of acid for the shoot, while the explicit sex scenes were not faked—much to the frustration of Pallenberg's partner of the time, Keith Richards, who had to be kept away from the set—adding a controversial degree of vérité to the kaleidoscopic madness.

Critics today prefer to judge *Performance* as a classic moment in British cinema, perfectly capturing the late 1960s *zeitgeist* without sinking into parody. **SG**

▶

Mick Jagger plays up the confusion created by Roeg's clever use of shadow and flickering candlelight to distort his character. Identities are exchanged with wigs, costumes, and mirrors.

This is Harold
Fully equipped to deal with life.

This is Maude
Harold's girlfriend.

Paramount Pictures Presents

Harold and Maude

Starring

Ruth Gordon   Bud Cort

Co-starring
VIVIAN PICKLES   CYRIL CUSACK   CHARLES TYNER   ELLEN GEER
Produced by COLIN HIGGINS and CHARLES B. MULVEHILL
Executive Producer MILDRED LEWIS   Written by COLIN HIGGINS
Directed by HAL ASHBY   Songs by CAT STEVENS
Colour by TECHNICOLOR®
 A Paramount Picture Distributed by Cinema International Corporation

HAROLD AND MAUDE 1971 (U.S.)

Director Hal Ashby **Producer** Colin Higgins, Charles Mulvehill, Mildred Lewis
Screenplay Colin Higgins **Cinematography** John Alonzo **Music** Cat Stevens
Cast Bud Cort, Ruth Gordon, Vivian Pickles, Cyril Cusack, Charles Tyner, Ellen Geer,
Eric Christmas, G. Wood, Judy Engels, Shari Summers, Susan Madigan

Harold and Maude has a terrific cult reputation as one of the blackest of black comedies. A preppy young heir to a fortune, Harold (Bud Cort), obsessed with funerals, suicide, and death (all varieties), consistently puts off all the debs his mother (Vivian Pickles) churns out for him through his bizarre antics. Then he meets Maude (Ruth Gordon), a woman more than sixty years his senior, and they begin one of the oddest, yet most affecting, screen romances Hollywood's ever come up with. If you saw Michelle Obama's mother on TV recently, think *great grandmother*—and then some. Ashby intended to film a scene of Harold and Maude making love, but Paramount dismissed it in a rare attack of good taste. The movie's all the better for flouting conventions so thoroughly and for its mordant wit.

Harold defies the combined efforts of psychiatrist (G. Wood), priest (Eric Christmas), and general (Charles Tyner), a Buñuelian trio if ever there was one—not to mention his despairing socialite mother—to put him on the straight and narrow. (In the scenes between Harold and the psychiatrist, both wear matching clothes, down to the ties and handkerchiefs.) Meanwhile, Maude continues on her blithe way, dispensing a mixture of anarchy

◀
Deservedly a cult movie for its black humor and, seemingly, the epitome of bad taste (but told ever so engagingly).

and cracker-barrel philosophy with the charming insouciance of the aging. Cort and Gordon are both magnificent in the title roles—in some ways, Cort's career never recovered from his initial vast success. For Gordon, it was a wonderful swan song, although Cort first wanted Swedish legend Greta Garbo to play Maude. Others considered included English thespian Dames Peggy Ashcroft, Gladys Cooper, and Edith Evans.

"A LOT OF PEOPLE ENJOY BEING DEAD. THEY'RE NOT DEAD, REALLY. THEY'RE JUST BACKING AWAY FROM LIFE." MAUDE

Cort was aware of the dangers. When considering the role of Harold (up against Elton John, among others), he asked his *M.A.S.H.* and *Brewster McCloud* mentor director Robert Altman's opinion. Altman cautioned the rising star that he might find himself forever typecast. Cort took it, but when offered the part of Billy Bibbit in *One Flew Over The Cuckoo's Nest* (1975), he turned it down, holding out for the role of McMurphy. No dice: Oscar for Nicholson. Cort's next film wasn't until 1977.

As an aside for those interested in the props as much as the plot, the hearse Harold originally drives is a 1959 Cadillac Superior three-way model, one of the most sought-after hearses among collectors today, but when the movie was made it was an undesirable gas guzzler. And in all the shots of Gordon driving the hearse, it's being towed because she'd never learned how to drive. **MH**

► Harold (Bud Cort) enjoys committing a series of fake suicides in this decidely dark-humored parlor game.

"two-lane blacktop"

STARRING

James Taylor • Warren Oates
Laurie Bird • Dennis Wilson

 Screenplay by RUDOLPH WURLITZER and WILL CORRY • Story by WILL CORRY • Directed by MONTE HELLMAN • Produced by MICHAEL S. LAUGHLIN
A MICHAEL S. LAUGHLIN PRODUCTION • DISTRIBUTED BY CINEMA INTERNATIONAL CORPORATION • A UNIVERSAL PICTURE • TECHNICOLOR •

TWO-LANE BLACKTOP 1971 (U.S.)

Director Monte Hellman **Producer** Michael S. Laughlin **Screenplay** Rudolph
Wurlitzer, Will Corry **Cinematography** Jack Deerson **Music** Billy James (uncredited)
Cast James Taylor, Warren Oates, Laurie Bird, Dennis Wilson, David Drake,
Richard Ruth, Rudolph Wurlitzer, Harry Dean Stanton

Heard in milliseconds, the sound of a V-8 engine presents a
growl and a roar, a cough and a murmur. The crankshaft purrs
as eight metal pistons ram through their thousands of
revolutions a minute, belching petroleum blood into black fans
of exhaust. It's a gear head's fantasy in so many moving parts
that send cars and trucks racing across asphalt prairies in the
illusion of earthbound flight.

Built upon the V-8 muscle cars then popular on American
roads, *Two-Lane Blacktop* is a 1971 road movie directed by
Monte Hellman. Its dramatic arc sketches the paths of
inexpressive men, all but cut off from the mainstay of a
changing world. Its feel and attraction, however, is all
testosterone, as expressed through a pair of cars that symbolize
their drivers, inasmuch as cars are often more important to
people than any expression of an inner life not nearly as vivid as
the growl of a V-8 engine.

Starring singer-songwriter James Taylor, an emerging folk
superstar, Beach Boys drummer Dennis Wilson, longtime
character actor Warren Oates, and the debut of Laurie Bird,
soon to be Hellman's girlfriend, the film concerns the

◄

**The classic road
movie where
dialogue is
at a minimum,
and edits rely
on long takes
and thoughtful
observation. Kris
Kristofferson's
version of
"Me and Bobby
McGee" fuels the
soundtrack, but
the point of the
film is watching
those muscle cars.**

aimlessness of unplanned discovery. Sometimes cited as the inspiration for the *Cannonball Run*, a cross-country race through America and a Burt Reynolds vehicle from 1981, *Esquire* magazine declared *Two-Lane Blacktop* movie of the year, although Universal executives hated the film and pulled marketing support to help ensure a commercial failure. But this road movie struck a chord despite very little reliance on classic

"YOU GUYS AREN'T LIKE THE ZODIAC KILLERS OR ANYTHING?" *GIRL* "NOPE. JUST PASSIN' THROUGH." *MECHANIC*

rock, a mainstay of similar pictures like *Easy Rider* (1969), which is especially remarkable in light of the participation of musician-actors Taylor and Wilson, who contributed no music at all.

The film traces Driver (Taylor) and Mechanic (Wilson), who live in their '55 Chevy 150 and challenge townies to race wherever they go. They journey east along Route 66 from Needles, California, and pick up a hitchhiking Girl (Bird) before they bump into another drag racer, GTO (Oates), who drives a 1970 Pontiac GTO Judge. He challenges them to a cross-country race to Washington, D.C., pink slips on the line, and so sets in motion a road movie through the American midwest and southeast. As per many movies of the period, the nostalgic journey is characterized by male competition, female chattel, and the mourning for lost icons, in this case Route 66 just before the Interstate Highway System opened up the route. **GC-Q**

► The American dream transferred from *Easy Rider's* two-wheel choppers to the iconic '55 V-8 Chevy, with Driver (Taylor) and Mechanic (Wilson) and their pickup Girl (Bird).

Jess Franco's
Lesbos
Soledad Miranda
Ewa Stroemberg
Heidrun Kussin
Dennis Price
Victor Feldmann
Michael Berling
Paul Mueller
Musik:Manfred Hubler & Siegfried Schwab

VAMPYROS LESBOS 1971 (WEST GERMANY • SPAIN)

Director Jesus Franco   **Producer** Artur Brauner   **Screenplay** Jaime Chávarri
Cinematography Manuel Merino   **Music** Jesus Franco, Manfred Hübler, Siegfried
Schwab   **Cast** Soledad Miranda, Ewa Strömberg, Dennis Price, Heidrun Kussin,
Michael Berling, Jesus Franco, Andris Monales, Paul Muller

With almost 200 films to his name, Jesus (Jess) Franco is one of
the most important directors of cult and exploitation cinema.
Vampyros Lesbos, his 1971 version of the vampire mythos, owes
more to the Sapphic vampires of Sheridan Le Fanu's *Camilla*
(1872) than Bram Stoker's *Dracula,* although it is loosely based
on Stoker's short story *Dracula's Guest* (1914).

Told in a nonlinear fashion, *Vampyros Lesbos* focuses on the
obsession and desire of a young woman, Linda (Ewa Strömberg),
for the beautiful and captivating female vampire, Countess
Nadine Carody (Soledad Miranda), who she meets when she is
sent by her firm, Simpson & Simpson, to sort out the Countess's
estate. In this revision of the Dracula myth, the paternal vampire
hunter—here Dr. Seward (Dennis Price)—seeks to join rather
than defeat the vampire, while Nadine only takes beautiful
women as her prey. However, despite the homoerotic overtones,
the film reasserts heterosexuality with Linda eventually choosing
her lover, Omar (Andris Monales), over the Sapphic pleasures
offered by the Countess. The Countess is not a conventional
vampire. When we first meet her in a fevered dream recounted
by Linda to Dr. Steiner (Paul Muller) , she is an exotic dancer in

◄

**Like a dream told
by a deranged
madman, this
is a classic of cult
cinema and a high
point in the prolific
career of Franco.
Despite its shlock
title, the movie was
an international
success when
released.**

a nightclub in Istanbul, whose sensual dance includes a section playing with her reflection in a mirror. The Countess is not vulnerable to sunlight, a she lives in a modern villa rather than Gothic ruins, and it is a stake through the head rather than the heart that finally defeats her.

The sets and costumes are meticulously designed: carefully placed fishing nets in the villa are a modern substitute for the

"HEAVING FLESH, WRITHING SCORPIONS, AND FLUTTERING BUTTERFLIES." TOTAL FILM

spiderwebs typically found in Dracula's castle; shots of a floating red kite are used as a metaphorical signifier of female desire; and drops of blood on panes of glass metonymically signal danger. Repeated insets of a scorpion and a butterfly are used artfully to mirror the changing relationship between the Countess and Linda, predator and prey. While the addition of a *giallo*-esque serial killer, Memmet (played with aplomb by Franco), who tortures and kills young women, might seem superfluous to the plot, it adds to the feverish and hallucinatory landscape against which this gender inversion of Dracula is played out. The experimental psychedelic soundtrack to the film by Manfred Hübler and Siegfried Schwab adds impact to the surreal imagery and sexual pathology central to this retelling of the *Dracula* myth. **CB**

▶
The camera certainly loved both the vampire, Countess Nadine Carody (Soledad Miranda), and her chosen prey, Linda (Ewa Strömberg).

VANISHING POINT 1971 (U.S.)

Director Richard C. Sarafian   **Producer** Norman Spencer   **Screenplay** Guillermo Cain (story by Malcolm Hart)   **Cinematography** John A. Alonzo   **Music** Jimmy Bowen   **Cast** Barry Newman, Cleavon Little, Dean Jagger, Victoria Medlin, Paul Koslo, Bob Donner, Karl Swenson, Severn Darden

Unmistakably of its time, this counterculture, high-speed car chase across the American southwest exposes extreme ideals of personal freedom in a post-Woodstock United States. Heavily laden with symbolism and often interpreted as an existentialist movie, *Vanishing Point* draws upon a starkly basic plot in which Barry Newman's car delivery driver, enigmatically known only as Kowalski, places a bet that he can drive from Denver to San Francisco in fifteen hours. Without sleep and pumped full of Benzedrine, Kowalski takes to the open road; he is a man driven by the need for speed to control his inner demons.

Driving a superfast 1970 white Dodge Challenger, Kowalski's improbable mission is rendered obsolete after attracting the attention of two motorcycle cops, running one off the road. His aim now is to stay free from the clutches of the law, a cause taken up by the blind D.J., Super Soul (Cleavon Little) at K.O.W. Radio. Able to intercept police frequency reports, Super Soul begins communicating with Kowalski on air, offering messages of support for a man he exuberantly describes as "the last American hero." The director, Richard C. Sarafian, had originally cast Gene Hackman as Kowalski, but the relatively unknown

◄

Reminiscent of the antiauthoritarian road movie, *Easy Rider* (1969), tragedy also awaits our hero, Kowalski (Barry Newman). Is he on an extended suicide drive? Or does he believe the sliver of light in the bulldozer's barrier offers a way through?

Newman was preferred by studio executive Richard Zanuck. He brings a world-weary demeanor to a character that, as we discover through a series of flashback scenes piecing his life story together, has been chewed up and spat out by the system. Kowalski was wounded in Vietnam, winning the Medal of Honor for bravery in battle, and then worked as a detective in the San Diego police force before being dishonorably

> ## "THE QUESTION IS NOT WHEN'S HE GONNA STOP, BUT WHO IS GONNA STOP HIM." *SUPER SOUL*

discharged—a flashback alluding that this was linked to once preventing a fellow cop from indecently assaulting a young girl. Kowalski is a man of conscience marginalized by society, forced to exist on the fringes after rejection by the establishment he once so dutifully served. He has lost everything he once held dear, including a beautiful lover drowned while surfing; what's left is the car and all the freedom that allows.

If the car is the real star, then John A. Alonzo's breathtaking cinematography runs it a very close second. Sweeping panoramic shots effortlessly capture the American west in all its unspoiled majestic glory, interspersed with hypnotic car chases through desert and mountains. The film certainly left an impression on Quentin Tarantino; his faux-exploitation movie *Death Proof* practically fawns in deference to *Vanishing Point*— right down to using a replica of Kowalski's Dodge. **SG**

▶
Naked girl on a motorbike—the fallback of choice for a director seeking an existentialist twist.

SERGE SILBERMAN présente

le charme discret
de la bourgeoisie

avec par ordre
d'entrée en scène
FERNANDO REY
PAUL FRANKEUR
DELPHINE SEYRIG
BULLE OGIER
STEPHANE AUDRAN
JEAN-PIERRE CASSEL
JULIEN BERTHEAU
MILENA VUKOTIC
MARIA GABRIELLA MAIONE
CLAUDE PIEPLU
MUNI
FRANÇOIS MAISTRE
PIERRE MAGUELON
MAXENCE MAILFORT

scénario de
LUIS BUNUEL
avec la collaboration de
JEAN-CLAUDE CARRIERE

décors de
PIERRE GUFFROY
Directeur de la Photographie
EDMOND RICHARD
Directeur de la Production
ULLY PICKARD
un film produit par
SERGE SILBERMAN
PANAVISION SPHERIQUE
EASTMANCOLOR
Distribué par 20th Century Fox

UNE PRODUCTION
GREENWICH FILM PRODUCTION
© COPYRIGHT MCMLXXII

UN FILM DE LUIS BUNUEL

THE DISCREET CHARM
OF THE BOURGEOISIE 1972 (FRANCE • SPAIN)

Director Luis Buñuel **Producer** Serge Silberman **Screenplay** Luis Buñuel, Jean-Claude Carrière **Cinematography** Edmond Richard **Music** Luis Buñuel, Jacques Carrere **Cast** Fernando Rey, Delphine Seyrig, Bulle Ogier, Stéphane Audran, Paul Frankeur, Jean-Pierre Cassel, Julien Bertheau, Milena Vukotic, Muni, Michel Piccoli, Claude Piéplu

One of the most individual directors in movie history, Luis Buñuel must have appreciated the jest life played on him by showering awards as he entered his forty-fifth year of filmmaking: he'd been a permanent thorn in the establishment's side since making *Un Chien Andalou* (1928) with surrealist artist, Salvador Dalí. Now, as he was beginning to wind down—there were only two more films, *The Phantom of Liberty* (1974) and *That Obscure Object of Desire* (1977) before his death in 1983— the film establishment, at least, embraced him. His belief in the arbitrary, dreamlike quality of life was vindicated. The film won the Oscar for Best Foreign Film.

Although Buñuel preferred to be allusive, he wasn't afraid to be direct, writing *Los Olvidados* (1950), a fiery neo-documentary onslaught on those responsible for the dreadful social conditions prevailing in Mexico at that time. His normal style, however, was to launch a withering dissection of more general social evils with surgical precision, concentrating on the vices of the Church, the Army, the aristocracy, and the bourgeoisie.

◄

Surrealist director Buñuel ridicules the middle classes mercilessly in this bizarre tale of thwarted diners.

It's not quite true that plot isn't important for Buñuel—we find snatches of one from time to time—but it's fair to say he was more interested in exploring themes based around central connecting ideas. In *The Exterminating Angel* (1962), he shows the rapid collapse of social mores among the wealthy when they are prevented by inexplicable forces from leaving their Madrid party mansion. Interspersed with terrorist outrages

"WE ARE NOT AGAINST THE STUDENTS, BUT WHAT CAN YOU DO WITH A ROOM FULL OF FLIES?" *DON RAFAEL ACOSTA*

(a leitmotif of his 1970s films), *The Discreet Charm of the Bourgeoisie* (*Le Charme Discret de la Bourgeoisie*) offers us the joys attendant on a group of six outwardly respectable bourgeois and their constantly thwarted attempts to dine together. It's ever-shifting, a spiral of dreams within dreams within dreams—the interruptions becoming more surreal as the movie develops. Magnificently served by his central six—feckless, beautiful women Delphine Seyrig, Stéphane Audran, and Bulle Ogier counterpointing corrupt, charming men Fernando Rey, Jean-Pierre Cassel, and Paul Frankeur—Buñuel also draws fine performances from his regular troupe of supporting actors, such as Milena Vukotic and Julien Bertheau. And the scene where a curtain is drawn back to reveal to the diners' total disorientation that they are on stage with lights, a prompter, and an audience is a high point in surreal cinema. **MH**

►

Buñuel successfully shocks and bemuses his audience with unexpected surreal scenes, as seen here with Bulle Ogier.

THE HARDER THEY COME 1972 (JAMAICA)

Director Perry Henzell **Producer** Perry Henzell, Jeff Scheftel **Screenplay** Perry Henzell, Trevor D. Rhone **Cinematography** Peter Jessop, David McDonald, Franklyn St. Juste **Music** Jimmy Cliff, Desmond Dekker, The Slickers **Cast** Jimmy Cliff, Janet Bartley, Carl Bradshaw, Ras Daniel Hartman, Basil Keane, Bob Charlton

A major production in terms of Caribbean culture, *The Harder They Come* was the first feature-length Jamaican film, and the movie that has been credited with popularizing reggae. This low-budget production was made at a time when the American blaxploitation genre, or black action film, was having a marked impact on independent filmmaking with gritty urban stories of crime, corruption, gangsters, and violence. Within this wave of black consciousness, *The Harder They Come* drew on local culture and the Jamaican popular figure of the rebel hero, and incorporated scenes of poverty and class struggle to establish what can be viewed as a social problem film.

Its cult status was initially set on the circuit of midnight film screenings in the United States, where it became a staple of this alternative form of film exhibition. In contrast, in Jamaica, the film was politicized and briefly banned under the late administration of Hugh Shearer, with the argument that it could incite delinquent behavior. The film's cult status is largely due to its music. Like many blaxploitation films, *The Harder They Come* presents a distinctive musical identity through a score of contemporary sounds. Such is *The Harder They Come*'s musical

◄
A rich tapestry of Jamaican shanty town life buoyed by an uplifting reggae soundtrack.

importance that over the years the film has been preceded by its soundtrack, which includes performances from reggae legend Desmond Dekker, among others. Famously, the soundtrack also features four original songs by Jimmy Cliff: "Many Rivers to Cross," "You Can Get it if You Really Want," "The Harder They Come," and "Sitting in Limbo." An iconic reggae musician, a young Cliff takes the lead role in the film as Ivan

"THE HARDER THEY COME, THE HARDER THEY FALL, ONE AND ALL."

JIMMY CLIFF, FROM THE TITLE SONG

Martin, a man with few funds who travels from the country to the Jamaican capital, Kingston, with a hope of breaking into the record industry. He makes a record but is exploited by a corrupt record producer, and then turns to drug dealing, shoots a policeman, and becomes a fugitive from the law.

It's based on the true story of Ivanhoe "Rhygin" Martin, a criminal of the Jamaican ghettos who was in a gunfight with police in 1948 that left two people dead. Ivanhoe was obsessed with the Wild West and cowboys and was eventually killed by a police marksman, but not before his escapades had dominated the local media and had given this antihero an aura of invincibility. Director Perry Henzell, a maker of commercials, also wrote the screenplay with subtitles to help understand the Jamaican patois. He imbues a roughness and amateurishness to the film, which has become part of its cult appeal. **IC**

► Jimmy Cliff as country boy adrift in Kingston who kills a cop involved in the ganja trade.

PINK FLAMINGOS 1972 (U.S.)

Director John Waters **Producer** John Waters **Screenplay** John Waters
Cinematography John Waters **Music** John Waters **Cast** John Waters,
Divine, Mink Stole, Edith Massey, David Lochary, Mary Vivian Pearce, Danny
Mills, Cookie Mueller, Paul Swift

While Hollywood continued to churn out big-budget art films under the aegis of United Artists and its followers, a new movement was taking hold in America of which the impact would be felt across the cultural spectrum for some years to come. It could be that the first great volley of the real American "indie" began with John Waters's still shocking *Pink Flamingos*.

Babs Johnson (played to the somewhat monotone hilt by Waters regular Divine) is the head of the family who currently holds the title of "The Filthiest People Alive." But not all is well in Baltimore: the Marbles (Mink Stole and David Lochary), operators of a white-slave baby-making operation, are contesting the title. *Pink Flamingos* depicts the epic bad taste showdown between these two families.

There are some notable standouts in this battle, but few assaults seem either more perfect or more amusing than Babs Johnson and her son Crackers salivating all over their rivals' house, supported by some sensationally deadpan lines. Having finally won, Babs and Crackers try the Marbles in an outdoor Kangaroo Court and execute them, a shocking finale of which the antiestablishment ethos could hardly be dared

◄

Pink Flamingos **is a prototypical midnight movie, and definitely among the first to be marketed as such. Its transgressions are legion: the queerness, the filth, the overall bad taste.**

in our more cautious times; one wonders if the director himself would dare repeat a movie ending this severe.

Pink Flamingos is very much a film borne of a scene that has existed in isolation: its humor is obscure, it's full of inside jokes, and everything is personal. The language of the film is entirely unique and owes its idiosyncrasies to the company. It is played by a cast almost utterly without skill—nothing schooled in

"MAMA, NOBODY SENDS YOU A TURD AND EXPECTS TO LIVE. NOBODY!"

CRACKERS

sight, no smear of professionalism to strain credibility. The defiant placement of *Pink Flamingos* in irrelevant Baltimore might also be an early instance of hometown art, ignoring the prominence of New York and L.A., and in this context *Pink Flamingos* reads almost as a manifesto against those polished, austere, and often bogus auteur American films of the art house scene. But that scene was always an approximation of something well honed and European, and not native to American spirit as *Pink Flamingos* can be said to be: aggressive, flamboyant, and in your face, John Waters might very well have rescued American cinema for America.

Pink Flamingos cemented its status as an era-defining moment of exuberant, excessive, pure, homemade cinema. It is definitely, defiantly democratic: one has the sense almost that *Pink Flamingos* had to be made. **GS**

► **Divine is the filthiest person alive as this scene attests. Much of Waters's later work has not come close to matching it in vitality and freshness.**

SUPER FLY 1972 (U.S.)

Director Gordon Parks, Jr. **Producer** Sig Shore **Screenplay** Phillip Fenty
Cinematography James Signorelli **Music** Curtis Mayfield **Cast** Ron O'Neal,
Carl Lee, Sheila Frazier, Julius Harris, Charles MacGregor, Nate Adams, Polly Niles,
Yvonne Delaine, Henry Shapiro, K. C., James G. Robinson, Make Bray

Melvin Van Peebles wrote, directed, produced, and starred in *Sweet Sweetback's Baadasssss Song;* he also funded it and in the spring of 1971 began promoting the film. His purpose was to circumvent the Hollywood distribution system and offer a story made by, and for, black people. His story of a sex worker-turned-revolutionary who confounds "the Man" was a great success among minority spectators. Its imagery and themes helped frame a subsequent wave of Hollywood action films dubbed "blaxploitation" that rooted to Gordon Parks, Sr.'s studio movie, *Shaft*, beginning in the summer of 1971. One year later, Parks's son, Gordon Parks, Jr. directed his own seminal blaxploitation film, *Super Fly*, which was partly financed by Parks, Sr.

As in all blaxploitation movies, *Super Fly* critiques a white mainstream society in the midst of post-Civil Rights transitions. It shows corruption within the police force and humanizes inner city people, but especially inner city black criminals as a subtle, and commercially calculated, response to the endemic poverty and limited opportunity for black Americans in the early 1970s.

◄

Cocaine dealer Priest (Ron O'Neal) does truly embody "super fly" style with that fedora, those sideburns, and that turtleneck sweater so prominent on the poster.

Curtis Mayfield, a newly turned solo artist after his star-making turn with The Impressions, supplied the soundtrack and top-forty hooks in such songs as "Freddie's Dead" and the title track. A customized 1971 Cadillac Eldorado features large, too, and became iconic as the basis of later pimp mobiles with its unique color and ornaments, and then there are the flamboyant costumes of drug lords and pimps, dressing

"NOTHING, NOTHING BETTER HAPPEN TO ONE HAIR ON MY GORGEOUS HEAD. CAN YOU DIG IT?" *PRIEST*

up blaxploitation with a sensual balance of attitude and style. Movie critics were quick to disparage the production, however, because it centers on drug peddling and avoids answering the question of whether the film uplifts, or helps denigrate, black America.

As the film opens, Youngblood Priest (Ron O'Neal) is on his way to an uptown "meet" when he's mugged by two junkies. Realizing he's culpable in this crime of personal violence, for Priest is a cocaine dealer, he decides to leave "the life" after one last huge sale to live happily on the profits for the rest of his days. He wants out of the drug trade because he feels guilty for his participation in the high-stakes game of addiction. But this doesn't keep him from selling a million dollars worth of coke in Harlem, a scene that is brilliantly synched across photo montage to Mayfield's "Pusherman." **GC-Q**

▶
Priest (O'Neal) is the dealer with a conscience, but that doesn't prohibit him from playing kickbacks—taking cops against his underworld contacts.

SISTERS 1973 (U.S.)

Director Brian De Palma **Producer** Edward R. Pressman, Lynn Pressman
Screenplay Brian De Palma, Louis Rose **Cinematography** Gregory Sandor
Music Bernard Herrmann **Cast** Margo Kidder, Jennifer Salt, Charles Durning,
Bill Finley, Lisle Wilson, Barnard Hughes, Mary Davenport, Dolph Sweet

Critics have long targeted *Sisters* as the motion picture in which
De Palma emerged as an auteur with a predilection for thrillers,
and thus as a work that marks a transformative moment in the
director's long and storied career. However, if one considers
Sisters in relation to his two previous, quasi-Godardian features,
Greetings (1968) and *Hi, Mom!* (1970), *Sisters* can be understood
as less of a "turning point" in the director's oeuvre, and as more
of an important yet logical step in a career that explores the
voyeuristic drive as a primary element of moviemaking.

Furthermore, *Sisters* disallows viewers from settling into a
comfort zone in which they can embrace a tonal consistency or
anticipate the narrative's trajectory. Humorous moments
conflict with, and at times accompany, visceral shocks, a trait
that can be found throughout some of De Palma's more recent
and better known works like *Blow Out* (1981), *Scarface* (1983),
Body Double (1984), and *The Untouchables* (1987). In short, for a
director whose career arc reveals an obsession with the
complex relationships that exist between the filmmaker, the
film, and the audience, *Sisters* is an essential component in an
increasingly extensive and diverse filmography.

◄

**In this movie, De
Palma sealed his
style as a director
who seduces his
audience
voyeuristically into
a psychological
and emotional
investment
with the often
nightmarish events
transpiring on
the screen.**

Sisters' plot builds from the tensions that develop when a reporter named Grace Collier (Jennifer Salt) begins to investigate a murder that she suspects may have been committed by Dominique Breton. There is, however, one crucial, uncanny catch: Dominique is dead, having perished on the operating table a year earlier while being separated from her conjoined twin, Danielle, who is now a beautiful model.

"DID YOU KNOW THAT GERMS CAN COME THROUGH THE WIRES? IT'S A GOOD WAY TO GET SICK." CRAZY WOMAN

What follows is a complex series of unexpected twists and unnerving turns that explore the power invested within the act of spectatorship (the film opens with a hidden camera program called Peeping Toms, a murder is witnessed through a window, and a character remembers events experienced by an entirely different person). Additionally, *Sisters* examines the politics of identity. Danielle— once physically linked with the deceased Dominique—suffers from multiple personality disorder. If components of this narrative seem like derivations of Hitchcock films, such as *Rear Window* (1954) and *Psycho* (1960)—the use of split screen and the distinctive musical compositions of Bernard Hermann, who scored several of Hitchcock's masterpieces—it is because such cinematic echoes are intentional and have become defining elements of De Palma's style. **JMcR**

► **Reporter Grace (Jennifer Salt) finds that her investigation is steadily compromising the integrity of her own psyche.**

Was one man's life worth 1 million dollars and the death of 21 men?

SAM PECKINPAH'S

"BRING ME THE HEAD OF ALFREDO GARCIA"

A MARTIN BAUM—SAM PECKINPAH PRODUCTION

WARREN OATES · ISELA VEGA in "BRING ME THE HEAD OF ALFREDO GARCIA"

Produced by MARTIN BAUM · Executive Producer HELMUT DANTINE · Screenplay by GORDON T DAWSON and SAM PECKINPAH · Story by FRANK KOWALSKI and SAM PECKINPAH

Music Composed and Arranged by JERRY FIELDING · Directed by SAM PECKINPAH · COLOR · United Artists

BRING ME THE HEAD OF ALFREDO GARCIA 1974 (U.S.)

Director Sam Peckinpah **Producer** Martin Baum **Screenplay** Sam Peckinpah,
Gordon Dawson **Cinematography** Alex Phillips Jr. **Music** Jerry Fielding
Cast Warren Oates, Isela Vega, Robert Webber, Gig Young, Helmut Dantine,
Kris Kristofferson, Emilio Fernández, Chano Urueta, Don Levy

Sam Peckinpah was no stranger to controversy—indeed his career was bathed in the stuff—but with the release of *Alfredo Garcia* in 1974, controversy turned into outright revulsion with this unflinchingly bleak parable of greed and revenge. It's a film that pounds with nihilistic fury and drips with grimy, unsentimental characters, yet it contains moments of profound poetry, jet black humor, and, lurking somewhere beneath the shower of bullets and lacerating violence, a love story.

This unique film begins with a deceptively serene image of a young pregnant woman, basking in the sun by a river's edge. The idyllic scene is brutally disrupted by two gunmen who march the young girl before her father, El Jefe, a rich Mexican warlord. The daughter is tortured, revealing the father's identity to be that of Alfredo Garcia, a man whom El Jefe claimed "was like a son to me." Shamed and consumed by rage, El Jefe offers $1 million for anyone who can deliver Alfredo's head, a bounty that leads two hitmen (Gig Young and Robert Webber) into a Mexico City bar, where they encounter the lowlife, washed-up,

◄

Alfredo Garcia was an intensely personal film for Peckinpah; it is his one and only movie made without compromise and is as defiantly anti-Hollywood as they come.

gringo alcoholic piano player, Bennie. Warren Oates reportedly based Bennie on Peckinpah—even donning the director's clothes and sunglasses while on-screen—and despite his countless flaws, Bennie's emotional vulnerability and relentless suffering invokes great sympathy from the audience.

Bennie learns from his prostitute lover, Elita, who had been having an affair with Alfredo, that he has recently died in a car

"THERE AIN'T NOTHING SACRED ABOUT A HOLE IN THE GROUND OR THE MAN THAT'S IN IT." BENNIE

crash. Despite the hurt that this confession brings, Bennie now sees salvation in Alfredo as a means to a better life. When he takes up the derisory reward of $10,000 from the two hitmen to find Alfredo's head, he defiantly responds to being labeled a loser by another bounty hunter with "nobody loses all the time." But this is a Peckinpah flick—and nobody wins in Sam's cruel world.

On a road trip Bennie confesses to Elita his plans to find Alfredo's grave; she begs him to return home and start a new life together. He won't allow it, triggering a Jacobean tragedy with death befalling almost everyone Bennie comes into contact with, including Elita herself, who is gruesomely buried alive in Alfredo's grave. Consumed by guilt at his own greed that had blinded him to the unconditional love he once had, Bennie unleashes his fury in a deranged killing spree. **SG**

▶
A dark humor engulfs the film as Bennie (Oates) befriends Alfredo's decomposing, fly-infested head, chatting to him all the way to the denouement.

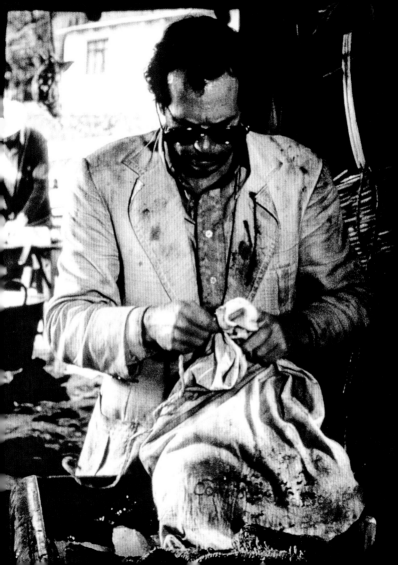

FEAR EATS THE SOUL 1974 (GERMANY)

Director Rainer Werner Fassbinder **Producer** Rainer Werner Fassbinder
Screenplay Rainer Werner Fassbinder **Cinematography** Rainer Werner Fassbinder
Music Rainer Werner Fassbinder **Cast** Brigitte Mira, El Hedi ben Salem,
Barbara Valentin, Irm Hermann

Rainer Werner Fassbinder was one of the leading figures of the *Neuer Deutscher Film* (New German Cinema) movement of the 1970s. Influenced by the French New Wave, from the end of the 1960s this new generation of directors emerged with a highly personalized vision of modern Germany, sparking a renaissance in the nation's cinema. Fassbinder was a deeply complex figure. Almost unfeasibly prolific in a professional career that lasted barely fifteen years, he completed forty feature-length films as well as numerous stage productions, TV series, and radio plays. Moreover, he routinely took on every imaginable role: not *merely* writer, producer, and director, but actor, cameraman, composer, designer, editor, and even theater manager.

It's almost impossible to dissociate Fassbinder's work from his personal life. His filmmaking took place within a closed social circle. Blurring private and professional life, family, friends, and lovers invariably appeared in his films. He formed close emotional—often sexual—ties within his surrogate "family," but heavy drug use and a wild, self-destructive promiscuity often resulted in abuse or violence. Invariably entangled in multiple relationships, while openly homosexual, he often

◄
The two lead roles are played by Mira and Salem with heartbreaking poignancy as their need to be accepted by their own friends and families begins to corrupt their bond.

formed deeply intense liaisons with women in his group. In 1970 he even married Ingrid Caven, one of his actresses. Brutish tendencies aside, his films were often tender affairs, exhibiting deep sensitivity to social outsiders, a hatred of institutionalized violence, and German bourgeois society.

In 1971, Fassbinder fell in love with El Hedi ben Salem, a Moroccan Berber. Salem quickly found himself on-screen,

"RAINER WAS A HOMOSEXUAL WHO ALSO NEEDED A WOMAN. IT'S THAT SIMPLE . . . THAT COMPLEX." *INGRID CAVAN (RAINER'S WIFE)*

eventually cast as the lead in *Fear Eats The Soul* (*Angst essen Seele auf*). Ali (Salem) is a Moroccan "Gastarbeiter" in his thirties who strikes up an unlikely friendship with a sixty-year-old cleaner, Emmi (Brigitte Mira). Facing discrimination at every turn, Ali's life is a tough one; when they decide to marry, Emmi finds *herself* shunned by her family and friends. Craving their acceptance, she begins to make racial slurs about him in public. But when she visits him at work, he pretends to his colleagues that he doesn't know her—and they all openly mock her age.

▶
Brigitte Mira in a doomed love affair with an Arab half her age exposing the hypocrisy of modern West Germany's middle classes.

One influence on *Fear Eats The Soul* is the 1955 Douglas Sirk melodrama *Life And All That Heaven Allows*. In a direct homage, we see Emmi's son kicking in the TV after discovering his mother has married an Arab. But unlike Sirk's oeuvre, there is nothing overblown about this film. Tragically, a lethal combination of sleeping pills and cocaine took Fassbinder's life in 1982. **TB**

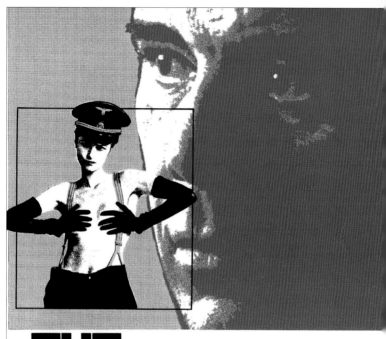

THE NIGHT PORTER x

JOSEPH E. LEVINE presents for ITAL NOLEGGIO CINEMATOGRAFICO
The ROBERT GORDON EDWARDS / ESA DE SIMONE Production of
A Film by LILIANA CAVANI starring DIRK BOGARDE · CHARLOTTE RAMPLING in"THE NIGHT PORTER", with PHILIPPE LER
and with GABRIELE FERZETTI in the role of 'Hans' · Screenplay by LILIANA CAVANI and ITALO MOSCATI
Produced by ROBERT GORDON EDWARDS for Lotar Film s.r.l. · Directed by LILIANA CAVANI
TECHNICOLOR* AN AVCO EMBASSY RELEASE

THE NIGHT PORTER 1974 (U.K.)

Director Liliana Cavani **Producer** Esa De Simone, Robert Gordon Edwards
Screenplay Barbara Alberti, Liliana Cavani, Italo Moscati, Amedeo Pagani
Cinematography Alfio Contini **Music** Dirk Bogarde, Charlotte Rampling,
Philippe Leroy, Gabriele Ferzetti, Isa Miranda, Giuseppe Addobbati

Max Adolfer (Dirk Bogarde) is a self-contained and understated night porter working in an elegant Viennese hotel. The arrival of Lucia (Charlotte Rampling), the elegant wife of an American composer, reveals that Max was, in fact, an S.S. Officer at a wartime concentration camp, where she was a prisoner and seemingly an object he commandeered to satisfy his sexual desires. That she tacitly accepted her part in a kind of Faustian bargain in order to save her life is at the core of the film's narrative arc. The fact that she survives her ordeal is miraculous enough, but her reunion with Max is full of ambiguities. Despite the past—or perhaps because of it—they quickly fall back into their intense sadomasochistic relationship, each rapidly readopting the role of aggressor and submissive.

The Night Porter was extremely controversial upon release. The film was nearly banned in Italy and met critical opprobrium in the United States, where critics tended to focus on what they saw as the sadomasochistic nature of Max and Lucia's relationship. In part this lies with the salacious, exploitative way in which it was advertised, but the film endures because it is more nuanced and more complex than critics initially allowed for.

◄
Despite the salacious advertising, this is not an S&M fest but really a challenging exploration of the complex nature of good and evil, of the cost of surviving at all odds.

Lucia's relationship with Max is ambiguous in as much as it is unclear exactly what she feels toward him. Director Liliana Cavani refuses to make things easy for the audience, fudging any simple designation of tormentor or victim. Instead it is unclear whether Max is—in however twisted a fashion—in love with Lucia or simply taking pleasure in his control of her pain. For Lucia it is hard to know whether she is suffering from

"REPORTEDLY BASED PARTLY ON [CAVANI'S] OWN INTERVIEWS WITH A HOLOCAUST SURVIVOR." THE NEW YORK TIMES

a form of Stockholm syndrome or, perversely, she has genuine feelings for Max (despite the way in which they met).

Bogarde lends Max a calm but threatening air that recalls his earlier work on Joseph Losey's *The Servant* (1963), while Rampling is quietly, stoically focused as someone who finds it impossible to shake off the dangers of her past. It's not an easy film to watch, its themes of power, abuse, and dependency nestling thornily against the backdrop of the Holocaust and its aftermath. The decadence of postwar Vienna is also expertly evoked by Cavani, and notably Max still meets with a small cadre of Nazis, who gather to keep the spirit of their beliefs alive, underlining that the end of the war did not mean an end to either the ideas that drove it or the evil that made it possible. As an exploration of the dark side of human nature and desire, *The Night Porter* is undoubtedly disturbing. **RH**

► Bogarde and Rampling, who developed a lifelong friendship after working together on the film, exude an on-screen chemistry that is at once electrically charged and terrifyingly intense.

he sold his soul for rock n'roll

PHANTOM OF THE PARADISE

HARBOR PRODUCTIONS PRESENTS A PRESSMAN WILLIAMS PRODUCTION
PAUL WILLIAMS · WILLIAM FINLEY IN BRIAN DE PALMA'S PHANTOM OF THE PARADISE
CO-STARRING GEORGE MEMMOLI · HAROLD OBLONG · ARCHIE HAHN
JEFFREY COMANOR · GERRIT GRAHAM AND INTRODUCING JESSICA HARPER
EXECUTIVE PRODUCER GUSTAVE BERNE · PRODUCED BY EDWARD PRESSMAN · WRITTEN AND DIRECTED BY BRIAN DE PALMA
WORDS AND MUSIC BY PAUL WILLIAMS · COLOR BY MOVIELAB · ORIGINAL FILM SOUNDTRACK ON A&M RECORDS

PHANTOM OF THE PARADISE 1974 (U.S.)

Director Brian De Palma **Producer** Edward R. Pressman **Screenplay** Brian De Palma **Cinematography** Larry Pizer **Music** Paul Williams **Cast** William Finley, Paul Williams, Jessica Harper, Gerrit Graham, George Memmoli, Archie Hahn, Jeffrey Comanor, Peter Elbling

More decadent and perverse, and far funnier than either Ken Russell's *Tommy* (1975) or *The Rocky Horror Picture Show* (1975), Brian De Palma's *Phantom of the Paradise* is a rock opera that gives new meaning to the prefix meta. It is a musical mash-up, primarily of "Phantom of the Opera" and "Faust," in which a disfigured composer named Winslow Leach (William Finley) unknowingly bargains away his Faust-based sonata to record producer Swan (played by preeminent 1970s songsmith Paul Williams, who also wrote the Oscar-nominated score) for the opening of Swan's new rock venue, The Paradise. After his beloved singer, Phoenix (Jessica Harper), is seduced away as well, Leach haunts The Paradise in an attempt to destroy Swan, who, it is revealed, has signed an immortal deal with the devil.

Besides the Phantom and Faust, there are elements of *The Portrait of Dorian Gray*, *The Cask of Amontillado*, silent slapstick films, and as many cinematic allusions that De Palma could muster; so not only does the film satirize rock, opera, rock operas, and literary forbears, it also pastiches famous films or filmmakers. De Palma is a well-recognized disciple of Hitchcock, whose influence shows up in, among other ways, effective point-of-

◄

Paul Williams was a a real-life music industry insider, and he manages to inject his Faustian Swan with just the right amount of insidious sleaze.

view long takes. But there is also an homage to the use of television screens and the assassination in John Frankenheimer's *Manchurian Candidate* (1962), as well as a clever take-off on the famous opening tracking shot of Orson Welles' *Touch of Evil* (1958), done here with two cameras in split screen.

De Palma has always been an ingenious filmmaker, fond of virtuoso scenes and trick shots, and there are many here that

"READ IT CAREFULLY, THEN SIGN AT THE BOTTOM IN BLOOD. MESSY, I KNOW, BUT IT'S THE ONLY WAY TO BIND." SWAN

go almost unnoticed beneath the satire: a long crane shot up the stairs of Swan's mansion over scores of female groupies, all practicing in cacophonous unison for auditions that will require less singing than swinging; or auditions done as a kind of memory play, with lights rising and dimming on acts that revolve around a giant 45 r.p.m. record-shaped desk, with Swan in the center hole.

There are funny transpositions from high art staidness to low art hipness, such as the Phantom's disfigurement in a record press machine, or the Dorian Gray portrait as a "picture" in the slang sense of a film. There is also a finale rock show that is part *Masque of the Red Death*, part Alice Cooper-like Guignol. Mention should be made, too, of the supporting cast that is committed to the operatic insanity, not least Gerrit Graham as prima donna rocker Beef, a cross between Liberace and Gary Glitter. **GC**

► **Finley (as the Phantom) contorts himself into gawky hysterics both in and out of his birdlike mask and cape.**

"Extraordinary. One of the oddest, most beautiful films ever."
The London Sunday Times

EDITH BOUVIER BEALE AND HER DAUGHTER EDIE
IN

A MAYSLES BROTHERS' FILM

GREY GARDENS

BY DAVID MAYSLES/ALBERT MAYSLES/ ELLEN HOVDE/ MUFFIE MEYER/SUSAN FROEMKE
FROM PORTRAIT RELEASING, INC.

NOW PLAYING 5th Avenue & 58th Street
MU 8-2013 PG

GREY GARDENS 1975 (U.S.)

Director Albert Maysles, David Maysles, Ellen Hovde, Muffie Meyer
Producer Albert Maysles, David Maysles **Screenplay** Albert Maysles, David
Mayslesen Hovde, Muffie Meyer, Susan Froemke **Cinematography** Albert Maysles,
David Maysles **Cast** Edith Bouvier Beale, Edith "Little Edie" Bouvier Beale

In the mid-1970s a storm was brewing in genteel, reclusive
Georgica Pond, East Hampton. Tucked up in the wealthy climes
of Long Island, this community was rallying behind a move to
push out the tenants of Grey Gardens, a twenty-plus-room
mansion on the Atlantic. Articulate women, descended of
America's ruling class (and with the accents to prove it), Edith
Bouvier Beale and her daughter, "Little Edie" Bouvier Beale,
presided over their estate with reverent indifference. "When're
you going to learn, Edie," asks Edie of her daughter, "you're in
this world, you know; you're not out of this world?"

Questions of abuse are obvious: to what extent has Big Edie
drawn her daughter down the rabbit hole into their warren of
condemned rooms populated by feral cats and vermin? "The
hallmark of aristocracy is responsibility, is that it?" Little Edie,
with a stinging, studied glance to her mother, quotes the
family motto. This is a class bred to draw blood, then lick it off
quietly with manicured paws. Occasionally, through all the
clatter, they really get each other, and in these flashes we see
that their madness is as much a ruse as anything else—a kind
of cladding that protects them from being too exposed to the

◄
**Stranger than
fiction, as a cliché,
often comes to
mind: few could
have invented a
pair so wholly
abstruse as Little
and Big Edie. *Grey
Gardens*, the house,
is haunted, and by
the Beales
themselves.**

true horror of their circumstances. Their twin theatricality is astonishing, depressing, and evinces the absolute worst of stage ambitions and their earned neuroses, the self-destructiveness of a need to be seen.

The Beales let the Maysles in wholesale, and this tale of a dysfunctional, decrepit, and starstruck pair makes *Whatever Happened To Baby Jane* seem milquetoast. Their love for one

"THEY CAN GET YOU IN EAST HAMPTON FOR WEARING RED SHOES ON A THURSDAY, THAT SORT OF THING." *LITTLE EDIE*

another is real but destructive, and their misapprehension of reality feeds their shared malaise. They are each other's prison, sharing their room with twin beds, miscellaneous elements piled everywhere, always relatively in reach. It is a way many of us sometimes dream of living, like children without supervision and meals of canapés spread with mayonnaise and tinned meats chased by ice cream. But as Little Edie throws herself at the camera with hideous gusto, there are cats relieving themselves behind the oil portrait of Big Edie propped against the wall, and we know that this definitely is not "cute."

▶ **Even more haunting is the clear resemblance between Little Edie and her first cousin, Jackie Kennedy Onassis, who eventually stepped in and helped out the odd couple.**

Grey Gardens has perhaps fascinated generations of cinephiles exactly because it depicts the reclusive lives of these ultimate outsiders, who slipped out of their rarefied world into one of their own, their eccentricities taking center stage and reality fading far from view. **GS**

GIVE YOURSELF OVER
to Absolute Pleasure

TWENTIETH CENTURY FOX presents A LOU ADLER-MICHAEL WHITE PRODUCTION "THE ROCKY HORROR PICTURE SHOW"
STARRING TIM CURRY SUSAN SARANDON BARRY BOSTWICK ORIGINAL MUSICAL PLAY MUSIC AND LYRICS BY RICHARD O'BRIEN SCREENPLAY BY JIM SHARMAN and RICHARD O'BRIEN
MUSICAL DIRECTION AND ARRANGEMENTS BY RICHARD HARTLEY ASSOCIATE PRODUCER JOHN GOLDSTONE EXECUTIVE PRODUCER LOU ADLER PRODUCED BY MICHAEL WHITE
SOUNDTRACK AVAILABLE ON ODE RECORDS DIRECTED BY JIM SHARMAN www.rockyhorror.com

THE ROCKY HORROR PICTURE SHOW

1975 (U.K.)

Director Jim Sharman **Producer** Michael White **Screenplay** Jim Sharman, Richard O'Brien **Cinematography** Peter Suschitzky **Music** Richard O'Brien, Richard Hartley **Cast** Tim Curry, Susan Sarandon, Barry Bostwick, Richard O'Brien, Meat Loaf, Peter Hinwood, Charles Gray

---

Still being shown in cinemas decades after its release, *The Rocky Horror Picture Show* has become a cult classic thanks to great rock 'n' roll songs, a superb cast, and a tradition of audience participation that makes for a wacky night out.

Based on a musical written by Richard O'Brien, the film is directed by Jim Sharman, who directed the original stage productions of *The Rocky Horror Show* in London in 1973. (Sharman had also directed the stage musicals *Hair* in 1969 and *Jesus Christ Superstar* in 1972.) The movie's cast includes actors from the original London musical, including Tim Curry as the crazy transvestite Transylvanian scientist, Dr. Frank-N-Furter, added to which are Susan Sarandon and Barry Bostwick as the naive young couple, Janet Weiss and Brad Majors. A deliberate homage to Hammer Horror films, *The Rocky Horror Picture Show* revels in its B-movie schlock, coupling crossdressing, and cannibalism in an outrageous plot in which the innocent Weiss and Majors seek help after their car breaks down and stumble upon a Transylvanian convention held at a castle. Their innocence does not last long because they

◄

The promotional materials for the movie's release parodied the contemporary action movie *Jaws* (1975), and the red lips were touted as being "a different set of jaws."

are initiated into the bizarre world of the debauched Dr. Frank-N-Furter who attempts to seduce each of them in turn.

When it was first released, the film found a lukewarm response as its edgy content, with its trashy celebration of hedonism and wicked humor, failed to appeal. But it went on to find a niche at midnight showings, particularly among students, who loved its transgressive nature and rocky tunes. Soon

"SWIM THE WARM WATERS OF SINS OF THE FLESH, EROTIC NIGHTMARES BEYOND MEASURE." DR. FRANK-N-FURTER

viewers began to dress up as characters from the movie and a ritual evolved as audiences joined in chanting, dancing, and talking back to the screen. What began with ad-libbing became almost a script for the participants, and as people returned to watch the film again and again, watching the movie became an event. Soon the audience started to bring props and customs—throwing rice at the screen during the wedding scene, for instance, became an expected rite.

The glitzy mix of glitter and fishnets, line dancing, anarchic chaos, and carnal frenzy may seem dated to a twenty-first-century viewer less inclined to 1970s glam rock, but it's undoubtedly a phenomenon: Curry belts out tunes like Freddie Mercury, O'Brien's hunchback butler Riff-Raff gives Boris Karloff a run for his money, and Sarandon's fresh-faced ingenue who loosens up helped make her a household name. **CK**

► Curry's brilliant performance as Frank-N-Furter was his film debut. His powerful singing and rendition of the evil madcap scientist made him a star.

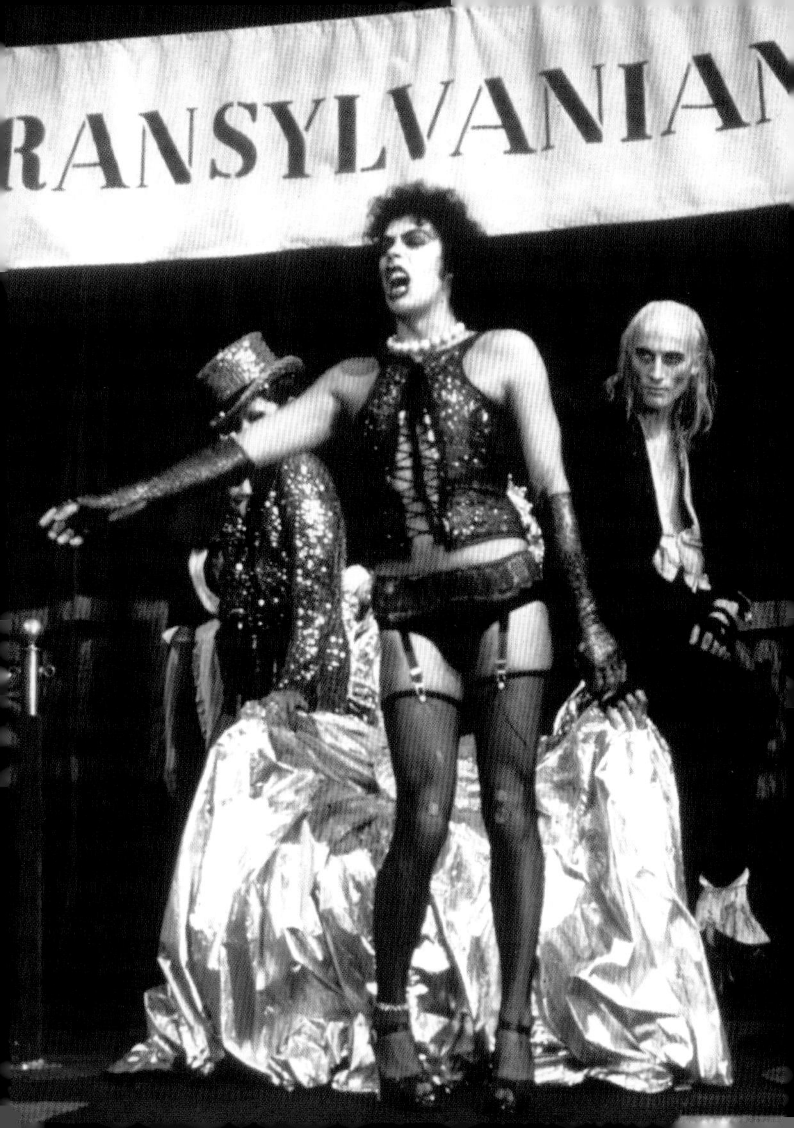
RANSYLVANIAN

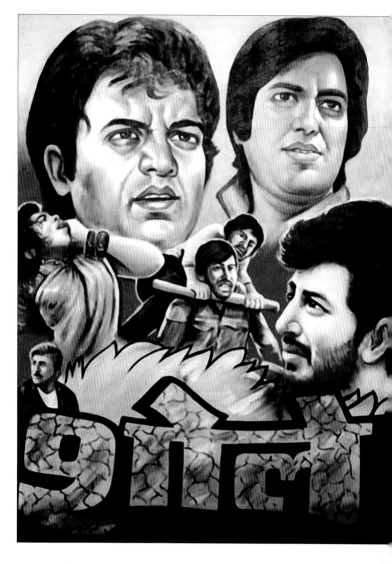

SHOLAY 1975 (INDIA)

Director Ramesh Sippy **Producer** G. P. Sippy **Screenplay** Javed Akhtar, Salim Khan **Cinematography** Dwarka Divecha **Music** Rahul Dev Burman **Cast** Amitabh Bachchan, Dharmendra, Hema Malini, Amjad Khan, Sanjeev Khumar, Jaya Bhaduri, A. K. Hangal, Sartyendra Kapoor

An epic Western set in a dusty, mountainous region of India, remote enough that the producers notoriously built a road for better access to Bangalore, it took more than two years to make and was a flop upon its release. Word of mouth quickly spread and *Sholay* became a "sleeper," occupying a place in the canon not unlike James Cameron's *Titanic* (1997). But it's not just Indians who so revere *Sholay*. *Sholay*, quite simply, set the record, and makes the best entry into this genre as both serious and silly, and it is for this reason that its name is passed on.

The story is epic: two thieves—one dressed as Robert Redford (Dharmendra), the other as John Travolta (Amitabh Bachchan)—are summoned to aid Thakur (Sanjeev Khumar) in apprehending a ruthless bandit, Gabbar Singh (Amjad Khan). Gabbar massacred Thakur's entire family in revenge for his having had him imprisoned. It is clear that frontier justice will rule the day, and at the end of it all, after many die, songs are sung and dances danced, and the armless Thakur confronts his nemesis, proclaiming "one uses his feet, not his hands, to crush the snake," and the audience is treated to a sort of *Star Wars*-on-the-subcontinent showdown.

◀

Sam Peckinpah meets Merchant Ivory in this frontier Western in which the relationship to the Empire is referenced constantly.

After a long absence, the police arrives and eventually the narrative ends where it began—the train station of Ramgarh.

The ritual of daily life is present, and the characters of India are true, amplified as they are but refined unexpectedly. The occasional indelicacy of the performances will no doubt deter some Western viewers, but it's precisely this broadness that develops its own delicacy. The joyous pastiche of R. D. Burman's

"HOW DO YOU PLAN TO FIGHT ME THAKUR? I'VE LONG CUT OFF, AND DISCARDED, YOUR ARMS." *GABBAR SINGH*

score blends the loucheness of Lee Hazelwood and Isaac Hayes funk with a new kind of Filmi. The musical numbers are simply ravishing and the film, piece by piece, achieves its perfection. The film's duration allows us to revel in some fun, increasing the Shakespearean symmetry. That our heroes are mechanicals is another clever trick, poised between the two forces whose motives, in absolute terms, overlap.

The scenery is unexpected, and must have been a revelation to many Indians. It's also didactic: we are well away from the city, therefore absent are most sights associated with the subcontinent; what we see, then, is the country stripped bare: culture and colonization, the leftover infrastructure of an occupying power alongside the traditional lives of a frontier village. This is Peckinpah territory, suggesting the Wild West of dreamland America and a similar fame for India in the future. **GS**

▶

Sholay, for a critical failure, set the bar extremely high.

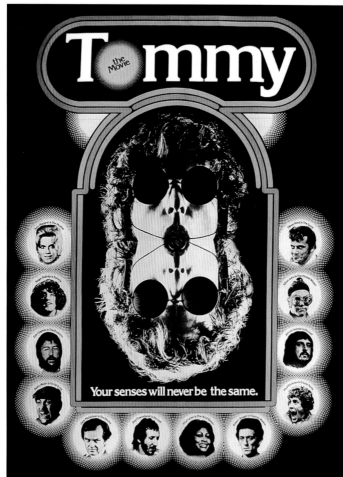

Tommy
the Movie

Your senses will never be the same.

Columbia Pictures and Robert Stigwood Present A Film By Ken Russell "Tommy" By The Who Based On The Rock Opera By Pete Townshend
Starring Ann-Margret As The Mother Oliver Reed As The Lover Roger Daltrey As Tommy And Featuring Elton John As The Pinball Wizard
Guest Artists Eric Clapton, John Entwistle, Keith Moon, Paul Nicholas, Jack Nicholson, Robert Powell, Pete Townshend, Tina Turner & The Who
Associate Producer Harry Benn, Musical Director Pete Townshend, Screenplay By Ken Russell, Executive Producers Beryl Vertue And Christopher Stamp
Produced By Robert Stigwood And Ken Russell, Directed By Ken Russell, Original Soundtrack Album on Polydor Records and Tapes
© 1975 The Robert Stigwood Organisation Limited

TOMMY 1975 (U.K.)

Director Ken Russell **Producer** Ken Russell, Robert Stigwood **Screenplay** Ken Russell, Pete Townshend **Cinematography** Dick Bush, Ronnie Taylor **Music** Pete Townshend (The Who) **Cast** Roger Daltrey, Ann-Margret, Elton John, Tina Turner, Keith Moon, Eric Clapton, Jack Nicholson

A couple says farewell during the dark days of the Blitz: he is an air force pilot playing his part in the war; she (Ann-Margret) is pregnant and remains home. A report arrives of his presumed death and the mother takes up with a new man. Her husband returns and is murdered in front of young Tommy's eyes (Roger Daltrey). In song, his mother and stepfather insist, "You didn't hear it, you didn't see it, you won't say nothing to no one." With this, Tommy loses all sensitivity and is psychosomatically deaf, dumb, and blind. After years of attempts at drawing him out, including treatments of sex, drugs, and the occult (the rock 'n' roll is implied), mother and stepfather employ relatives for his care, including torturing cousin Kevin and molesting uncle Ernie.

Staring into a mirror for the bulk of his day, Tommy is finally met by his own inverse, who exhorts him to "step into the mirror." Once inside, he is taken to an abandoned lot where an old pinball machine stands. Soon Tommy is a "sensation" on the pinball circuit, safely on the other side of the mirror, and his celebrity rises astronomically. The commercial apparatus springs up around him, but his own goals are altruistic. A holiday camp is erected for his new cult, and he, its messiah,

◄

***Tommy* is revered by cult audiences and cinephiles alike as perhaps the most authentic rock opera brought to the screen, and the music of Townshend played by The Who is unlikely to ever be rivaled.**

delivers missives exhorting their adherence to a regimen of sensory deprivation akin to his own. The piece is an extremely personal one, conceived as a whole by The Who guitarist Pete Townshend. Early performances of the work were purely musical as a concept concert, the songs flowing into each other and generally telling the story without dialogue. The dialogue itself is often extraneous, but Russell's film adapts to its medium

"THAT DEAF, DUMB, AND BLIND KID SURE PLAYS A MEAN PINBALL."

THE PINBALL WIZARD

and employs several expansions, drafted by himself with Townshend, which afford the film its overall cohesion.

Much of *Tommy*'s beauty is in its transitions: Russell lingers over them oddly, the smears from song to scene to song. The music is the story, and any actualization of it for the stage or screen cannot but be a filling out and expression of a reading of what the musical material contains. Much of the energy of *Tommy* seems to be aimed in achieving a sensation of true catharsis for its protagonist and, presumably, for its author. Commending *Tommy* further is its reputation for excess. Several images resonate: the TV vomiting baked beans is especially haunting. A pageant of poor taste that nonetheless exposes potent truths of the England that bore it, *Tommy* strains against all of the genres that could be invoked to pigeonhole it and make it somewhat more mainstream. **GS**

► Roger Daltry (lead singer of The Who) and budding actor in the making. In Russell's *Tommy*, innocence is destroyed; family destroys and exploits; and society only wants to be delivered from its bleak conformity by new forms of conformity.

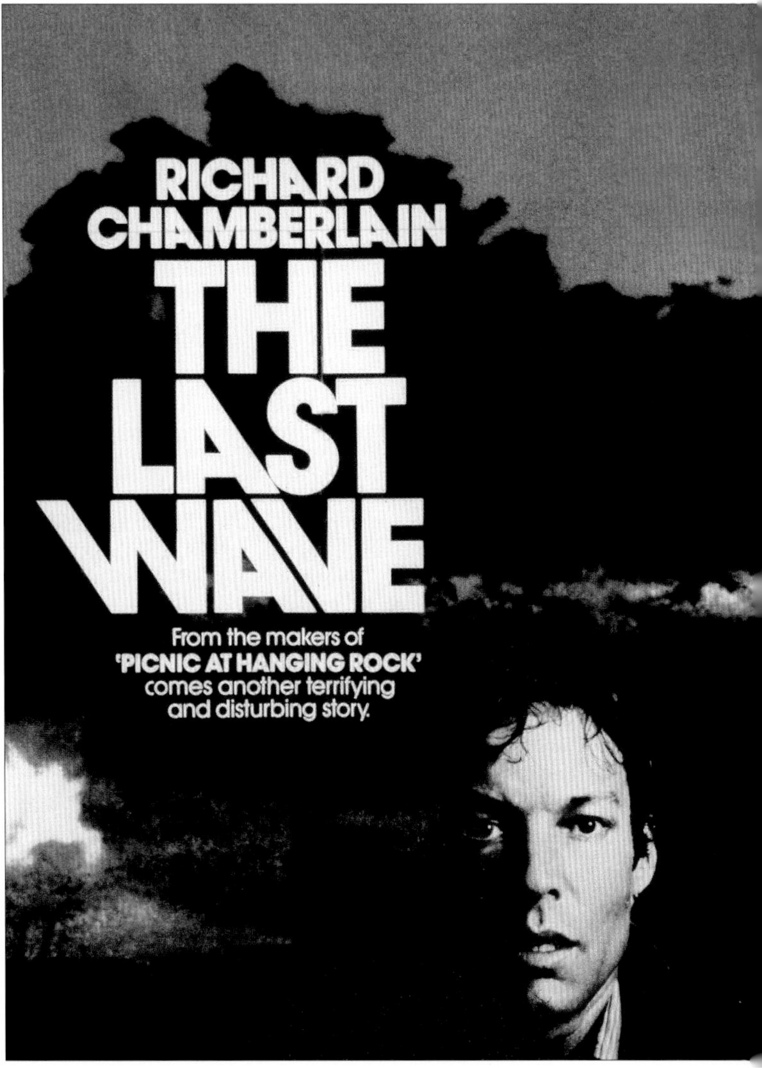
RICHARD
CHAMBERLAIN
THE
LAST
WAVE
From the makers of
'PICNIC AT HANGING ROCK'
comes another terrifying
and disturbing story.

THE LAST WAVE 1977 (AUSTRALIA)

Director Peter Weir **Producer** Hal McElroy, James McElroy **Screenplay** Peter Weir, Tony Morphett, Petru Popescu **Cinematography** Russell Boyd **Music** Charles Wain **Cast** Richard Chamberlain, Olivia Hamnett, David Gulpilil, Frederick Parslow, Vivean Gray, Nandjiwarra Amagula

The Last Wave is a very wet movie. During a brief opening sequence set in the dry Australian desert, a suspenseful thrum from the sky gives way to a major downpour that not only includes sluices of rain but a dangerous shattering of softball-size hail. From this initial storm, the rain doesn't let up for what feels like forty days and forty nights.

Hailstorms and eternal rain are just a few of the biblical allusions in director Peter Weir's dream thriller about a white Australian corporate tax lawyer (Richard Chamberlain) hired to defend a group of aborigines accused of murdering one of their own; other allusions include a rain of frogs, plenty of sacrificial imagery, and the apocalyptic prophecy of the title.

The movie has the look and feel of a kind of primitive urban surrealism. Even though the action takes place in a modern city, this setting merely serves as the externalization of forces much deeper and older. While David, the lawyer, is the adopted son of a minister, it is soon revealed that he has indelibly personal links with the aboriginal tribes. He begins having prophetic dreams and visions about one of his clients, Chris (David Gulpilil), a spiritually charged aboriginal Ramone in a dirty

◄

More than drenched, this movie is practically made of water, as if director Weir exteriorizes his own ninety percent makeup.

leather jacket and jeans. In the primary vision, Chris offers David an engraved bloodstained stone, which is related to an old gray-bearded oracle named Charlie (Nandjiwarra Amagula).

Since much of the film involves David's visions, and thus the sometimes literal flooded contents of his mind, the question posed by this waterlogged conflation of the biblical and tribal is less of a straightforward mystery—was the death a murder,

"WE'VE LOST OUR DREAMS. THEN THEY COME BACK AND WE DON'T KNOW WHAT THEY MEAN." *DAVID BURTON*

an accidental drowning or magic?—than the much more primal, existential "Who are you?," a phrase that Charlie chants to David in an effort to conjure the lawyer's deeper identity. Are both Charlie and Chris merely human conduits for unexplained forces, or beings from another reality? And is David one of them? These notions send David on an explicitly downward quest. The remnants of the tribe are literally buried beneath the city—not only in the sewers, but under them.

Great effects are achieved through simple means: long shots of wide-open skies streaked with clouds or double suns; production design dominated by both industrial and aboriginal ruins; a soundtrack that is at times like a chorus of mewling babies, at others the low guttural moan of someone humming through a didjeridoo implanted in their throat; and, most prominently, a profusion of water, from faucets to floods. **GC**

▶
Through dank, dripping, waste-filled tunnels, David (Chamberlain) makes his own dark journey of the soul in order to wash away one identity and uncover another, and to face the prophecy depicted on the subterranean walls.

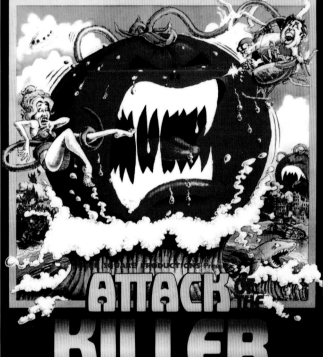

ATTACK OF THE KILLER TOMATOES!
1978 (U.S.)

Director John De Bello **Producer** John De Bello, Steve Peace, Mark L. Rosen
Screenplay John De Bello, C. J. Dillon, Steve Peace, Rick Rockwell **Cinematography**
John K. Culley **Music** Gordon Goodwin, Paul Sundfor **Cast** David Miller, George
Wilson, Sharon Taylor, J. Stephen Peace, Ernie Meyers, Eric Christmas

In this exchange we see the basics of good bad movie writing. There's willfully misunderstood euphemism heightened through profane insensitivity and naturalized into a punch line, thereby rendering the joke funny "haha." John De Bello's movie *Attack of the Killer Tomatoes!* is a knowing sendup of B movies developed to give moviegoers the impression they'd been properly entertained for the price of admission. Quentin Tarantino and Robert Rodriguez reprised the impulse in their collaboration *Grindhouse* (2007), but the earlier *Tomatoes* makes the point with a much smaller budget and even cheaper thrills.

Produced for less than $100,000, the movie is a satire of Hollywood thrillers and horror movies, and of topical concerns of late-1970s America. There are clear references to *The Birds* (1963) and to *Jaws* (1975), as well as inside jokes about the Carter administration, stagflation, and Eastern Bloc sports fraud. The film opens with a tomato rolling out of a garbage disposal truck and killing a woman. This is followed by other attacks, causing the president (Ernie Meyers) to assemble a

◄
The original *Tomatoes* led to three sequels, *Return of the Killer Tomatoes!* (1988), *Killer Tomatoes Strike Back!* (1990), and *Killer Tomatoes Eat France!* (1991), and a children's animated TV series.

crackerjack team of special agents, headed by Mason Dixon (David Miller), to investigate this new danger. And Dixon's team is that idealized cross section of America: Sam Smith (Gary Smith), a Black undercover expert; diver Greg Colburn (Steve Cates); Russian Olympic swimmer Gretta Attenbaum (Benita Barton); and soldier Wilbur Finletter (J. Stephen Peace). The group investigates the tomatoes while shadowed by

"WE HAVE TO CONVINCE [HER] THAT THE TOMATO THAT ATE THE FAMILY PET IS NOT DANGEROUS!" TED SWANN

newspaper reporter Lois Fairchild (Sharon Taylor). Government misdirection ensues as Dixon closes in on the tomatoes, only to uncover a plot headed by the president's press secretary, Jim Richardson (George Wilson), who intends to use the tomatoes for nefarious purposes. Fortunately, the tomatoes are vulnerable to the song "Puberty Love," which also helps Dixon declare his love for Fairchild while the tomatoes are literally squashed underfoot.

► This satire of America works only once we accept that the fruit-come-vegetable, the tomato, is a killing monster in search of human flesh.

Newspaper advertisements from 1978 ignored the film's satire to instead play up the ridiculous premise that a popular fruit hunts and kills people. Audiences of the time were vexed by the premise, or else unaware the movie even existed, seeing how this was the year of *Superman*, but the fact of De Bello's creative risk demonstrates both sheer gumption and high concept inspiration. This is cult as kitsch. **GC-Q**

I SPIT ON YOUR GRAVE 1978 (U.S.)

Director Meir Zarchi **Producer** Meir Zarchi, Joseph Zbeda **Screenplay** Meir Zarchi
Cinematography Nouri Haviv **Music** No soundtrack **Cast** Camille Keaton, Eron
Tabor, Richard Pace, Anthony Nichols, Gunter Kleemann, Alexis Magnotti, Tammy
Zarchi, Terry Zarchi, Traci Ferrante

Often named one of the most controversial films of all time, the
brutal and unflinching violence of *I Spit on Your Grave* horrified
critics such as Roger Ebert at the time of its release. Caught up
in the video nasty debate, *I Spit on Your Grave* was banned in the
U. K. for more than twenty years and then released with more
than seven minutes of cuts in 2001. There is little doubt that *I
Spit on Your Grave* is a brutal film, unflinchingly showing the
rape of its female protagonist, Jennifer Hills (Camille Keaton), at
the hands of a group of dispossessed white men who seek to
reinforce their superiority over the educated and self-sufficient
Jennifer through the violation of her body.

While Jennifer is a successful writer who is on a working
vacation to the country, the male rapists are situated in inferior
socioeconomic positions. Johnny (Eron Tabor) is an ex-marine
who works at a service station, while both Andy (Gunter
Kleemann) and Stanley (Anthony Nichols) are unemployed.
The fourth member—marginal to the group itself—is the
retarded and childlike Matthew (Richard Pace), who works as a
delivery boy at the local grocer. In *I Spit on Your Grave*, as in real
life, rape is an assertion of male potency and power. This is

◄
**Keaton's powerful
performance as the
traumatized and
vengeful Jennifer
garnered her the
Best Actress Award
at the 1978
Catalonian Film
Festival.**

made clear through the repeated and extended assaults on Jennifer—twice in the woods and the final time in her rented house. Without the emotional dynamic of music, the brutalization of Jennifer reaches an intensity and horror that is almost unwatchable at times. In the second half of the film, Jennifer takes her violent and equally brutal revenge against the male group, including the now notorious scene of Johnny's

"THIS IS A FILM WITHOUT A SHRED OF ARTISTIC DISTINCTION."

ROGER EBERT (FILM CRITIC)

seduction and castration. It is significant that Jennifer, unlike many of her female counterparts in the rape-revenge genre, including Thana in Abel Ferrara's *Ms. 45* (1981), does not die at the film's conclusion. Jennifer is a survivor of male oppression rather than merely a victim, whose death is necessary to restore patriarchal order.

To dismiss the film as morally reprehensible, as film critic Roger Ebert and other critics did at the time, is to overlook its deliberate strong feminist message and corresponding explicit condemnation of the men's actions. By demonstrating the sheer horror of rape through extended and explicit scenes in the first forty minutes, *I Spit on Your Grave* provides a powerful condemnation of individual and societal violence against women. *I Spit on Your Grave* is an essential, although not pleasurable, viewing experience. **CB**

▶
Much reviled at the time of its release, this seemingly misogynistic exploitation piece is actually a loaded revenge movie where men get what's comin'.

THE WIZ 1978 (U.S.)

Director Sidney Lumet **Producer** Rob Cohen **Screenplay** Joel Schumacher (based on the book *The Wiz* by William F. Brown) **Cinematography** Oswald Morris **Music** Charlie Smalls, Quincy Jones **Cast** Diana Ross, Michael Jackson, Nipsey Russell, Ted Ross, Mabel King, Theresa Merritt

Imagine a clinic in post-Civil Rights sensitivity and cynical opportunism. "Let's redo *The Wizard of Oz.*" "Why?" "The Brown/ Smalls musical won the Tony and it's doing boffo business on the Great 'White' Way. You've got songs, dancing, pedigree, the right kind of distance from Garland. The script is basically written, and Motown Productions wants a piece of the action. It can't miss." "Oh," says the Universal executive, and soon there was a new vehicle for Berry Gordy's superstar, Diana Ross.

The outline is familiar. Introverted Harlem schoolteacher Dorothy Gale (Ross) lives with her Aunt Em (Theresa Merritt) and Uncle Henry (Stanley Greene). Cleaning up from a Thanksgiving party, Dorothy's dog Toto runs away into a snowstorm, and a magical whirlwind transports them both to the land of Oz. Dorothy accidentally kills the Wicked Witch of the East, and must visit the Wiz (Richard Pryor) to return home. She meets a Scarecrow (Michael Jackson) in need of a brain, a Tin Man (Nipsey Russell) in need of a heart, and a Cowardly Lion (Ted Ross) in need of courage. To receive these gifts, the Wiz requires that they first kill Evillene, the Wicked Witch of the West (Mabel King). They accomplish the task, learn

◄
Recalling the 1939 classic, *The Wiz* includes memorable songs like "Ease On Down the Road," "Don't Nobody Bring Me No Bad News," and "If You Believe In Yourself," with Quincy Jones as music supervisor.

that the Wiz is a fraud, and finally Glinda (Lena Horne), the Good Witch of the South, assists Dorothy in her return home.

Debuting in 1978, which was a few years after the emergence of blaxploitation, *The Wiz* attempts to redirect an aspect of black image-making in America that was closely associated with masculine stereotype, crime, profanity, and R & B music. Helmed by Sidney Lumet, a white establishment director, and

"BARNUM SAID THERE'S A SUCKER BORN EVERY MINUTE." *SCARECROW*
"I WAS THERE WHEN HE SAID IT." *TIN MAN*

catapulted forward by the success of other early 1970s stage musicals such as *Raisin*, *The Wiz* adapted the beloved novel-turned-movie-turned-Broadway smash *The Wonderful Wizard of Oz* to carve out new racially aware myths from bedrock Americana. Despite best laid plans, however, the film was a commercial and critical failure.

► **Diana Ross replaced the theatrical first choice Stephanie Mills, depite being way older, partly because she claimed she could bring Michael Jackson on board if she was cast.**

With passing years, *The Wiz* has become an unusually powerful time capsule. This is because Oz is rendered as Manhattan, including sequences in the sewer and subway systems, and at the public library. In particular, The Emerald City is the World Trade Center, then newly built and half empty. Since 9/11, such images of New York City have taken on an acute grade of nostalgic fascination, and *The Wiz* is central to this remembering that also features Michael Jackson's impressive pre-"Thriller" movie debut. **GC-Q**

ZOLTAN, HOUND OF DRACULA
1978 (U.S.)

Director Albert Band **Producer** Philip Collins **Screenplay** Frank Ray Perilli
Cinematography Bruce Logan **Music** Andrew Belling **Cast** José Ferrer, Michael
Pataki, Arlene Martel, Jan Shutan, Libby Chase, John Levin, Reggie Nalder, Clero
Harrington, Tom Gerrard, Gordon McGill

On the surface *Zoltan, Hound of Dracula* is a fairly unremarkable
horror cheapy, taking the vampire tradition and melding it with
the 1970s vogue for uncontrollable killer animals—*à la Jaws*.
Indeed, a film like this could *only* have been made in the 1970s.

Set in contemporary Romania, soldiers digging a road set off
a series of explosives in the middle of a field, accidentally
unearthing a hidden subterranean crypt. During the night, an
earthquake shakes loose two coffins from the crypt, sending
one of them sliding down and landing at the feet of a confused
guard. Too curious for his own good, he opens the coffin and
discovers the body of a dog impaled by a wooden stake.
Removing the stake, the hound reanimates and rips out the
soldier's throat. Meet Zoltan, the canine vampire!

In scenes oddly reminiscent of the TV series *Skippy the Bush
Kangaroo*, Zoltan proceeds to prise open the other coffin, this
time revealing human remains in a similar condition. The dog
removes the stake and the body comes to life. Who is this
mysterious figure? No, it's not Dracula. A flashback takes us to
the eighteenth century, where we find a woman being attacked

◄

The film was
released in the
United States with
the comically
prosaic title of
Dracula's Dog. For
all its low-budget
schlock, *Zoltan,
Hound of Dracula*
makes for a rather
diverting hour and
a half for any fan
of 1970s horror.

by a bat. Zoltan intervenes and the woman escapes intact. Of course, the bat is Dracula, and he is not a happy camper; indeed, he's so angry that he bites the dog, sending it into the realm of the undead. Zoltan is then taken under the wing of Dracula's faithful servant, Veidt. Yes, *he's* the one in the other coffin.

Back to the present, still loyal to the Dracula clan, Veidt and Zoltan go in search of living descendants. There is only one

"MAN'S BEST FRIEND IS NOW MAN'S WORST FRIEND. THERE'S MORE TO THE LEGEND THAN MEETS THE THROAT!" *TAGLINE*

remaining: mild-mannered Californian psychiatrist, Michael Drake, who is unaware of his heritage. The evil duo proceed to America, where Zoltan embarks on a wild animal killing spree, creating his own army of vampire hounds as they seek out their new master. This is what makes *Zoltan, Hound of Dracula* such an appealing movie. Unlike other postwar vampire flicks, it's free of ironic nods and winks, to the point where it could almost be called po-faced. It's this fact, that such a ridiculous premise should take itself so seriously, that helps to make it such fun. Production values are typically low, yet some of the pack attacks toward the end of the movie are genuinely quite chilling. In fact, director Albert Band manages to maintain the right amount of tension throughout. And although the denouement can be spotted a mile away, it's no less satisfying when it arrives. **TB**

► Special effects are par for the low budget and consist of little more than vampire hounds with glowing eyes.

Produced by
BYRON KENNEDY

Directed by
GEORGE MILLER

With
MEL GIBSON

Music by
BRIAN MAY

Written by
JAMES McCAUSLAND and **GEORGE MILLER**

MAD MAX 1979 (AUSTRALIA)

Director George Miller **Producer** Byron Kennedy **Screenplay** James McCausland, George Miller **Cinematography** David Eggby **Music** Brian May **Cast** Mel Gibson, Joanne Samuel, Hugh Keays-Byrne, Steve Bisley, Tim Burns, Roger Ward, Lisa Aldenhoven, David Bracks

Mad Max is set in a bleak Australia "a few years from now" after an unexplained apocalypse has destroyed the society we know, leaving a violent world where gangs of thugs speed along deserted roads to terrorize the few remaining citizens, pursued by leather-clad cops who have only a tenuous grasp on justice. Mel Gibson (aged just twenty three and baby-faced) plays Max Rockatansky, the star of the highway police, the Main Force Patrol (MFP), cool and sensible, but with killer instincts in a car.

Though it became one of the most profitable movies of all time, this first installment of George Miller's Mad Max trilogy was made on a shoestring budget and it often shows. The plot is shaky at best, the score straight out of an old-fashioned melodrama, and some of the acting so bad you're left wondering if Miller was aiming for parody rather than real action-thriller. Gibson coasts through the movie with a lack of expression, which is presumably intended to convey self-possession, and the only time he displays any other expression, viewing the burned body of his friend Goose (Steve Bisley), his contorted outrage is laughable. Some of the effects are less than perfect, too: the scene where the eyes of brutal gang

◄

The road-biker-dystopian-disaster film that launched Mel Gibson (after Aussie TV soap *Neighbours***).**

leader Toecutter (Hugh Keays-Byrne) pop out of their sockets as he realizes that he is about to be hit by a truck is so cartoonish it detracts from the horror of the moment.

The first two-thirds of the movie are action-packed with thrilling, perfectly staged car and bike chases, but the plot is confused and directionless and the characters sketchy. It's only late in the movie, when Toecutter's gang targets Max's

> "WELL DAMN THEM! YOU AND ME MAX, WE'RE GOING TO GIVE THEM BACK THEIR HEROES." FIFI (ROGER WARD)

wife and child, that plot and characters begin to develop. Max dons his black leather and sets out in an all-black, super-charged car on a mission of vengeance. Max commented to his boss earlier that there wasn't much difference between him and the thugs, and now we see him descend to their brutal level, hunting and killing each gang member, no questions asked. As the movie ends, Max drives off into the no-go zone, leaving his old life behind him. Mad Max has a very different feel from its big-budget sequels. The postapocalyptic future presented here is far more like the present, or even the not-too-distant past than the later movies. In spite of its patchy moments, Mad Max's striking visual effects make it a movie that sticks in the memory. Moments of bleakness exploited by the later movies stand out: such as the gang scrambling over a moving tanker to steal fuel. **GC-Q**

▶
Max (Gibson) lies injured on the highway, his gun just out of reach and two thugs waiting to finish him off—just one of the film's many powerful visual moments.

THE SECOND COMING OF
MONTY PYTHON'S
LIFE OF BRIAN
MONTY PYTHON'S 'LIFE OF BRIAN'
Written by & Starring GRAHAM CHAPMAN JOHN CLEESE TERRY GILLIAM ERIC IDLE TERRY JONES MICHAEL PALIN
Executive Producers GEORGE HARRISON & DENIS O'BRIEN Produced by JOHN GOLDSTONE Designed by TERRY GILLIAM Directed by TERRY JONES
© 1979 Python (Monty) Pictures Limited. All Rights Reserved.
www.PythOnline.com
A Rainbow Release
www.rainbowreleasing.com

MONTY PYTHON'S LIFE OF BRIAN

1979 (U.K.)

Director Terry Jones **Producer** John Goldstone **Screenplay** Graham Chapman, John Cleese, Eric Idle, Michael Palin, Terry Jones **Cinematography** Peter Biziou **Music** Geoffrey Burgon **Cast** Graham Chapman, John Cleese, Eric Idle, Michael Palin, Terry Jones, Sue Jones-Davies, Spike Milligan, Chris Langham

---

In breaking away from their groundbreaking TV series *Monty Python's Flying Circus*, *Monty Python's Life of Brian* was the comedy team's second film after *The Holy Grail* (1975). As with *The Holy Grail*, the Pythons both wrote their own material and played multiple roles, with Graham Chapman taking the lead role of Brian, a simple resident of Judea who gets mistaken for Jesus Christ. Born at the same time and in the same place as Jesus (the Three Wise Men initially mistake Brian's crib for that of Jesus as he is next door), through a series of unfortunate events the adult Brian is mistaken for the Messiah and is hounded by believers. After joining a local revolutionary group intent on overthrowing Roman rule in Judea, Brian is pursued by a crowd believing him to be "the chosen one" before finally being arrested and crucified by the Romans.

The film is full of memorable scenes, from revolutionary leader Reg's speech asking, "What have the Roman's ever done for us?" (which presented such a historically accurate overview of the benefits of Roman rule that it has featured in school history textbooks) to a Roman centurion correcting the

◄

Beatle George Harrison helped to bankroll the film and had an uncredited part as Mr Papadopoulos.

grammatical accuracy of Brian's anti-Roman graffiti and making him write it out a hundred times across the forum, to a chirpy convict leading Brian and a host of others on the cross in singing "Always Look on the Bright Side of Life."

The film was controversial from the start. The Monty Python team was accused of blasphemy by religious groups, even though the film does not mock the figure of Jesus and makes a

"SHUT UP ALL OF YOU. I'M TELLING YOU HE'S NOT THE MESSIAH, HE'S A VERY NAUGHTY BOY." *MANDY COHEN*

clear distinction between him and Brian, with early scenes representing him as another quite serious figure. Nonetheless, many British local authorities banned the film or placed a restrictive X certificate on it. The effect of all the controversy meant that it was accorded a high profile in the U.K., ending up as the fourth-highest grossing film of 1979. Indeed, the film's Swedish distributors, in true Python tradition, made full use of what became an international controversy by advertising it with posters stating, "So funny it was banned in Norway!"

► Terry Jones as Simon The Holy Man, a hermit vowed to a life of silence that doesn't last long.

The Life of Brian satirizes the unthinking devotion and desperation to believe in something—anything—at all costs. This is beautifully caught when Brian, addressing a large crowd of disciples, tells them they don't need anyone to tell them what to think and that they "are all different," only to hear "yes, we are all different" ringing back to him in terrifying unison. **RH**

THESE ARE THE ARMIES OF THE NIGHT.

They are 100,000 strong. They outnumber the cops five to one.
They could run New York City. Tonight they're all out to get the Warriors.

Paramount Pictures Presents A Lawrence Gordon Production "THE WARRIORS"
Executive Producer Frank Marshall Based Upon the Novel by Sol Yurick
Screenplay by David Shaber and Walter Hill Produced by Lawrence Gordon
Directed by Walter Hill Read the Dell Book

THE WARRIORS 1979 (U.S.)

Director Walter Hill **Producer** Lawrence Gordon **Screenplay** David Shaber, Walter Hill (from the novel by Sol Yurick) **Cinematography** Andrew Laszlo **Music** Barry de Vorzon **Cast** Michael Beck, James Remar, Dorsey Wright, Deborah Van Valkenburgh, David Patrick Kelly, Thomas G. Waites, Brian Tyler, David Harris, Roger Hill

---

Set across one night, director Walter Hill used the Greek writer Xenephon's *Anabasis* as his muse to create a tale of courage, survival, and loyalty in a perilous environment—and from the opening scenes of gloriously attired street gangs descending in their thousands to a midnight summit in the Bronx, it's apparent that *The Warriors* is no ordinary tale of inner-city lawlessness.

At the summit, Cyrus (Roger Hill), leader of the city's most powerful gang, the Gramercy Riffs, implores the attendant gangs to come together as one force, using their superior numbers to overcome the N.Y.P.D. and gain full control of the city. In the process he is assassinated by the Rogues' leader, Luther, but the blame is pinned on the Coney Island gang, the Warriors. With a bounty subsequently declared on the Warriors, they must negotiate a way home, stranded twenty-seven miles behind enemy lines and with the combined forces of New York's gangs and police force all in hot pursuit.

It's an incredibly simple plot, but one capable of creating extended suspense as we follow the Warriors, led by Swan (Michael Beck), through the mean streets of a hostile New York. Escape for the gang is only possible via the New York City

◄

No mention of *The Warriors* would be complete without reference to one of cinema's most memorably creepy catchphrases: "Warriors, come out to play-ay."

subway system, shot entirely on location, which becomes the unrelenting beating heart of the movie, taking on a sinister presence where danger lurks at every station.

Newcomers to the film often find the unrealistic nature of the fight scenes bemusing for a film that caused such controversy on its initial release. The Warriors was held responsible for inciting extreme acts of violence in cinemas, subways, and the

"WARRIORS COME OUT TO PLAY. WARRIORS COME OUT TO PLA-AY. WARRIORS COME OUT TO PLA-AY." *LUTHER*

playground, culminating with Paramount severely reducing their advertising campaign. For Hill, the violence on-screen was always designed to have a balletic quality that could reproduce most efficiently the comic book style he originally intended for the film, but was only able to achieve with the addition of splash panels in the later director's cut.

▶
The dialogue is perhaps the film's greatest legacy, judging by the countless musicians who have incorporated elements of the script into their work. "Can you dig it?" Oh yeah.

Remarkably, for a film shot almost exclusively at night, the screen lights up in almost every shot, a testament to Andrew Laszlo's wonderfully creative cinematography, including his deliberate wetting of pavements to create light reflection. The highly stylized uniforms and face paint of the street gangs also contribute a riot of color against the nighttime backdrop. The final scene between Luther and Swan on a deserted beach in the early morning lends heavily from Westerns; the Warriors walk off into the sunset, exhausted, vindicated, and finally home. **SG**

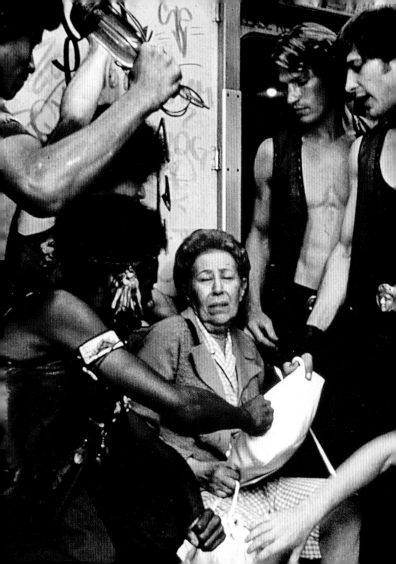

They'll never get caught.
They're on a mission from God.

JOHN BELUSHI   DAN AYKROYD

THE BLUES BROTHERS

JAMES BROWN · CAB CALLOWAY · RAY CHARLES · CARRIE FISHER
ARETHA FRANKLIN · HENRY GIBSON
THE BLUES BROTHERS BAND
Written by DAN AYKROYD and JOHN LANDIS
Executive Producer BERNIE BRILLSTEIN
Produced by ROBERT K. WEISS · Directed by JOHN LANDIS

Original Soundtrack Recording on ATLANTIC Records and Tapes.

Read the JOVE BOOK

A UNIVERSAL PICTURE
1980 UNIVERSAL CITY STUDIOS, INC. ALL RIGHTS RESERVED

THE BLUES BROTHERS 1980 (U.S.)

Director John Landis **Producer** John Landis **Screenplay** Dan Ackroyd, John Landis **Cinematography** Stephen M. Katz **Music** Elmer Bernstein **Cast** John Belushi, Dan Ackroyd, Ray Charles, Aretha Franklin, Cab Calloway, James Brown, Steve Cropper, Donald Dunn, Carrie Fisher, Henry Gibon, John Candy, Twiggy,

This is a tale of redemption, and of the cool versus the uncool. Jake (John Belushi) and Elwood (Dan Ackroyd) Blues are on a quest. They plan to reform their rhythm and blues band, The Blues Brothers, and stage a concert to raise the money needed to save the Catholic orphanage where they were brought up. This may be a "Mission from God," but the brothers leave a trail of destruction and pick up plenty of enemies en route, including the law, neo-Nazis, a country western band, and a mysterious woman (Carrie Fisher) who is out to annihilate them.

Dan Ackroyd and John Belushi first developed the characters Jake and Elwood Blues for the TV show *Saturday Night Live*, inspired by their love of R & B. Their comic double act holds the movie firmly together, in spite of its slack structure and simplistic plot. The movie rushes along at a relentless pace through a series of slapstick comedy sketches and lively musical episodes. Most of the slapstick violence is directed at cars. In a series of wildly inventive (and since there was no C.G.I. back in 1980, very expensive) car chases, cars are smashed up in every conceivable way, including falling from an immense height from the end of an unfinished flyover. *The Blues Brothers* held the world record

◄

It's a one-joke movie, but it works because it's charming and silly and joyful. It's excess-all-areas also reflected the 1980s *zeitgeist*.

for most cars destroyed in one movie until it was beaten by its own (very lame) sequel, *Blues Brothers 2000*. There is yet more slapstick in Carrie Fisher's cartoon-style vengeance as Jake's jilted fiancée, working her way through bombs, flame throwers, and missile launchers in her attempts to kill him. The humor relies on Ackroyd and Belushi's ability to remain deadpan while surrounded by chaos.

"WE GOT A TANK OF GAS, HALF A PACK OF CIGARETTES, IT'S DARK AND WE'RE WEARING SUNGLASSES." *ELWOOD*

The music is fabulous. Numbers from R & B and soul legends James Brown, Aretha Franklin, Ray Charles, and Cab Calloway are lovingly interwoven into the plot. Bluesman John Lee Hooker is left rather oddly singing "Boom Boom" in the street, but who cares, he's great and he's there. None of them can act except Cab Calloway, but that really doesn't matter either. The music is energetic, brilliantly performed, and soul stirring.

The Blues Brothers has been accused of being self-indulgent— just think of that incredibly long opening scene as Jake leaves jail; think of the pointless inclusion of some of the star cameos (what is Twiggy's character for?); think of all those destroyed cars. But the movie hits exactly the right nerve with audiences, who relish its zany individuality, daft comedy, exuberant music, and of course, those ever-cool brothers in their trademark black suits, hats, and Ray-Bans. **CW**

► It's overlong, rambling, and self-destructive, but in between there are fabulous comic moments, sublime musical performances, and the iconic cool-looking dudes.

MS. 45 1981 (U.S.)

Director Abel Ferrara **Producer** Richard Howorth, Mary Kane, Rochelle Weisberg
Screenplay Nicholas St. John **Cinematography** James Lemmo **Music** Joe
Delia **Cast** Zoë Lund, Editta Sherman, Albert Sinkys, Darlene Stuto, Nike
Zachmanoglou, Abel Ferrara, Helen McGara

Thana is a young seamstress working for a high-class fashion
designer in the garment district of Manhattan. Beautiful but
mute, she dresses conservatively and fades into the background
in contrast to her vibrant and vivacious coworkers. Her life is
shattered forever when she is violently attacked twice on the
same day while walking home from work. Her assailant is
wearing a mask and drags her into a dark alleyway and rapes
her. He lets her go and she flees back to her apartment home,
only to interrupt a burglary and be sexually assaulted for a
second time. Using a paperweight and an iron, she fights off
her attacker and kills him. Thana then proceeds to dismember
his body, refrigerating the pieces while she disposes of them
one by one at various locations throughout the city.

Using the gun that her second attacker brought with him,
Thana prowls the city at night, shooting men indiscriminately
in revenge for her multiple violations. The gun becomes a
substitute for her lost voice and virginity. Men in *Ms. 45* are
portrayed as inherently predatory, with perverted desires and
pedophilic tendencies. Even Thana's boss (Albert Sinkys), who
seems sympathetic toward her throughout the film, uses his

◀
**Zoë Lund (born
Tamarlis) once
claimed to have
been fired at by
a sniper and was
wounded as a
result of this movie.**

position of power to attempt to force her into having sex with him. A powerful central performance by Zoë Lund makes Thana's transformation from shy wallflower to femme fatale/ psychotic killer believable, even when she is dressed as a nun with a gun in the fancy dress party at the end of the film. Above all, Abel Ferrara makes sure the film does not disintegrate into clichés around male fantasies.

"WE DON'T USUALLY WIN THINGS . . . I'VE BEEN LAUGHED OUT OF VENICE WITH MY FILMS." ABEL FERRARA

With its strong feminist sentiments, *Ms. 45* is one of the best early rape-revenge films—a subgenre that emerged from 1970s exploitation cinema with films such as *Lipstick* (1976) and *I Spit on Your Grave* (1978). Editing and sound add to the powerful and lasting impact of *Ms. 45*, with slow motion effectively used in the scene of Thana's eventual demise, contrasting to the documentary style approach of *I Spit on Your Grave*. Thana's muteness functions as a powerful symbol of the conflict between second-wave feminism and the deeply puritanical and patriarchal American society of the time. The forerunner of the "girls with guns" subgenre, *Ms. 45* is both a feminist statement against male oppression and an effective psychological horror film. *Ms. 45* might be exploitation cinema, but it is never exploitative due to both Lund's mesmerizing performance and Ferrara's fine direction. **CB**

► Thana's (Lund) inability to kill either another woman or the dog of her landlady means that she retains an essential humanity even as she descends into total psychosis.

TIME BANDITS

STARRING

JOHN CLEESE SEAN CONNERY SHELLEY DUVALL
KATHERINE HELMOND IAN HOLM MICHAEL PALIN
RALPH RICHARDSON PETER VAUGHAN DAVID WARNER

WITH

DAVID RAPPAPORT KENNY BAKER JACK PURVIS MIKE EDMONDS
MALCOLM DIXON TINY ROSS AND CRAIG WARNOCK

TIME BANDITS 1981 (U.K.)

Director Terry Gilliam **Producer** Terry Gilliam, George Harrison, Denis O'Brien
Screenplay Terry Gilliam, Michael Palin **Cinematography** Peter Biziou
Music Mike Moran, George Harrison **Cast** John Cleese, Sean Connery, Shelley
Duvall, Ralph Richardson, Ian Holm, Michael Palin, David Warner, Craig Warnock

Written by ex-Pythons Terry Gilliam and Michael Palin, *Time Bandits* is a shambolic time travel comedy that transcends its episodic structure and not quite up to the mark comedy thanks to Gilliam's ability to bring his remarkable imaginative vision to the screen. Historical sets have a level of detail that lends them great authenticity, while fantasy sets are startlingly inventive. The low-budget homemade special effects hold their own against modern technical wizardry.

Kevin (Craig Warnock) lives with his parents who are too concerned with their own lives to take much notice of their son. One night, six dwarves rush out of Kevin's closet and carry him away to the hero-filled lands of his dreams. The dwarves have a map that enables them to travel through holes in time and space. "We're international criminals," they claim, but they clearly haven't had much practice yet. They are being hunted by their former employer, the Supreme Being, from whom they have stolen the map (Ralph Richardson's Oz-like first as a huge fiery head and then a bumbling old man). The dwarves lead Kevin through history, stealing treasure from a size-obsessed Napoleon (Ian Holm), then losing it when Robin Hood (John

◄
A schoolboy's fantasy-adventure that marked Gilliam's transition from wacky Python animator to director with an original vision.

Cleese) takes it to give to the poor, with wonderfully vague noblesse oblige. Stranded without the dwarves in ancient Greece, Kevin meets a valiant king (Sean Connery) who wants to adopt him. He is furious when the dwarves carry him off along with the king's treasure, which they immediately lose as the ship they land on turns out to be the Titanic. Meanwhile, trapped in the Fortress of Ultimate Darkness by the Supreme

"WHY DO WE HAVE TO HAVE EVIL?" KEVIN
"IT'S GOT SOMETHING TO DO WITH FREE WILL." SUPREME BEING

Being, Evil (played with exaggerated panache by David Warner) wants to get his hands on the map. To entice the dwarves into his lair, Evil makes them believe that their hearts' desire, The Most Fabulous Object in the World, lies there. Once the dwarves and Kevin are in his clutches, Evil grabs the map and locks them in a cage hanging over an endless void. With some daring circus acrobatics complete with cymbal rolls, the band escapes and regroups to challenge Evil. Some of the movie's most stunning visual effects come in here, as Evil laughs at their efforts, morphing into a merry-go-round and a giant pincushion to shrug off their weapons.

Time Bandits ultimately may be trying to deliver a message about materialism and technology, but the Supreme Being never offers any convincing alternative, leaving the message muddy and unconvincing. **GC-Q**

► The boy hero Kevin (Warnock) with one of the dwarves who's been turned into a pig by Evil.

THE TENANT IN ROOM 7 IS VERY SMALL, VERY TWISTED, AND VERY MAD

BASKET CASE

an IEVINS / HENENLOTTER production   starring KEVIN VanHENTENRYCK   TERRI SUSAN SMITH
BEVERLY BONNER   Director of Photography BRUCE TORBET   Music GUS RUSSO
Executive Producers ARNIE BRUCK   TOM KAYE   Production Executive RAY SUNDLIN
Produced by EDGAR IEVINS   Written and Directed by FRANK HENENLOTTER

DISTRIBUTED BY
RUGGED FILMS INC.

BASKET CASE 1982 (U.S.)

Director Frank Henenlotter **Producer** Edgar Ievins **Screenplay** Frank Henenlotter **Cinematography** Bruce Torbet **Music** Gus Russo **Cast** Kevin Van Hentenryck, Terri Susan Smith, Beverly Bonner, Robert Vogel, Ruth Neuman, Diana Brown, Lloyd Pace, Bill Freeman

Basket Case is dedicated to gore pioneer Herschell Gordon Lewis, so one can safely assume director Frank Henenlotter harbors a passion for peculiarity. While his contemporaries were learning in film schools, Henenlotter received his film education in the dingy grindhouses of 1970s New York City. With a steady diet of kung fu films, cheap horror, B-grade action, and sexploitation pictures stewing in his head, Henenlotter gave birth to this horror-comedy that defines the midnight movie.

Arriving from upstate New York, young Duane Bradley (Kevin Van Hentenryck) moves into a fleabag hotel in sleazy downtown New York City with a locked wicker basket in his arms. The curious container is secured for a reason, as inside is Belial, an angry, twisted mass of flesh that is Duane's Siamese twin brother. Sharing a telepathic link, the brothers have come to the rotting Big Apple to enact revenge on the doctors who separated them and left Belial for dead.

Made for a budget (roughly $30,000) that wouldn't cover a week of Hollywood craft services, *Basket Case* is the type of movie that lives or dies on its ability to shock and offer something original. The film succeeds with its vengeful

◄

Henenlotter eventually created a *Basket Case* trilogy with two tamer sequels in the early 1990s. He also served as an archivist and restorer for premier cult film distributors, Something Weird Video.

conjoined twin story line—displaying the sideshow appeal of Tod Browning's *Freaks* (1932)—and the bizarre beast, Belial. With his glowing eyes and razorlike nails, Belial might appear to be just another movie monster. Henenlotter, however, actually makes the monstrosity sympathetic. Sure, he likes to kill violently, but you can't help but feel sorry for the little guy when he is thrown out with the garbage postsurgery.

"THERE'S SOMETHING I'VE BEEN DYING TO ASK YOU. WHAT'S IN THE BASKET?" CASEY

Appropriately, Henenlotter stages memorable gore scenes (a father sliced in two and a doctor's face shoved into a tray of scalpels) that equally emphasize horror and comedy. Performances from mostly amateurs vary widely, brilliantly aiding to the grimy, real-life aesthetic. Also notable is the film's time capsule quality in capturing New York City at a squalid rock bottom (including a trip inside one of the seedy grindhouses Henenlotter frequented).

▶
This is the freak show revenge movie from a junk food-consuming and nasty little belching monster that goes off on a gory killing spree.

With accolades from trash-loving critics like Joe Bob Briggs, it's not surprising that *Basket Case* performed strongly on the midnight movie circuit. Henenlotter continued his "man versus a monster of his own making" theme with the hallucinogenic *Brain Damage* (1988) and the delirious in-title-and-execution *Frankenhooker* (1990), before returning with the offbeat love story *Bad Biology* (2008). **WW**

Klaus Kinski in
Fitzcarraldo
Der Film von Werner Herzog
KLAUS KINSKI
CLAUDIA CARDINALE
in »Fitzcarraldo«
mit JOSÉ LEWGOY · MIGUEL ANGEL FUENTES
PAUL HITTSCHER · HUEREQUEQUE ENRIQUE BOHÓRQUEZ
GRANDE OTHELO · PETER BERLING Kamera THOMAS MAUCH Musik POPOL VUH
Produziert von WERNER HERZOG und LUCKI STIPETIC
Eine Werner Herzog Filmproduktion mit der Pro-ject Filmproduktion
im Filmverlag der Autoren, München
FILMVERLAG DER AUTOREN

FITZCARRALDO 1982 (GERMANY)

Director Werner Herzog **Producer** Werner Herzog, Lucki Stipetić
Screenplay Werner Herzog **Cinematography** Thomas Mauch
Music Popol Vuh **Cast** Klaus Kinski, Claudia Cardinale, José Lewgoy,
Miguel Ángel Fuentes, Paul Hittscher, Grande Otelo

Even as cults go, the cult of Herzog is a fierce one, but it's to his golden period masterpiece *Fitzcarraldo* that the cult owes its real status. As with most Herzog productions, the lore of *Fitzcarraldo* is as large as the film itself. The effort of dragging a large river vessel over the crest of a mountain is of course the film's hero's prime challenge, but it's also the great achievement of his maker, Werner Herzog. Herzog himself is arguably the protagonist of folly in all of his films.

Colonial adventurer Brian Sweeney Fitzgerald (a familiarly wild-eyed Klaus Kinski) cannot make good of opportunity. A natural outcast, he is ever short of money, though his dreams are of absolute grandeur. Recently failed in the construction of the Trans-Andean Railway, Fitzgerald, in financial ruin, listens to phonographs of Italian tenor Enrico Caruso in a fevered state while trying his hand as a producer of ice.

His next dream: an opera house in his remote outpost of Iquitos, to be opened by the great singer himself. But the dream needs money, and the acquisition of money demands a greater dream. Having placed himself in a rubber-rich region of the Peruvian jungle, he expects that he, too, might attain the

◄

Fitzcarraldo is a unique amalgam of the madness of Herzog and Kinski, not Herzog's first choice for the role, but a reliable (and destructive) creative partner with whom he would never again collaborate.

extraordinary wealth of his cohorts and conceives of a trick by which he will open up a hitherto inaccessible territory all his own. He purchases a rusted-out boat with a drunk captain and procures a crew to man it, composed largely of superstitious natives to whom he is known as Fitzcarraldo.

The scenery is literally astonishing, and indeed one of the great boons of Herzog's Amazonian period is the footage we

"I WILL OUTNUMBER YOU. I WILL OUTBILLION YOU. I AM THE SPECTACLE IN THE FOREST." *FITZCARRALDO*

have of this wild terrain and its boundless river. Almost immediately, we feel irretrievably lost, even before we have ventured from the confines of the river community he dwells in. As in his earlier conquistador movie masterpiece *Aguirre: Wrath of God* (1972), everything and everyone is unhinged by the jungle and holds together by will and will alone, and Herzog's vision remains a complete invention all on its own. Herzog branded himself "Conquistador of the Useless" upon reflection of his great feat, feeding the legend that his entire oeuvre is, in many ways, summed up by the man Fitzcarraldo.

► The whole tortuous production of hauling a 340-ton steamship without special effects over a mountain was documented in Les Blank's *Burden of Dreams* (1982).

The strenuous role is so wholly Kinski's that it seems perverse to wonder that Herzog seriously flagged Jason Robards, Jack Nicholson, and, tellingly, himself for the part beforehand. One wonders if Herzog might not have regretted the final product had any of these earlier castings come to pass. **GS**

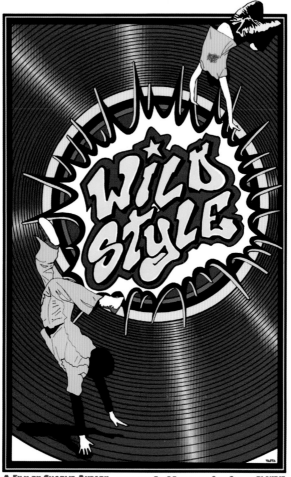

A FILM BY CHARLIE AHEARN ORIGINAL MUSIC FAB 5 FREDDY AND CHRIS STEIN of BLONDIE
FEATURING GRAND MASTER FLASH COLD CRUSH BROTHERS ROCK STEADY CREW
FAB 5 FREDDY CHIEF ROCKER BUSY BEE DOUBLE TROUBLE
STARRING 'LEE' QUINONES FRED BRATHWAITE PATTI ASTOR SANDRA 'PINK' FABARA
GRAFFITI LEE DAZE CRASH DONDI WILD STYLE LOGO ZEPHYR

WILD STYLE 1983 (U.S.)

Director Charlie Ahearn **Producer** Charlie Ahearn **Screenplay** Charlie Ahearn
Cinematography Clive Davidson, John Foster **Music** Fab Five Freddy, Chris Stein,
Rock Steady Crew, The Cold Crush Brothers, Grandmaster Flash **Cast** Easy A. D., A. J.,
Almighty K. G., Patti Astor, Busy Bee, Grandmaster Caz

Some time in the late 1970s, various poor, racial minority kids in
the Bronx began combining a new style of dance based on
disjointed, rhythm-centered movements with songs that clung
to rhyme over melodies and sentimental lyrics. Brown skin
meant legitimacy, and coming from the 'hood gave respect.
Combined with a D.J. to order musical selections and an M.C.
to bridge gaps in songs and comment on dancers and
audiences, the culture of hip-hop was born as economically
disenfranchised youth sprayed graffiti on the public facades of
New York buildings, subway cars, and bus stops.

White baby boomer Charlie Ahearn bumped into this
burgeoning movement after arriving in New York in the early
1970s. In particular, he became enamored of the graffiti artist
Lee Quinones. As he developed an interest in moviemaking, he
gradually met various art world figures, thereby establishing a
pattern that persists through today: white "detectives" uncover
brilliant minority culture producers and bring those cultural
products to a wider audience than was possible without the
detective-turned-promoter. When Ahearn made a martial arts
movie that debuted alongside work by Keith Haring and

◀
**Lead guitarist,
songwriter, and
cofounder of
Blondie, Chris Stein
had a hand in the
music of this film.**

Jean-Michael Basquiat, his profile was raised and one day he met the artist who would become world famous as Fab Five Freddy. Work formally began on a feature film about hip-hop in 1980. Freddy and Quinones participated in the planning and logistics of Ahearn's picture, and the documentarylike structure aped the lives of participants asked to perform their lives as if they were fictional characters. The story spins around Quinones

> ## "WE'RE SHOOTING IN THE SOUTH BRONX . . . IT LOOKED LIKE BERLIN AFTER WORLD WAR II." *CHARLIE AHEARN*

as Zoro, an elusive graffiti artist who struggles to express himself through his work while managing a relationship with another artist named Rose (Sandra Fabara) just as the moment he's thrown into the New York gallery scene and flanked by a reporter named Virginia (Patti Astor).

People don't watch *Wild Style* for scintillating enactment or a fast-paced plot. Instead, the movie's best qualities are its slow passage across a soon-to-blow-up scene. At that time, in that place (exclusively New York), no one knew that hip-hop would revolutionize the music and fashion industries, and prove to be the world's dominant art form at the close of the twentieth century precisely because it promotes ambitious self-expression as the badge of a new age. Standout moments include "Stoop Rap" by Double Trouble and an extraordinary scene in a band shell that gives the film its finale. **GC-Q**

► A tremendously fresh-faced film of New York's subway graffiti art and the birth of break dancing.

Beings from Another Dimension have invaded your world
You can't see them...but they can see you.

Your only hope
is Buckaroo Banzai.

Peter Weller
as Buckaroo

Ellen Barkin
as Penny Priddy

Jeff Goldblum
as New Jersey

Christopher Lloyd
as The Alien Lectroid

...and

John Lithgow
as Dr. Lizardo

THE ADVENTURES OF
BUCKAROO
BANZAI™
ACROSS THE 8TH DIMENSION!

SHERWOOD PRODUCTIONS PRESENTS A SIDNEY BECKERMAN PRODUCTION THE ADVENTURES OF BUCKAROO BANZAI
Starring PETER WELLER   JOHN LITHGOW   ELLEN BARKIN
Also starring JEFF GOLDBLUM   CHRISTOPHER LLOYD   Executive Producer SIDNEY BECKERMAN
Produced by NEIL CANTON AND W. D. RICHTER   Written by EARL MAC RAUCH
Directed by W. D. RICHTER   Now in Paperback from POCKET BOOKS

THE ADVENTURES OF BUCKAROO BANZAI ACROSS THE 8TH DIMENSION 1984 (U.S.)

Director W. D. Richter **Producer** Neil Canton, W. D. Richter **Screenplay** Earl Mac Rauch **Cinematography** Fred J. Koenekamp **Music** Michael Boddicker
Cast Peter Weller, John Lithgow, Ellen Barkin, Jeff Goldblum, Christopher Lloyd, Lewis Smith, Rosalind Cash, Clancy Brown, Robert Ito, Vincent Schiavelli

For many it's hard to enjoy a movie that demonstrates a perversely dense backstory while suggesting that its characters live far beyond the silver screen. Added to this excess is a deliberate homage to movie serials, comic books, and the 1980s resurgence of action movies centered on handsome polymaths, who are able to solve arcane problems, get the girl, and think through lectures and bar rooms equally. Indiana Jones may be the era's prototypical hero but then there's *The Adventures of Buckaroo Banzai Across the 8th Dimension* (1984), W. D. Richter's pastiche of sci-fi and action conventions that allude to some magnificent, but never spoken, private joke.

What's left is Peter Weller in the title role with a backup cast of movie character-actors, including Rawhide (Clancy Brown), Reno Nevada (Pepe Serna), Perfect Tommy (Lewis Smith), New Jersey (Jeff Goldblum), and Pinky Carruthers (Billy Vera). The six all play musical instruments. They do physics. They wear cool

Fans of the movie point to the winks and nudges that maintain ironic distance from these pulpy materials while also lavishing love upon them.

clothes. They have adventures. They are, in short, Renaissance men, although Dr. Banzai is undoubtedly their champion, considering that he is not only a scientist and musician, but also a samurai and test pilot-driver whose actions open up a hole into the 8th dimension where lots of bad stuff happens.

The movie's plot centers on Banzai's efforts to learn the extent of an overlap he's created with the 8th dimension that

> ## "NO, NO, NO, DON'T TUG ON THAT. YOU NEVER KNOW WHAT IT MIGHT BE ATTACHED TO." BUCKAROO BANZAI

▶
Banzai himself places the movie in the most appropriate milieu when he says, "You remind me of someone I once knew." And so he does, the beloved pop hero as media-aided messiah, from our ever-consuming pop frenzy.

depends on a high-speed, dimension-shifting car that can travel through solid objects. The bottom line is that a group of aliens, the Red Lectroids, trapped in the 8th dimension, recognize an opening into this world, courtesy of Emilion Lizardo (John Lithgow), a presumptively insane Italian scientist who has his mind colonized by the Red Lectroids. An overlap with The Mercury Theater of the Air broadcast of "The War of the Worlds" blurs fact and fiction, leaving the safety of the world in Banzai's capable hands. Oh, and there's a girl, too, named Penny Priddy (Ellen Barkin) who is the twin sister of Banzai's dead wife. Coincidence? No. The movie is actually the collected notations of years in the life of screenwriter Earl Mac Rauch, who produced enough false starts, character and plot outlines, notations, and parallel adventures to produce a book to assist during production. **GC-Q**

"THE FUNNIEST ROCK MOVIE EVER MADE."

Merrill Shindler—Los Angeles Magazine

"HILARIOUS...SENDS UP WHAT THE BEATLES STARTED WITH 'A HARD DAYS NIGHT.'"

Bruce Williamson—Playboy

"DON'T MISS IT...ONE OF THE FUNNIEST MOVIES"

Stephen Shaefer—US Magazine

THIS IS

Spinal Tap

CHRISTOPHER GUEST · MICHAEL McKEAN · HARRY SHEARER · ROB REINER
JUNE CHADWICK · TONY HENDRA & BRUNO KIRBY · KAREN MURPHY
CHRISTOPHER GUEST & MICHAEL McKEAN & ROB REINER & HARRY SHEARER · ROB REINER

THIS IS SPINAL TAP 1984 (U.S.)

Director Rob Reiner **Producer** Karen Murphy **Screenplay** Christopher Guest, Michael McKean, Harry Shearer, Rob Reiner **Cinematography** Peter Smokler **Music** Christopher Guest, Michael McKean, Harry Shearer, Rob Reiner **Cast** Rob Reiner, Michael McKean, Christopher Guest, Harry Shearer, Fran Drescher, Bruno Kirby

The brainchild of director, writer, composer, and performer Rob Reiner, *This Is Spinal Tap* is probably the best spoof rocumentary ever. It follows the heavy metal Spinal Tap as the band embarks on a comeback tour in the United States—while being filmed for a fly-on-the-wall documentary. Such is the realistic nature of the rock group's excesses and divalike pretentiousness, some even thought the film was a real documentary when it was released. Reiner—whose directorial credits include *When Harry Met Sally* (1989) and *The Princess Bride* (1987)—plays documentary-maker Marty DiBergi, and the faux English band is acted by Christopher Guest as lead guitarist Nigel Tufnel, Michael McKean as lead singer David Ivor St. Hubbins, and Harry Shearer as Derek Smalls the bassist. The motley crew lacks a drummer and the post has been filled by a string of musicians, all of whom have died in weird circumstances; the drummer who joins them on tour explodes on stage.

The movie's success is down to its deadpan humor, as it is packed with wonderful one-liners, often ad-libbed by Reiner and his costars and a convincing backstory for the group as the documentary traces their origins in the skiffle and then flower-

◄
The poster's 1980s heavy metal look and quotes from critics do not reveal that the band is not a real one. The movie achieved cult following when released on video.

power era with the aid of interviews and old footage. Most compelling is the credibility of the plot as the band members cope with an intrusive girlfriend, deal with accusations of sexism, argue with their manager, and struggle with the idea that their popularity is on the wane. Reiner handles such rock industry clichés with a verve and irreverent wit that verges into pastiche. The performance of its stars as the band members is

> ## "AS LONG AS THERE'S SEX AND DRUGS, I CAN DO WITHOUT ROCK AND ROLL." *MICK SHRIMPTON*

convincingly spot-on as they capture the posturing, preening swagger, and affectation of metal-head musicians. Bare-chested or satin-shirted, they bulge out of their pants and cod-metal ruminations: "We've got armadillos in our trousers, it's really quite frightening." Their belief in their "art" is charming: the dim-witted Tufnel explains the secret of their success is that the band has a guitar amp that goes to eleven rather than ten.

This Is Spinal Tap was a slow burner at the box office but achieved its cult following when it was released on video. Since then, the band has taken on a life of its own, doing rock concerts, performing on David Letterman's TV show, and Guest even giving an interview in character as Tufnel on the National Geographic Channel. Reiner created a fiction in *This Is Spinal Tap* that has spawned a reality and created a fan following. Truth really is stranger than fiction. **CK**

► **Christopher Guest in full-on metal pose. It's a long way from *Best In Show* (2000) or *For Your Consideration* (2006).**

THE TOXIC AVENGER 1984 (U.S.)

Director Michael Herz, Lloyd Kaufman **Producer** Michael Herz, Lloyd Kaufman
Screenplay Joe Ritter, Lloyd Kaufman **Cinematography** Lloyd Kaufman, James A.
Lebovitz **Music** Mark Hoffman, Dean Summers **Cast** Mitchell Cohen, Andree
Maranda, Gary Schneider, Robert Prichard, Cindy Manion, Mark Torgl

Roughly ten minutes into *The Toxic Avenger*, there is a scene where some jocks in a Trans-Am run over a twelve-year-old on a bicycle for kicks, crushing his head like a melon. The two female passengers exit the car, run over to the body, and begin taking pictures. "This is fun," exclaims the blonde bimbo of the two. Nothing could sum up this film and the wild world of Troma Entertainment better.

Troma Entertainment is a New York-based indie that originally found success with homegrown T&A productions and exploitation film distribution in the late 1970s. Everything involving blood, beasts, and babes drew its attention— basically anything that could earn money and deliver on the promise of offering the "Aroma of Troma."

The action unfolds in Tromaville, New Jersey ("Toxic waste dumping capital of the world"), where bullied gym janitor Melvin Junko (Mark Torgl) ends up in a pink tutu and headfirst in a vat of toxic waste thanks to a prank gone awry. The chemicals transform his body and he morphs into the grotesque Toxic Avenger (Mitchell Cohen), a muscle-bound, mop-wielding superhero monstrosity with an instinctive sense to fight evil.

◀

This is the same film company that produced the deliciously titled horror-comedy-musical *Poultrygeist: Night of the Chicken Dead* (2006).

And Tromaville is overflowing with evil from the aforementioned thrill-kill jocks to corrupt Mayor Belgoody (Pat Ryan), who hopes to turn the toxic waste dump Melvin now calls home into condos.Playing upon the early 1980s nuclear hysteria and box office success of gore films, Troma produced *The Toxic Avenger*, a mishmash of goofy comedy, satire, sexploitation, violence, and splatter that resembles *MAD* magazine brought to life.

"I GO OUT AND I MASH PEOPLE. I TEAR THEM APART AND I CAN'T STOP."

THE TOXIC AVENGER

Proudly relying on a do-it-yourself low-budget aesthetic, anything goes in the anarchist world of Troma filmmaking. No one is safe from harm in *The Toxic Avenger* as the elderly, men, women, children, babies, midgets, and even dogs all receive some form of abuse (amusingly, Troma head Lloyd Kaufman has said the dog death garnered the most outcry). Naturally, the exploitation factor is high as nudity battles with realistically realized gore for on-screen dominance.

Troma struck gold among cult audiences with *The Toxic Avenger,* and the character — lovingly dubbed Toxie—became synonymous with the company as its official mascot. He returned for three more sequels and, believe it or not, a cartoon series. Troma continued to mine the successful gore-n-girls formula over the next twenty-five years, producing titles such as the Shakespeare send-up *Tromeo & Juliet* (1996). **WW**

► **Shapely forms vie with gory freaks for dominance in the decidely weird Toxic Avenger series.**

"BLUE VELVET is a mystery...a masterpiece...
a visionary story of sexual awakening,
of good and evil, a trip to the underworld."
—David Thompson, CALIFORNIA MAGAZINE

"A nightmarish, intensely disturbing exploration
of the hidden side of the soul. It is sure to cause a sensation."
—Ken Turan, GQ

"Brilliant and unsettling...this is the work of
an all-American visionary—and a master film stylist."
—Stephen Schiff, VANITY FAIR

Blue Velvet

DE LAURENTIIS ENTERTAINMENT GROUP
PRESENTS
A DAVID LYNCH FILM
"BLUE VELVET" KYLE MACLACHLAN ISABELLA ROSSELLINI DENNIS HOPPER
AND LAURA DERN WITH HOPE LANGE GEORGE DICKERSON AND DEAN STOCKWELL
Director of Photography FREDERICK ELMES Sound Design ALAN SPLET Production Designer PATRICIA NORRIS Edited by DUWAYNE DUNHAM
Music Composed by ANGELO BADALAMENTI Executive Producer RICHARD ROTH Written and Directed by DAVID LYNCH

BLUE VELVET 1986 (U.S.)

Director David Lynch **Producer** Fred C. Caruso **Screenplay** David Lynch
Cinematography Frederick Elmes **Music** Angelo Badalamenti
Cast Kyle MacLachlan, Isabella Rossellini, Dennis Hopper, Laura Dern, Hope Lange,
Dean Stockwell, George Dickerson, Brad Dourif, Jack Nance, Priscilla Pointer

When David Lynch's *Blue Velvet* was released in 1986, it was generally well received by critics. Another sentiment was that it was "weird." And "weird" is certainly the key word in describing David Lynch's career. But, looking at *Blue Velvet* nearly a quarter-century later, and in hindsight with Lynch's subsequent works, it's actually one of his most accessible, straightforward, normal films. There's very little here that even compares to the "Look how wildly eccentric I am!" obfuscation of many of his later films. After all this time, what was flamboyantly weird to 1986 eyes looks refreshingly quaint and, at times, almost old-fashioned, with fairly obvious symbolism about the evil that lurks underneath a picture-perfect façade, such as a small town straight out of Norman Rockwell.

College student Jeffrey Beaumont (Kyle MacLachlan) has returned home to Lumberton after his father suffers a stroke. Walking home from the hospital, he finds a severed human ear in a field. Reporting it to a detective (George Dickerson), Jeffrey ends up getting friendly with his daughter, Sandy (Laura Dern). It's Sandy who tells Jeffrey what she's overheard her father discussing, and that leads him to the apartment of sultry,

◄

This film continues Lynch's inventive subversion of small-town America, already dissected in his TV series *Twin Peaks*.

masochistic nightclub singer Dorothy Vallens (Isabella Rossellini), whose husband (the owner of the ear) and son have been kidnapped by psychotic Frank Booth (Dennis Hopper) as a means of forcing her to cater to Frank's sadistic sexual whims. As it is one of Lynch's best films, *Blue Velvet* would have a fervent cult following anyway, but it's Hopper's legendary performance that everyone still talks about. From the moment he appears

"IN DREAMS I WALK WITH YOU. IN DREAMS I TALK TO YOU. IN DREAMS, YOU'RE MINE ALL THE TIME." *BOOTH*

on-screen (not until nearly forty-five minutes in; he makes such an unforgettable impression that it's surprising how little screen time he really has), Hopper simply takes over. 1986 was a comeback year for the newly clean and sober actor, with equally memorable turns in *The Texas Chainsaw Massacre Part 2*, *River's Edge*, and his Oscar-nominated role in *Hoosiers*, but all of those take a backseat to Hopper's Frank Booth and whatever it is he's huffing from that oxygen mask.

Early in the film, Jeffrey remarks, "It's a strange world, isn't it?" Indeed. Whether you look at the film from an oedipal standpoint, or with the notion that Jeffrey and Frank are two sides of the same coin, or as a haunting tale of innocence lost, it's a film that stays with you, much like the darkness stays with the characters even as they go about their normal lives. It's always there, even if you don't see it. **MT**

▶
Isabella Rossellini plays a heartbreaking femme fatale, smoldering with sexual tension.

The terror starts the moment he stops.

THE HITCHER

Never pick-up a stranger.

HBO PICTURES in association with SILVER SCREEN PARTNERS Presents A FELDMAN MEEKER PRODUCTION
"THE HITCHER" RUTGER HAUER · C. THOMAS HOWELL · JEFFREY DeMUNN · JENNIFER JASON LEIGH
Director of Photography JOHN SEALE A.C.S. · Editor FRANK J. URIOSTE, A.C.E. · Music by MARK ISHAM · Co-Producer PAUL LEWIS
Executive Producers EDWARD S. FELDMAN and CHARLES R. MEEKER · Written by ERIC RED
Produced by KIP OHMAN and DAVID BOMBYK · Directed by ROBERT HARMON

THE HITCHER 1986 (U.S.)

Director Robert Harmon **Producer** David Bombyk, Kip Ohman **Screenplay** Eric Red **Cinematography** John Seale **Music** Mark Isham **Cast** Rutger Hauer, C. Thomas Howell, Jennifer Jason Leigh, Jeffrey DeMunn, John M. Jackson, Billy Green Bush, Jack Thibeau, Armin Shimerman, Gene Davis

More than a decade before torture porn became a fashionable label for films preoccupied with evildoers inflicting pain on victims just for the heck of it, *The Hitcher* laid down the law for this subgenre. And it didn't need fancy effects or masks to do it —just a solid enigmatic maniac with charisma and an open road.

The Hitcher is the story of Jim (C. Thomas Howell), a young man delivering a car from Chicago to San Diego. He picks up hitchhiker, Ryder (a truly satanic Rutger Hauer), who soon announces he is going to kill him. Jim rids himself of Ryder a few times, but Ryder keeps coming back, killing anyone who stands between him and Jim. He even shoots down a police helicopter and frees Jim from a jail to get to him. "What do you want?" asks a desperate Jim. "I want you to stop me," answers Ryder. Jim only finds relief with waitress Nash (Jennifer Jason Leigh). After Ryder murders her, too, Jim finally confronts Ryder. But by then there is no more redemption—he has become Ryder.

The Hitcher stands in between the tradition of the demonic road movie and the high-concept thriller of the 1990s. But it contains much more violence than both of these traditions put together. In fact, there is so much relentless violence that it

◄

The byline for this movie might have been Hauer's immortal line in *Blade Runner* (1982): "Time to die."

becomes the story. Ryder never gives a reason for his killing, nor does he kill Jim when he gets the chance. Like a cat playing with a mouse, he loves the run-up to the violent act too much. Ryder's tricks are so elaborate that they command respect. Audiences really only have one single way of enjoying *The Hitcher*: admire Ryder's cleverness and relentlessness as he hunts for Jim. Two images stand out: the little detail of the

"ACTUALLY WE'RE ALL FROM MARS AROUND HERE; WE KEEP OUR SPACESHIP OUT BACK." NASH

finger in Jim's burger (a nice dig on fast food), and the ornate construct of Nash tied between two trucks, ready to be torn in two—a scene that gives the word tension new meaning.

Because of the cult reputation of Dutch actor Rutger Hauer (*Turkish Delight* (1973), *Blade Runner* (1982), and *Flesh+Blood* (1985), in which Hauer had had some kinky scenes with Jennifer Jason Leigh), *The Hitcher* did not go unnoticed upon its release, but it really only reached its true audience through the video market, where it became a solid hit.

In true cult-sleeper fashion, it took years for the film to develop a firm fan base. After that fandom had fully emerged, a TV series was developed, and in 2007 Michael Bay produced a sequel. None of these, however, have the eerie menacing power, or Hauer's maniacal grin, that make the original one of the most unsettling movies of the 1980s. **EM**

► **Rutger Hauer in truly menacing form as the scheming hitcher who gets his kicks from the promise of violence as much as from the violence itself.**

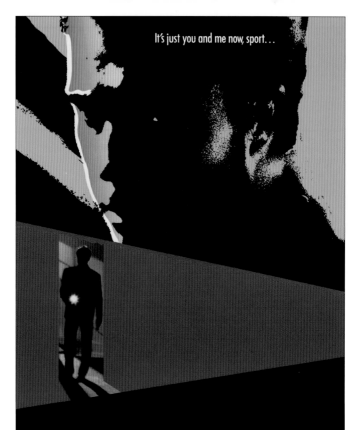

MANHUNTER 1986 (U.S.)

Director Michael Mann **Producer** Dino De Laurentiis, Richard Roth
Screenplay Michael Mann, Thomas Harris (novel) **Cinematography** Dante
Spinotti **Music** The Reds, Michel Rubini **Cast** William Petersen, Brian Cox,
Tom Noonan, Kim Greist, Joan Allen, Dennis Farina, Stephan Lang

Adapted by Michael Mann from Thomas Harris's best-selling novel, *Red Dragon*, *Manhunter* was a box office flop upon initial release. It was only with the later success of *The Silence of the Lambs* (1991) that the film was "rediscovered." The chance of a reassessment proved beneficial to Mann's film, and it is now thought by many to be superior to Jonathan Demme's *The Silence of the Lambs*. The original screen incarnation of Hannibal Lecktor (as opposed to the later spelling Lector), Brian Cox is far less "cuddly" than Anthony Hopkins' subsequent version of the same character. Although the *Silence of the Lambs* was a box office success in a way that *Manhunter* never managed to be, for many Cox's portrayal of Lecktor as an intensely darkly brooding and physically intimidating presence is both far closer to the Lecktor of Thomas Harris's novels and a far scarier figure for it.

William Petersen, who would later find greater fame playing Gil Grissom in *C.S.I.*, is perfectly cast as the F.B.I.'s top criminal profiler Will Graham, a man who attempts to get inside the mind of the killers he is employed to track down. Since catching the infamous Dr. Hannibal Lecktor, a psychopathic killer with a genius level I.Q., family-man Graham has been in self-imposed

◄
The film was later remade by Brett Ratner as *Red Dragon* (2002), but it lacked both the intensity of Cox's Lecktor and the coolness of Mann's direction.

retirement, the trauma of inhabiting the mind of a killer as potent as Lecktor's having caused a breakdown. But when a new family-murdering serial killer, quickly dubbed "The Tooth Fairy" (Tom Noonan) by the press, comes on the scene, Will's old boss Jack Crawford (Dennis Farina) asks him to return for one last time. To address both his own demons and to get his assistance in tracking down The Tooth Fairy, Graham visits Lecktor in his

"AND IF ONE DOES WHAT GOD DOES ENOUGH TIMES, ONE WILL BECOME AS GOD IS." DR. HANNIBAL LECKTOR

high-security prison cell and what ensues is a cat-and-mouse game of bluff and counter-bluff between the two men, with Lecktor seeking to manipulate Graham and—by extension The Tooth Fairy—to his own, unknown ends. Graham manages to use one serial killer in order to catch another and ends up finding both peace of mind and solace with his own family.

Manhunter is both brilliantly moody and utterly typical of Mann at his best. The stark, clinically lit interiors of Lecktor's prison cell contrasts with the murky interiors of both the victims' houses and The Tooth Fairy's own hideout. Typically the city and its modernist milieu are as important as the on-screen characters. And, although the clean lines of the flat white buildings set against the scorching Californian sun and the urgent soundtrack date the movie as very 1980s Los Angeles, they also add an oddly expressionistic feel to the film. **RH**

► **Tom Noonan as Francis Dollarhyde, a.k.a. "The Tooth Fairy"—a suitably scary serial killer.**

HANDMADE FILMS PRESENTS

Withnail and I

"WITHNAIL AND I"
EXECUTIVE PRODUCERS GEORGE HARRISON AND DENIS O'BRIEN
PRODUCED BY PAUL HELLER CO-PRODUCED BY DAVID WIMBURY
WRITTEN AND DIRECTED BY BRUCE ROBINSON

WITHNAIL AND I 1987 (U.K.)

Director Bruce Robinson **Producer** Paul Heller **Screenplay** Bruce Robinson **Cinematography** Peter Hannan **Music** David Dundas, Rick Wentworth **Cast** Richard E. Grant, Paul McGann, Richard Griffiths, Ralph Brown, Michael Elphick, Michael Wardle, Eddie Tagoe

This film is a true classic of British cinema that reserves a special place in the heart of anyone who considers a lost afternoon in an alcoholic daze time well spent. Like any cult film worthy of the name, *Withnail and I* entered the world with barely a flicker of interest. Its popularity grew from a committed word-of-mouth campaign, particularly among students, that has elevated the film to something approaching the mainstream.

Withnail's enduring appeal lies in Bruce Robinson's intelligent screenplay, which fizzes with achingly funny and quotable dialogue, beautifully executed by the film's four main characters. Robinson based the story around his own experiences as an out-of-work actor in north London during the dying embers of the 1960s. Richard E. Grant, as Withnail, delivers a mesmerizing performance full of bitterness and frustration for his own current demoralized state and the part in it of those around him. He is a ridiculous coward and a prancing pompous thespian, self-deluded in his own ability. It's a tribute to Grant—eternally associated with this his first role, despite an extremely successful career—that we love him despite all the flaws and are unable to take our eyes away from this car crash of a man.

◄

George Harrison was an executive producer (the company Handmade Films being his), and the poster featured a droll caricature by Gerald Scarfe.

Paul McGann as "I"—later identified as Marwood—narrates the film, infused with paranoia and struggling to keep a grip on reality. Out of his depth when trying to keep up with Withnail's prodigious alcohol and substance intake, he is longing for an opportunity to escape this protracted adolescence.

In search of rejuvenation, the pair stay at a cottage belonging to Withnail's Uncle Monty in the Lake District. Hopelessly inept

"THE GREATEST DECADE IN . . . HISTORY . . . IS COMING TO AN END AND WE HAVE FAILED TO PAINT IT BLACK." DANNY

at heating and feeding themselves, they traipse the countryside with polythene bags on their feet, drink vigorously, and upset the locals. There is little in the way of plot or action; the suspense hinges around the prospect of hearing another memorable line from Withnail's alcohol-soaked mouth such as, "I demand some booze," or "We want the finest wines available to humanity." The supporting cast is no less explosive: Richard Griffiths is superb as Uncle Monty with his infectious *joie de vivre*, designs on Marwood, and glorious turn of phrase—"As a youth, I used to weep in butcher's shops"—and Ralph Brown excels as Danny the drug dealer, who offers a series of hilarious amphetamine-charged philosophical musings. The final scene is doused in melancholy: Marwood, finally employed, leaves Withnail behind in the driving rain, bottle in hand, quoting Hamlet to a bemused caged wolf. Cinematic endings rarely come more moving. **SG**

► **Withnail (Grant) and Marwood (McGann) embark on another boozy outing: "We've gone on holiday by mistake."**

AMAZON WOMEN ON THE MOON
1987 (U.S.)

Director Joe Dante, Carl Gottlieb, Peter Horton, John Landis, Robert K. Weiss
Producer Robert K. Weiss **Screenplay** Michael Barrie, Jim Mulholland
Cinematography Daniel Pearl **Music** Ira Newborn **Cast** Arsenio Hall, Donald F. Muhich, Lou Jacobi, Corey Burton, Joe Pantoliano, Rosanna Arquette, Archie Hahn

Omnibus movies pattern themselves on the medium that largely replaced cinema: TV. Often unrelated short stories hold together on the small screen precisely because they're interrupted by commercials and the private functions of spectators. When the bits fail, they fail spectacularly, but when they succeed there is an element of chancy surprise since the quality of bits isn't always apparent before broadcast. In movies, though, the failures and successes are magnified since so much more attention and effort folds into the construction of a singular entertainment.

Amazon Women on the Moon is a comic anthology featuring twenty-one skits directed by five name directors. The film's title refers to a film-within-the-film spoof, a mishmash of sci-fi and schlock references, which gives a taste of what the overall movie is trying to accomplish. The frame is about a dynamic duo battling volcanoes and spiders on the moon, discussed in the film as a 1950s B movie, and it stitches together a grab bag of goofs, infomercials, trailers, and clips that suggest an evening in front of the boob tube flipping channels. By final credits

◄

Look out also for Michelle Pfeiffer, Kelly Preston, Ed Begley, Jr., Jenny Agutter, David Alan Grier, and Huey Lewis, alongside blues musician B. B. King, movie director Russ Meyer, and comedian Andrew Dice Clay.

there is a sense of having seen important chunks of "Amazon Women on the Moon," starring rip-away-bra, B-movie queen Sybil Danning. One is equally amused to have spent time with a former hooker who has become First Lady (Angel Tompkins) in "First Lady of the Evening," as well as a sexually frustrated teen boy hawking condoms (Matt Adler) in a skit called "Titan Man," both directed by Weiss. Other highlights include a man (Arsenio

"WHY DO JEWISH DIVORCES COST SO MUCH? THEY'RE WORTH IT."

HENNY YOUNGMAN (COMEDIAN)

Hall) who nearly dies through silly adventures inside his apartment, a woman (Monique Gabriell) who conducts all the affairs of her life in the nude, Joe Pantoliano extolling the virtues of stapled carpet as replacement hair for balding, a show called "Bullshit or Not?," and a funereal roast of an actor (Archie Hahn) who has been mauled to death. The formula for *Amazon Women* derives from the earlier success John Landis enjoyed with *The Kentucky Fried Movie* (1977). The same criticism that applied to that film applies here: it's uneven and half-baked, but when the humor flows, it flows with exactly the right balance of surprise and smart execution. Is it bad taste? Is it satire? Is it fun? Yes, yes, and yes. For most viewers now, the fun is in watching various then-prominent actors showcased in these sketches, including Rosanna Arquette, Griffin Dunne, Carrie Fisher, and Steve Guttenberg, to name a very few. **GC-Q**

► **Steve Forrest as Capt. Steve Nelson does his turn in the "Amazon Women on the Moon" segment.**

MICKEY ROURKE   FAYE DUNAWAY

BARFLY

THE CANNON GROUP, INC. FRANCIS FORD COPPOLA PRESENTS MICKEY ROURKE · FAYE DUNAWAY A GOLAN-GLOBUS PRODUCTION
A BARBET SCHROEDER FILM BARFLY ALICE KRIGE · J.C. QUINN · FRANK STALLONE ASSOCIATE PRODUCER JACK BARAN EDITED BY EVA GARDOS
DIRECTOR OF PHOTOGRAPHY ROBBY MULLER EXECUTIVE PRODUCERS MENAHEM GOLAN AND YORAM GLOBUS WRITTEN BY CHARLES BUKOWSKI PRODUCED BY BARBET SCHROEDER,
FRED ROOS AND TOM LUDDY DIRECTED BY BARBET SCHROEDER

CANNON
RELEASING CORPORATION

R RESTRICTED

BARFLY 1987 (U.S.)

Director Barbet Schroeder **Producer** Tom Luddy, Fred Roos, Barbet Schroeder
Screenplay Charles Bukowski **Cinematography** Robby Müller **Music** Jack
Baran **Cast** Mickey Rourke, Faye Dunaway, Alice Krige, Jack Nance, J. C. Quinn,
Frank Stallone, Sandy Martin, Roberta Bassin

Charles Bukowski was a writer, a drunk, and a postal worker. He
lived a unique version of the "I know best and sod you" school
of American manhood and achieved fame in middle age on
the basis of autobiographical stories about promiscuity, work,
impoverishment, and the trials of being a writer.

In the mid-1980s, after negotiating with the likes of Sean Penn
for the story of his life, Barbet Schroeder got the nod to direct
the Bukowski-penned roman à clef *Barfly* (1987) because he
commissioned the script and was a "comer" in the parlance of
Hollywood. Mickey Rourke was cast as the surrogate Bukowski
character, Henry Chinaski, fresh from his role in *9 ½ Weeks* (1986),
and Faye Dunaway was cast as Wanda Wilcox, just then settling
into her middle-aged marmdom in roles like the horrific *Mommie
Dearest* (1981) and this, despite her Oscar for *Network* (1976).

The story concerns a pivotal moment in Bukowski's life in
which he was committing to being a writer. For him, this
meant capturing words on paper by day, and abusing alcohol
and having fistfights by night. It was both a romantic and
destructive time that put into practice the idea of living for
one's art because art is worth the discomfort. Still, the fact

◄
**Bukowski fans take
apart *Barfly* for its
inaccuracies, but
the man himself
was happy to be
an uncredited bar
patron in the film
as well as writing
this fictionalized
version of his
life story.**

remains that Bukowski's life really did circle around wordplay and a highball of scotch, so it comes as no surprise that *Barfly* covers the same territory.

By day, Henry writes poems and stories, hoping to publish in literary magazines. By night, he drinks heavily and devotes himself to Wanda, although Wanda isn't fully committed to Henry and has an ongoing affair with bartender Eddie (Frank

"SOME PEOPLE NEVER GO CRAZY. WHAT TRULY HORRIBLE LIVES THEY MUST LEAD." HENRY CHINASKI

Stallone). Henry is discovered by Tully Wilcox (Alice Krige), an arts patron with means, and Henry is seduced into being her playmate and prize. Eventually discomfited by her polished and staid social circle, Henry leaves Tully for his old environs, takes up again with Wanda, and resigns himself to being a barfly, that combination of muse-devil to enable his peculiar art. During the final credits, he goes to blows with Eddie over what seems to be a bar tab alongside years of antipathy, although it's equally true that *Barfly* uses interpersonal violence, much as Bukowski did, as a sorting method to clarify and bind people together.

Biopic aficionados like the film because of its familiar tale of survival and struggle and warm to the Rourke-Dunaway pairing that is unexpected and totally fascinating—the feminine softness in Rourke and the slightly overlarge features of Dunaway. **GC-Q**

► Rourke fans see *Barfly* as the story of a talent on the rise, followed by the nadir of his early 1990s misadventures.

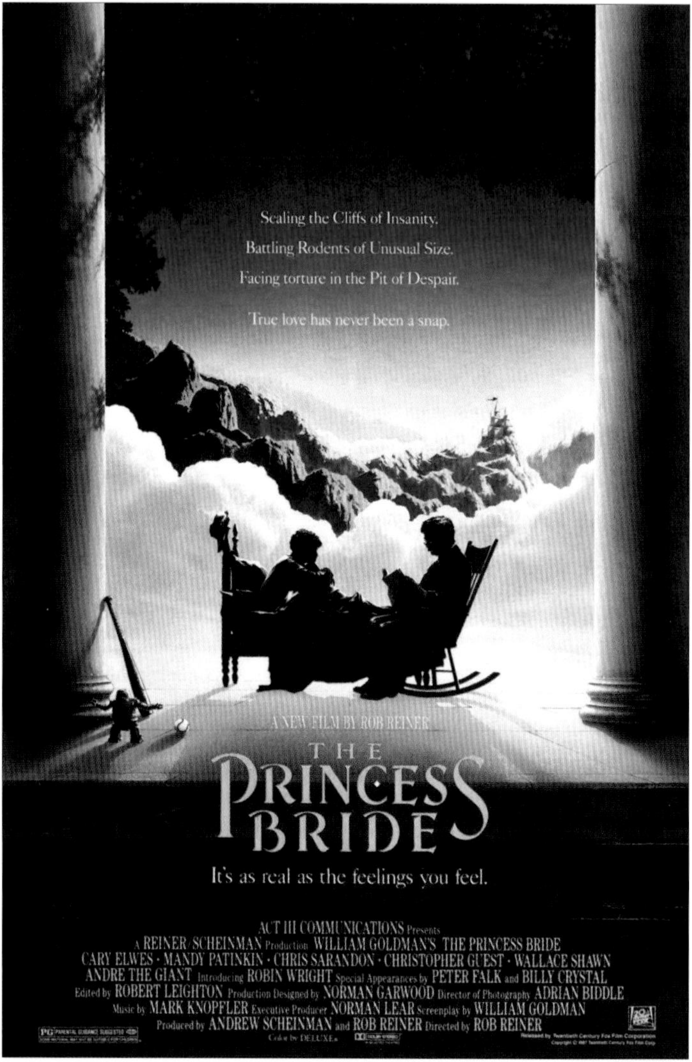
Scaling the Cliffs of Insanity.
Battling Rodents of Unusual Size.
Facing torture in the Pit of Despair.
True love has never been a snap.
A NEW FILM BY ROB REINER
THE PRINCESS BRIDE
It's as real as the feelings you feel.
ACT III COMMUNICATIONS Presents
A REINER/SCHEINMAN Production WILLIAM GOLDMAN'S THE PRINCESS BRIDE
CARY ELWES · MANDY PATINKIN · CHRIS SARANDON · CHRISTOPHER GUEST · WALLACE SHAWN
ANDRE THE GIANT Introducing ROBIN WRIGHT Special Appearances by PETER FALK and BILLY CRYSTAL
Edited by ROBERT LEIGHTON Production Designed by NORMAN GARWOOD Director of Photography ADRIAN BIDDLE
Music by MARK KNOPFLER Executive Producer NORMAN LEAR Screenplay by WILLIAM GOLDMAN
Produced by ANDREW SCHEINMAN and ROB REINER Directed by ROB REINER
Color by DELUXE

THE PRINCESS BRIDE 1987 (U.S.)

Director Rob Reiner **Producer** Andrew Scheinman **Screenplay** William Goldman
Cinematography Adrian Biddle **Music** Mark Knopfler **Cast** Cary Elwes, Robin
Wright Penn, Mandy Patinkin, Chris Sarandon, Christopher Guest, Wallace Shawn,
André the Giant, Peter Falk, Carol Kane, Billy Crystal, Fred Savage

In a fantasy medieval world of castles and forests and apparently
insurmountable obstacles like the Cliffs of Insanity and the Pit
of Despair, farm boy Westley (Cary Elwes) battles his way
through daring escapes, swordfights, wrestling matches,
battles of wits, torture, and even near-death for the sake of his
true love, Buttercup (Robin Wright Penn). Framing the fairy-tale
action, and occasionally intruding into it, a grandfather (Peter
Falk) reads the story to his sick grandson (Fred Savage). The boy
is not impressed at first, convinced that this is going to be a
"kissing book." But the grandfather persuades him to give the
book a chance, promising that it contains plenty of sports.
Before long, the boy is truly involved, asking his grandfather to
come back and read it again the next day.

◄
**The movie
manages to mock
the fantasy
adventure genre
and at the same
time relish it. To
misquote Miracle
Max (Billy Crystal):
"Not all perfect.
Just mostly
perfect."**

Adapted by William Goldman from his own 1973 novel (he
won two Oscars for Best Screenplay, in 1976 for *All the President's
Men* and in 1969 for *Butch Cassidy and the Sundance Kid*), *The
Princess Bride* is a romantic fantasy action-adventure with some
great comic cameos played with a tone of knowing, exaggerated
theatricality. The hero is dashing and apparently capable of
anything. The villains are all truly dastardly, almost inviting boos

and hisses like pantomime baddies. The romance may not be all that convincing, but the action is real with impressive swordplay and moments of nail-biting peril alongside the comic asides and catchphrases. There's a heart-stopping moment when Buttercup disappears into the sinking sand, and *twice* when she appears to have married the wicked prince. The water-powered Machine in the Pit of Despair looks a bit too Heath Robinson to

"FENCING. FIGHTING. TORTURE. REVENGE. GIANTS. MONSTERS. CHASES. ESCAPES. TRUE LOVE. MIRACLES." *GRANDFATHER*

be truly frightening, but Westley suffers real agony when he is tortured with it. Mandy Patinkin is a joy to watch as the revenge-driven Inigo, chanting, "My name is Inigo Montoya. You killed my father. Prepare to die," as he closes in on the six-fingered Count Rugen (Christopher Guest). The movie is not without flaws. At times the stunning landscapes (filmed in England and Ireland) seem a little too real, giving the fantasy dungeons, villages, and castles a two-dimensional stage set feel. Westley's battle with the deadly R.O.U.S. (Rodent Of Unusual Size) is probably more laughable than it is supposed to be. Watch the movie with children and you will see what it's trying to achieve. There'll be plenty of moments when you're laughing and they're not: they see just the fantasy adventure, while you see the movie's knowingness. And Goldman should know; he wrote the definitive *Adventures in the Screen Trade* after all. **CW**

▶
Mandy Patinkin appears as Inigo Montoya, a skilled swordsman on a quest to avenge his father.

Deutscher Filmpreis
1988

Festival de Cannes
Beste Regie 1987

Europäischer Filmpreis
Beste Regie 1988

BRUNO GANZ   SOLVEIG DOMMARTIN   OTTO SANDER
CURT BOIS und PETER FALK

DER HIMMEL ÜBER
BERLIN

Wiederaufführung 1986 – 2006

Ein Film von Wim Wenders

BRUNO GANZ SOLVEIG DOMMARTIN OTTO SANDER CURT BOIS und PETER FALK   JÜRGEN KNIEPER
PETER PRZYGODDA   HENRI ALEKAN   HEIDI LUDI, SFK   INGRID WINDISCH
WIM WENDERS und ANATOLE DAUMAN   WIM WENDERS   PETER HANDKE   WIM WENDERS
ROAD MOVIES FILMPRODUKTION GMBH und ARGOS FILMS S.A.
© 1987 REVERSE ANGLE LIBRARY GMBH   ℞   ARGOS FILMS S.A.   Im Verleih von Neue Visionen Filmverleih GmbH www.neuevisionen.de

WINGS OF DESIRE 1987 (GERMANY)

Director Wim Wenders **Producer** Wim Wenders **Screenplay** Wim Wenders, Peter Handke **Cinematography** Henri Alekan **Music** Jürgen Knieper

Cast Bruno Ganz, Solveig Dommartin, Otto Sander, Curt Bois, Peter Falk, Hans Martin Stier, Elmar Wilms, Sigurd Rachman

From early beginnings at the forefront of the German New Cinema movement, Wim Wenders had achieved widespread international acclaim in 1984 with *Paris, Texas*. Wenders's films have often dealt with alienation or individuals out of place in their surroundings (not unlike Peter Weir). Many of his early works could best be described as "mood" pieces.

Set in West Berlin two years before the actual fall of the wall and communism, *Wings of Desire* (*Der Himmel über Berlin*) follows two angels, Damiel (Bruno Ganz) and Cassiel (Otto Sander), as they roam the city unseen and unheard, observing and listening to the thoughts of ordinary Berliners. Damiel begins to fall in love with a beautiful but profoundly lonely trapeze artist, Marion (Solveig Dommartin). Actor Peter Falk (playing himself) arrives in Berlin to make a film about the city's Nazi past. It is revealed that he was once an angel who, tired of merely observing and never experiencing, renounced immortality to become mortal. Damiel, too, sheds his immortal existence, experiencing life for the first time: he bleeds, sees colors, tastes food, and drinks coffee. He runs into Marion at a bar, and they greet each other with the familiarity of long-standing friends.

◄

Unsurprisingly, Hollywood had its own take on Wenders's cult classic: relocating to L.A., *City of Angels***, starring Meg Ryan and Nicolas Cage, retained the basic premise of angels watching humans and ditched just about everything else.**

Immediately striking is the cinematography of Henri Alekan, who had worked on Jean Cocteau's *La Belle et la Bête*: his mastery of shooting in black and white enables us to see the human world through the eyes of the angels—monochrome, ethereal, and achingly out of reach. He achieved these effects by shooting through a filter made from a silk stocking. By contrast, the world when shown from the human perspective is in vivid color.

"ANY MOVIE THAT HAS THAT SPIRIT AND SAYS THINGS CAN BE CHANGED IS WORTH MAKING." WIM WENDERS

Although not a "difficult" film, *Wings of Desire* was nonetheless experimental in its creation. The angels, Ganz and Sander, were cast because they had been close friends for decades. Working to a minimal script, Wenders shot vast amounts of footage that remained unused, some of which would have altered the tone of the film: scenes with Damion and Cassiel humorously mocking human behavior and even a supposed pie fight in a bar. The director was also prepared to experiment with improvisation when it came to his characters: the significance of Peter Falk's drawings only came about when Wenders saw that the actor, famed for his portrayal of TV detective Columbo, was also an exceptionally talented artist. Without a doubt one of the standout European films of the 1980s, *Wings of Desire* is often found at the upper end of "greatest-of-all-time" lists. **TB**

► **Solveig Dommartin was cast as Marion and happened to be Wenders's girlfriend at the time. Impressively, she learned trapeze acrobatics from scratch, performing all of the high-wire stunts herself.**

It's more than music…it's a way of life

a Penelope Spheeris film
The Decline of Western Civilization Part II.
the Metal Years

featuring **Alice Cooper · Ozzy Osbourne · Poison** and members of
Aerosmith · Kiss · Motorhead

performances by **Megadeth · Faster Pussycat · Lizzy Bordon**
London · Odin · Seduce

NEW LINE CINEMA presents an IRS WORLD MEDIA PRODUCTION
'THE DECLINE OF WESTERN CIVILIZATION PART II, THE METAL YEARS'
edited by EARL GHAFFARI director of photography JEFF ZIMMERMAN line producer DANIEL RASKOV executive producers MILES COPELAND III and PAUL COLICHMAN
produced by JONATHAN DAYTON and VALERIE FARIS directed by PENELOPE SPHEERIS

 NEW LINE CINEMA

ORIGINAL SOUNDTRACK IS AVAILABLE ON RECORDS
CASSETTES AND COMPACT DISCS FROM CAPITOL RECORDS
 Capitol R RESTRICTED

THE DECLINE OF WESTERN CIVILIZATION PART II: THE METAL YEARS 1988 (U.S.)

Director Penelope Spheeris **Producer** Jonathan Dayton, Valerie Faris **Screenplay** Penelope Spheeris **Cinematography** Jeff Zimmerman **Music** Simon Steele, Alice Cooper, Aerosmith, Kiss, Ozzy Osbourne **Cast** Steven Tyler, Joe Perry, Alice Cooper, Gene Simmons, Ozzy Osbourne, Bret Michaels, Paul Stanley, Lemmy, Jeff Young

Musical epicenters change over time according to musical tastes and developing music recording and performance technologies. New York and Detroit score high in this regard (think Tin Pan Alley and Motown), but one of the more extraordinary subgenres of pop music is heavy metal, which coalesced in Los Angeles in response to disco and punk, and which became a mainstay in the sonic backdrop of hip-hop as the top forty moved in another direction.

   Director Penelope Spheeris first examined the dysfunction of troubled musicians in the late 1970s with her look at punk rock, *The Decline of Western Civilization* (1981). She followed up this underground hit with *The Decline of Western Civilization, Part II: The Metal Years* in 1988, a look at the Los Angeles heavy metal scene in the mid-1980s, particularly as it relates to a recognized connection between self-destructive behavior and musical success. The film features concert footage and interviews of legendary acts like Alice Cooper, Aerosmith, and Kiss, and spends

◄
Heavy metal as fly-on-the-wall documentary. Performances of particular note are Lizzy Borden's "Born to be Wild" and Megadeth's "In My Darkest Hour."

roughly equal time with emerging bands like Poison, Megadeth, Faster Pusscat, W.A.S.P, Odin, and Vixen. The sum of this exchange between musical vanguards is the contrast of youth and age in conflict over the power of amplifiers, the numbing effects of alcohol, and the level of personal excess an excitable group of troubled and largely white suburban kids will tolerate before they tune out and look forward to something new.

"I DON'T GET HIGH WHEN I'M PRACTICING AT HOME ALONE, SO WHY SHOULD I DO IT ONSTAGE?" JEFF YOUNG

History teaches us that these same white suburban fans grew up and turned into copies of their parents, or else into acolytes of the simultaneously developing world of hip-hop (consider the crossover "Walk This Way," featuring Run DMC and Aerosmith). Yet The Metal Years gives us an insider glimpse of four-piece bands with glamorously androgynous stage presence and bad behavior that now seem as cliché-ridden as it was then viscerally transgressive and brilliant.

The movie tackles these excesses, especially substance abuse, female objectification (sleazy means front of the line), and misogynistic promiscuity (Paul Stanley in bed surrounded by girls), alongside a consideration of the commodity nature of music as a corporate hedge against profit losses in the lead-up to grunge, the subject of Spheeris's third documentary in her triptych about L.A. music. **GC-Q**

► **Ozzy Osbourne displayed his substance abuse in the morning with a heavy dose of the shakes.**

1962...
JFK was in
The White House...
John Glenn was in orbit...
Cadillacs had fins...
Beehives were in...

And girls *really*
knew how to
tease!

"OUTRAGEOUS!"
—Bruce Williamson, PLAYBOY

A new movie by John Waters

HAIRSPRAY

The 60's Comedy That Shows No Mercy!

NEW LINE CINEMA PRESENTS IN ASSOCIATION WITH STANLEY F. BUCHTHAL A ROBERT SHAYE PRODUCTION
"HAIRSPRAY" STARRING SONNY BONO · RUTH BROWN · DIVINE · DEBBIE HARRY
RICKI LAKE AND JERRY STILLER · WITH SPECIAL APPEARANCES BY RIC OCASEK AND PIA ZADORA
CHOREOGRAPHER EDWARD LOVE EXECUTIVE PRODUCERS ROBERT SHAYE AND SARA RISHER
CO-PRODUCERS STANLEY F. BUCHTHAL AND JOHN WATERS PRODUCED BY RACHEL TALALAY
WRITTEN AND DIRECTED BY JOHN WATERS

PG PARENTAL GUIDANCE SUGGESTED
SOME MATERIAL MAY NOT BE SUITABLE FOR CHILDREN

SOUNDTRACK ALBUM AVAILABLE ON MCA
RECORDS, CASSETTES, AND COMPACT DISCS.

RECORDED IN
ULTRA·STEREO

 NEW LINE CINEMA

HAIRSPRAY 1988 (U.S.)

Director John Waters **Producer** Rachel Talalay **Screenplay** John Waters
Cinematography David Insley **Music** Kenny Vance **Cast** Sonny Bono, Ruth Brown,
Divine, Debbie Harry, Ricki Lake, Jerry Stiller, Colleen Fitzpatrick, Leslie Ann Powers,
Clayton Prince, Joann Havrilla, Pia Zadora, Ric Ocasek

Adapted from life experiences in and around his boyhood home
of Baltimore, Maryland, John Waters's 1988 comedy *Hairspray* is
about a fat girl who wants to fit in. It was a musical-dance "feel
good" movie quite unlike the normally outrageous John Waters
offerings and marked his entrée into the mainstream.

Tracy Turnblad (Ricki Lake) and her best friend, Penny
Pingleton (Leslie Ann Powers), audition for The Corny Collins
Show, a popular Baltimore dance show (think "Hand Jive" at
Rydell High). Despite her size, Tracy becomes a show regular,
frustrating the norms enforced by teen queen Amber Von Tussle
(Colleen Fitzpatrick), a conventionally gorgeous high school
classmate of Tracy's whose parents, Velma (Debbie Harry) and
Franklin (Sonny Bono), own a popular amusement park. When
Tracy woos away Amber's boyfriend, the dramatic tension really
engages, since overweight people aren't supposed to be happy
in the fantasy-scape of American movies.

Newly confident Tracy is hired as a plus-sized model but her
new fashion sense collides with conventional adult regulations.
She's put into special ed classes to both stifle and alter her
unusual behavior, and in her remediation she encounters black

◄

John Waters mixes
playful sensibility
typecasting to
ethnic stereotypes,
splashy costumes,
sentiment-laden
dialogue, and
earnest feeling
beneath all the
artifice to create
a vehicle for
considering serious
issues such as racial
intolerance.

kids who introduce her to Motormouth Maybelle (Ruth Brown), a record shop owner and host of the monthly "Negro Day" on The Corny Collins Show. Maybelle teaches Tracy and Penny how to really dance, and Penny begins romancing Maybelle's son, Seaweed (Clayton Prince). This doesn't play well with Penny's mother, Prudence (Joann Havrilla), who enlists the help of a psychiatrist (Waters) to "correct" her daughter's behavior.

"TRACY TURNBLAD, ONCE AGAIN YOUR RATTED HAIR IS PREVENTING ANOTHER STUDENT'S EDUCATION." *GEOMETRY TEACHER*

Ever the optimist and undeterred by these life and plot complications that stand in her way, Tracy uses her new popularity and cultural awareness to champion the cause of racial integration. With the help of her new friends and her overweight mother, Edna Turnblad (Divine), she participates in a race riot and is arrested at the Von Tussle's amusement park, after which Velma and Frank Von Tussle seek to smear Tracy once and for all. But things go right just when you'd expect them to go wrong, because the Von Tussle plot is uncovered in time for Tracy to integrate The Corny Collins Show and live happily ever after. In this case, the happy afterglow included a Tony Award-winning musical adaptation of her post-Civil Rights fairy tale and a Hollywood blockbuster remake, *Hairspray* (2007), albeit with a different ingenue in the starring role. **GC-Q**

► **Debbie Harry as pushy parent Velma, but it is Ricki Lake as Tracy who shows great charisma, and this was true long before she became a popular TV talk show hostess.**

NECO Z ALENKY
1988 (CZECHOSLOVAKIA • SWITZERLAND • U.K. • GERMANY)

Director Jan Svankmajer **Producer** Peter-Christian Fueter, Paul Madden, Michael Havas, Keith Griffiths, Hannes Bressler **Screenplay** Jan Svankmajer (based on a story by Lewis Carroll) **Cinematography** Svatopluk Malý **Sound** Robert Jansa, Ivo Spalj **Cast** Kristýna Kohoutová

Of the various film adaptations of Lewis Carroll's classic stories *Alice's Adventures in Wonderland* and *Through the Looking Glass*, *Neco z Alenky* is the darkest and most bizarre. Directed by Jan Svankmajer, a celebrated Czech experimental filmmaker, this adult fairy tale is a fantastic mix of stop-motion animation and live action that manages to brilliantly visualize an imaginary world. It embraces the essence of the children's books, despite Svankmajer seeing his film as less an adaptation and more of an interpretation. Carroll's Wonderland is found within a dream and Svankmajer regards his version as a dream of that dream. It is a poetic mix of illusion and reality, which emerges from Svankmajer's work within a Czech tradition of surrealism.

A leading figure of the Czech Surrealist Group, Svankmajer has been influenced by expressions of the avant-garde and modernism that are rooted in 1930s Czechoslovakia, and which have persisted within the local arts throughout the twentieth century. In particular, he draws upon traditions of folk puppetry and experimental theater, which have explored concepts of movement and abstraction. Svankmajer is also interested in a

◄

Disney meets Buñuel as the marketing men had it. The result is a series of extraordinary and abstruse experiences, which the viewer feels compelled to follow.

kinetic visualisation, the dramatic bringing to life of classic literature with an emphasis on the power of the image. This is a magical game of transformation in which surrealism can be seen as an alchemical process.

In *Neco z Alenky*, as in Carroll's stories, Alice (played here by Kristýna Kohoutová) changes size to such an extent that she is disturbingly out of proportion to her surroundings. But

"AN EXTRAORDINARY PIECE OF WORK: BRILLIANTLY INVENTIVE . . . A PIECE OF ORIGINAL VISION." *TERRENCE RAFFERTY (FILM CRITIC)*

Svankmajer's film unsettles where Carroll's story charmed. In *Neco z Alenky*, Alice follows the white rabbit through a slim drawer within a table, through which she improbably squeezes, leaving last her almost disembodied legs sticking in the air. Sound is accentuated in the film, with each creak of the rabbit's limbs, shifting of its sawdust stuffing, and nipping of its lethal front teeth defining the eerie form of this animated and humanized animal. Toys and dolls are given life through the film's stop-motion technique, which fantasizes such characters as a water rat in a sailor's outfit building a campfire in Alice's hair, and a caterpillar constructed from a sock, human teeth, and eyeballs, which sleeps by stitching its own eyes shut. Svankmajer motifs, such as a crawling slab of meat and an extended miniature toy theater, are also present as he searches his conscious and unconscious states for creative expression. **IC**

► The white rabbit that Alice follows is a stuffed animal, which awakens and wrenches itself free of its spiked positioning in a glass display cabinet before eating a bowl of sawdust to refill its weakened body.

MUJERES
al borde de un
ataque
de NERVIOS

un film de
ALMODÓVAR

Carmen Maura • Antonio Banderas • Julieta Serrano

María Barranco • Rossy de Palma • Guillermo Montesinos • Kiti Manver • Chus Lampreave
Yayo Calvo • Loles León • Ángel de Andrés López y la colaboración de Fernando Guillén
José Mª de Cossío • Gailles Ortion • Ester García • José Salcedo
Bernardo Bonezzi • José Luis Alcaine • Antonio Lloréns • Agustín Almodóvar

guión y *dirección* **Pedro Almodóvar**

WOMEN ON THE VERGE OF A NERVOUS BREAKDOWN 1988 (SPAIN)

Director Pedro Almodóvar **Producer** Pedro Almodóvar **Screenplay** Pedro Almodóvar **Cinematography** José Luis Alcaine **Music** Bernardo Bonezzi
Cast Carmen Maura, Antonio Banderas, Julieta Serrano, Rossy de Palma, María Barranco, Kiti Manver

Women on the Verge of a Nervous Breakdown (_Mujeres al borde de un ataque de nervios_) opens with beautiful mood-setting credits (kitsch straight out of a Doris Day/Rock Hudson comedy). "Soy Infeliz," a melodramatic heartbreak ballad, plays as we are introduced to TV actress Pepa (Carmen Maura). Distraught at being dumped by her married lover, she descends into depression. Refusing to take phone calls, her answering machine is burning up, but not, as she hopes, with messages from her ex, but from her best friend Candela, who arrives shortly afterwards in a state of panic and immediately attempts to jump off Pepa's balcony. Thereafter the plot gets _wildly_ out of hand in a series of intrigues that involve Shiite hijackers, chickens loose in a penthouse, a mambo-crazy taxi driver whose cab is done out like a brothel (a neat little cameo from Almodóvar himself), and a spiked gazpacho. Welcome to the implausible world of Pedro Almodóvar.

Spain after World War Two was dominated by the hard-line, right-wing dictatorship of General Franco. The years leading up to his death in 1975 and the gradual transition to democracy

◄
Almodóvar cemented his film festival following with this enchantingly subversive movie. Niche audiences that would find lesbian nuns shooting up smack amusing (as seen in _Entre Tinieblas_ in 1983) became mainstream filmgoers.

created a new mood of freedom and optimism among the youth of Spain. It was a time when countercultural arts—hitherto covertly conducted—began to flourish openly in Spain's major cities. This was the environment in which Pedro Almodóvar took his first strident steps into the world of moviemaking. Arriving in Madrid, but unable to study film—Franco had closed down Spain's National School of Cinema in 1967—Almodóvar took an

"WOMEN ARE STRONGER THAN US . . . AND ARE MUCH MORE SPECTACULAR TO TALK ABOUT." *PEDRO ALMODÓVAR*

admin job (one he would keep for the next twelve years) and taught himself. By the mid-1970s, he was showing his own experimental short films in bars and at parties. From the earliest beginnings, the components of a typical Almodóvar affair were already well in place: black comic farce, overwrought melodrama, convoluted narrative, irreverent humor, promiscuous sex, casual drug use, drag queens, prostitutes and nuns—all framed in the gaudiest and glossiest of colors.

Before the release of *Women on the Verge of a Nervous Breakdown,* Almodóvar did not enjoy a great reputation as a filmmaker. All of this changed with this breakout film, which toned down his natural tendency to juvenile excess while maintaining his stock-in-trade themes. Moreover, the cartoon emotional volatility of previous work was now augmented with genuinely touching and "human" moments. **TB**

► **A young, gawky Antonio Banderas (as Carlos) with María Barranco (as Candela).**

WINONA RYDER
CHRISTIAN SLATER
SHANNEN DOHERTY

Heathers

"Don't be surprised if it becomes a classic."
– Mike Clark, USA Today

HEATHERS 1989 (U.S.)

Director Michael Lehmann **Producer** Denise Di Novi **Screenplay** Daniel Waters **Cinematography** Francis Kenny **Music** David Newman **Cast** Winona Ryder, Christian Slater, Shannen Doherty, Kim Walker, Penelope Milford, Patrick Labyorteaux, Jeremy Applegate, Lance Fenton

The premise of this movie—high school girl inadvertently becomes involved in the murders of the popular kids she despises—could so easily have become a schlocky, tacky teen horror, but in the hands of director Michael Lehmann and writer Daniel Waters, *Heathers* turns out to be a dark comedy with unsettling surreal moments and vivid characters.

The opening scene places us firmly in the realms of the surreal. We see three girls, all called Heather, each dressed in a perfectly color-coordinated outfit, red, green, and yellow, like dancers in a musical. They're playing croquet and, as they do so, the hierarchy is laid out. Red Heather (Kim Walker) is Heather No. 1, the bitch queen in charge who will tolerate no challenges from Heathers 2 (Shannen Doherty) or 3. Right at the bottom of the pecking order is our heroine, Veronica (Winona Ryder), who appears to be buried up to her neck playing the target for the croquet balls. It's Alice in Wonderland 1980s-style.

The Heathers are the most powerful clique in the school, making life hell for everyone with cruel tricks and cutting comments. Winona Ryder is utterly convincing as Veronica, torn between working hard to keep her position as the only

◄

The bouffant hair and shoulder pads are so 1980s, but the dark humor is vividly timeless.

non-Heather and hiding her discomfort at the group's tyranny. New student J.D. (Christian Slater) eggs Veronica on when she rants about how she'd like to see Heather No. 1 dead. Intending to teach Heather a lesson by making her vomit, Veronica accidentally hands her a fatal cup of drain cleaner. Veronica is freaked, but J.D., who had noticed the mistake before Heather drank, helps Veronica cover up the murder by writing a touching

"THIS IS OHIO . . .IF YOU DON'T HAVE A BREWSKI IN YOUR HAND YOU MIGHT AS WELL BE WEARING A DRESS." *J.D.*

suicide note. Like a many-headed beast, as one Heather dies, another rises to take her place: Heather No. 2 dons Heather No. 1's red scrunchie, and takes on the role of supreme bitch. Veronica shrugs back into her role as Heather hanger-on, but behind the scenes J.D. is stoking the fires of her revenge fantasies. She's attracted by J.D.'s disregard for all that is held sacred in the peer-pressure-ridden high school universe.

During an elaborate prank to discredit a pair of jocks who have been spreading lies about her, Veronica is forced to shoot one of the boys dead. Suddenly she realizes J.D. has set her up and that he's using her to play out some psychotic scheme of his own. Appalled at her complicity, she rejects J.D. and sets out to save the school from an ending (a compromise foisted on the filmmakers by the studio) that is a little too neat and moralistic to sit comfortably with the rest of the movie. **CW**

► Slater's J.D. is charming, tortured, and creepily malevolent, a gravel-voiced Jack Nicholson imitation.

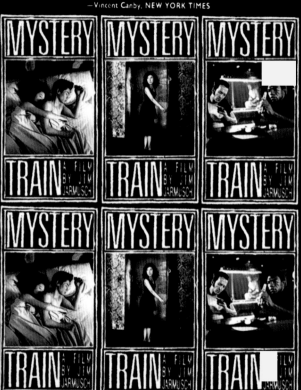

"...MYSTERY TRAIN is both brilliantly funny and subtle.
...MYSTERY TRAIN is thoroughly satisfying, a delight.
...MYSTERY TRAIN, an enchanting new comedy by Jim Jarmusch."
—Vincent Canby, NEW YORK TIMES

MYSTERY TRAIN 1989 (U.S.)

Director Jim Jarmusch **Producer** Jim Stark **Screenplay** Jim Jarmusch
Cinematography Robby Müller **Music** John Lurie **Cast** Masatoshi Nagase,
Youki Kudoh, Screamin' Jay Hawkins, Cinqué Lee, Rufus Thomas, Jodie Markell,
Tom Noonan, Elizabeth Bracco, Joe Strummer, Rick Aviles, Steve Buscemi

Jim Jarmusch's third feature, *Mystery Train* (1989), continues the director's exploration of outsider-ness and attaches this master theme to Memphis, Tennessee. Mixing comedy styles, wildly distinct emotional modes from deep pathos through slapstick, and a career-long use of long takes to simmer alongside performers—almost as if acting were a sport of patience rather than an explosion of emotive efficiency and narrative clarity—*Mystery Train* carves out the flesh of human experience as a journey through, and not the result of conquering, time.

Composed of three partly overlapping stories that occur on the same evening, *Mystery Train* is also about the often tenuous chance connections that create communities, even if for only one evening. "Far From Yokohama" is about a Japanese couple, Jun and Mitsuko (Youki Kudoh and Masatoshi Nagase), on a pilgrimage to the roots of rock 'n' roll (Sun Studios, downtown Memphis), as distilled from their pop cultural awareness of all things American. "A Ghost" is about an Italian widow, Luisa (Nicoletta Braschi), stranded in Memphis as she prepares for her return trip to Italy with the ashes of her dead husband; circumstances force her to share a room with talkative Dee Dee

◄
Three stories converge at a Memphis hotel and show off Jarmusch's attention to the super-ordinary, not the extraordinary—precisely why his stories work in movie after movie.

(Elizabeth Bracco) before she's visited by the ghost of Elvis Presley. "Lost In Space" focuses on Dee Dee's ex, an unemployed Brit named Johnny (Joe Strummer), and his friends Will and Charlie (Rick Aviles and Steve Buscemi), who drink and fight and rob a liquor store, which ends up forcing them to hide out until morning. Connecting each of the three stories is the Arcade Hotel, a flophouse managed by a night clerk (Screamin' Jay

"IF YOU TOOK AWAY SIXTY PERCENT OF THE BUILDINGS IN YOKOHAMA, IT WOULD LOOK LIKE [MEMPHIS]." *JUN*

Hawkins) with the help of his bellboy (Cinqué Lee), the thrice repeated Elvis song "Blue Moon," and a gunshot. Otherwise the movie is about overlap and coincidence, simultaneity, accommodation, and a very specific vision of America somehow devoid of corporate intrusion and sanitary packaging.

The movie frames a series of small moments and looks behind surfaces of polish and charm to the ordinary backdrop typically avoided by American movies. For critics, there is a sense that Jarmusch's films form a pose of reticence and cool, so detached from more conventional movies that he's an artist of negative action, a painter of boredom. Between these poles is the real Jarmusch of *Mystery Train*. This isn't a movie to satisfy fans of *Batman* or *Lethal Weapon 2*, two of the most commercially successful titles in 1989. Instead, it's a small canvas with smaller aims but potentially more thoughtful rewards. **GC-Q**

►

She (Kudoh) loves Elvis; he (Nagase) digs Carl Perkins. That brings them to the famous Memphis Sun Studios.

FRANKENHOOKER 1990 (U.S.)

Director Frank Henenlotter **Producer** James Glickenhaus, Edgar Ievins
Screenplay Frank Henenlotter, Robert Martin **Cinematography** Robert M.
Baldwin **Music** Joe Renzetti **Cast** James Lorinz, Joanne Ritchie, Patty Mullen,
J. J. Clark, Carissa Channing, Shirl Bernheim, Judy Grafe, Helmar Cooper, Louise Lasser

When it comes to cult movies, there are different gradations,
from foreign cult movies (which are really mainstream in their
own countries and tongues), dropping down through genuine
oddball movies (which may or may not have been successful
on first release), and ending up in deep cult underground.
Frankenhooker is near the bottom of this slope—and none the
worse for that. The plot is just an excuse for bags of frippery,
and eventual seminaked mass girl action.

A medical school dropout, Jeffrey Franken (James Lorinz)
loses his fiancée, Elizabeth (Patty Mullen), in a tragic lawnmower
incident, and decides—as he's a misunderstood science
genius—to bring her back to life. Unfortunately, he could only
save her head, so he hits the button marked "bright ideas,"
goes to the red-light district in the city, and lures prostitutes
into a hotel room to get body parts for his girlfriend. Testing
them turns out to be a lot of fun, of course, but the bad girls
are all frazzled in some vast electrical freak-out, leaving the
perspiring Jeffrey apologizing to the call girls just a little too
late, and stitching Elizabeth a body from the superior legs,
thighs, breasts, and bums on offer.

◀

**Henenlotter does
it again with this
tale of transplanted
hookers' heads,
limbs, breasts, and
torsos. Sleazy and
gory and never
more than the sum
of its body parts.**

Things, bizarre as they are, go pretty well, except the reformulated Elizabeth turns out to have distinct streetwalking tendencies. Distraught, Jeffrey pleads with her to change her ways, but he gets sizzled in another electrical storm, and wakens to find himself a man's head on a curvaceous woman's body. Poor old Elizabeth just had no other parts to work with. *Flesh for Frankenstein* (1973), the sex-crazed satire directed by

"MEDICAL SCHOOLS UPSET ME, MOTHER . . . I'M BECOMING DANGEROUSLY AMORAL." FRANKEN

Paul Morrissey under the aegis of Andy Warhol, and its companion piece, *Blood for Dracula* (1974), put together by the same partnership, are obvious reference points. Mel Brooks's *Young Frankenstein* (1975) is hilarious, but more in the tradition of homage with old-fashioned comedy. *The Rocky Horror Picture Show* (1975) is perhaps a more direct forbear.

Henenlotter pays his dues. There's a family in the movie called Shelley, after Mary Shelley (wife of brilliant Romantic poet Percy Bysshe Shelley and no mug with the pen herself), the original author of *Frankenstein*. The interior of the Franken family garage is intentionally four times larger than the exterior, as specified in the screenplay. Fans of the long-running English TV series *Doctor Who* will recognize the conceit. Henenlotter also references his own movies *Basket Case* (1982), *Brain Damage* (1988), and *Basket Case 2* (1990) with Beverley Bonner appearing as "Casey." **MH**

► "Want a date?" becomes more of a threat than a come-on as "Shelley" (Joanne Ritchie) wreaks havoc among the hookers and johns.

WINNER PALME D'OR CANNES 1991

WINNER BEST DIRECTION CANNES 1991

WINNER BEST ACTOR JOHN TURTURRO CANNES 1991

JOHN TURTURRO

JOHN GOODMAN

A film by JOEL & ETHAN COEN

CIRCLE FILMS presents a TED and JIM PEDAS, BILL DURKIN, BEN BARENHOLTZ production

BARTON FINK

JOHN TURTURRO JOHN GOODMAN "BARTON FINK" JUDY DAVIS MICHAEL LERNER JOHN MAHONEY JON POLITO
Music by CARTER BURWELL Costume Designer RICHARD HORNUNG Production Designer DENNIS GASSNER
Director of Photography ROGER DEAKINS B.S.C. Co-Producer GRAHAM PLACE
Executive Producers BEN BARENHOLTZ, TED and JIM PEDAS, BILL DURKIN
Written by ETHAN COEN and JOEL COEN Produced by ETHAN COEN Directed by JOEL COEN

BARTON FINK 1991 (U.S.)

Director Joel Coen **Producer** Ethan Coen **Screenplay** Ethan Coen, Joel Coen
Cinematography Roger Deakins **Music** Carter Burwell **Cast** John Turturro,
John Goodman, Michael Lerner, Judy Davis, John Mahoney, Tony Shalhoub,
Jon Polito, Steve Buscemi, Lance Davis, Richard Portnow, Christopher Murney

The Coen brothers are an anachronism in modern American cinema, sharing with David Lynch a unique ability to take what would otherwise be called "art house" product into the mainstream. Having produced such intelligent, quintessentially American works as *Raising Arizona* (1987) and *Miller's Crossing* (1990), they shifted into an altogether stranger dimension with *Barton Fink*.

Set in 1941, New York left-wing playwright Barton Fink (John Turturro) enjoys the critical acclaim of his Broadway debut when he discovers he has been offered a fortune to write Hollywood movie scripts. In L.A. he takes a room in a large art deco hotel that seems only to have one other guest—in the neighboring room. Barton meets Capitol Pictures movie mogul Jack Lipnick (a fast-talking parody of Louis B. Mayer) and is assigned to write a wrestling B picture. Back at his hotel, Barton composes a first line and is then beset by writer's block. He is distracted by noise coming from the adjoining room, which turns out to be Charlie Meadows (John Goodman), a seemingly affable insurance salesman who invites himself in for a drink. Barton's inability to write becomes increasingly acute and turns to panic, as the world surrounding him starts to take on a frighteningly surreal edge.

◄

This Coen brothers offering is a difficult film to categorize. Narrative events are ambiguous, but it remains endlessly fascinating and well suited to repeated viewings.

Barton Fink is sumptuous in appearance, tightly scripted, and features outstanding performances all around, but much of the real meat lies beneath the surface. It's a film comprising layer upon layer of dichotomy: art vies with commerce; wealth with poverty; east coast with west; and values prove to be malleable. Uneducated, crass, and venal, the mogul Lipnick represents everything Barton despises, but the writer is

"THERE IS A CERTAIN SORT OF SOMBER QUALITY TO IT THAT YOU WOULDN'T ASSOCIATE WITH A COMEDY . . ." *JOEL COEN*

neutered by the lure of money. Lipnick, on the other hand, knows that all who appear before him are ready to dance with the devil—they are compromised by their mere presence and he treats them with contempt. Fink, as an earnest intellectual whose stated ambition is to create a "theater of the common man," views a throwaway wrestling flick as beneath him . . . but evidence indicates that he may not be up to that job. And for all his talk of being a people's poet, when he meets Charlie, the genuine article, he is self-important, patronizing, and has little interest in what the man has to say. Eventually Charlie is revealed to be anything but "common," and as the film erupts in its surreal apocalyptic finale of blood, flames, and destruction, Barton is shown to be helplessly weak and hopelessly out of his depth. *Barton Fink* remains a darkly surreal comedy with its own internal logic. **TB**

▶
One strange meeting between the eponymous hero and Jack Lipnick (Michael Lerner), the boss of Capitol Pictures, leads to Lipnick kissing Fink's foot.

BRAINDEAD 1992 (NEW ZEALAND)

Director Peter Jackson **Producer** Jim Booth **Screenplay** Peter Jackson, Stephen Sinclair, Fran Walsh **Cinematography** Murray Milne **Music** Peter Dasent **Cast** Timothy Balme, Diana Peñalver, Elizabeth Moody, Ian Watkin, Brenda Kendall, Stuart Devenie, Jed Brophy, Stephen Papps, Murray Keane

Long before setting a world record when *The Lord of the Rings: Return of the King* (2003) won Academy Awards in every category it was nominated, director Peter Jackson held a different kind of world record—the world's bloodiest film. Combining over-the-top gore with Monty Python-style humor, *Braindead* (a.k.a. *Dead Alive* in the United States) is an all-in, gross-out horror-comedy that helped establish the cult following of one of today's most celebrated and innovative filmmakers.

Timid Lionel (Timothy Balme) finds his mother's overbearing behavior the least of his problems after she is bitten by a rare Sumatran rat-monkey at the zoo and quickly turns into a zombie. Lionel thinks he kept her resurrection a secret, until Mom bursts from the grave and starts chomping on the townsfolk. Unable to sever the maternity strings, Lionel hides his sedated zombie mother and her increasing flesh-hungry converts in the basement. Naturally, this proves tough on Lionel's blossoming relationship with unaware Paquita (Diana Peñalver) as the number of undead continues to grow.

Peter Jackson burst onto the filmmaking scene with low-budget exploitation such as the gory sci-fi *Bad Taste* (1987) and

◄

Peter Jackson's zombiefest set in 1950s surburbia is gory *in extremis* and very, very funny. *Shaun of the Dead* (2004) owes it big time.

the puppet-splatter musical-comedy *Meet the Feebles* (1989). *Braindead* tops them both as limbs fly and gallons of blood splash the screen, including an epic finale where Lionel dispatches of dozens of zombies by liquefying them with his trusty lawn mower. Slapstick comedy enhances the splatter as Jackson pushes the boundaries of tastelessness with a series of cinematic firsts. Highlights include his dying mother's ear falling

"THEY'RE NOT DEAD EXACTLY, THEY'RE JUST . . . SORT OF ROTTING."

LIONEL COSGROVE

off into her pudding, which she promptly eats; a kung fu priest ("I kick ass for the Lord!") who kicks off a zombie's head; a gaseous pile of intestines that attack our hero; a zombie coupling that results in cinema's first zombie baby; and a Freudian climax where Lionel is literally born again as he bursts from his gigantic mother's stomach after she swallows him whole.

More than just a gorehound's delight, *Braindead* showcases Jackson's expertise as a filmmaker who can get the most out of a tight budget ($3 million and partially financed by the New Zealand Film Commission). Jackson perfectly recreates a 1950s setting and fills the screen with acrobatic camera work and masterful slight-of-hand editing. A horror fan, Jackson also packed the film with movie references, including everything from George Romero's zombie films to *Psycho* (1960) to *King Kong* (1933), a film that he would later remake in 2005. **WW**

► Timothy Balme as the virgin who is having domineering mother problems of a gory yet humorous type.

It was the last day of school in 1976
A time they'd never forget
(If only they could remember)

Dazed and Confused

See It With A Bud

GRAMERCY PICTURES Presents An ALPHAVILLE Production In Association With DETOUR FILMPRODUCTION "DAZED AND CONFUSED"

PRODUCTION DESIGN JOHN FRICK   DIRECTOR OF PHOTOGRAPHY LEE DANIEL   CO-PRODUCER ANNE WALKER-McBAY   PRODUCED BY JAMES JACKS   SEAN DANIEL   RICHARD LINKLATER

WRITTEN AND DIRECTED BY RICHARD LINKLATER

DAZED AND CONFUSED 1993 (U.S.)

Director Richard Linklater **Producer** Sean Daniel, James Jacks, Richard Linklater
Screenplay Richard Linklater **Cinematography** Lee Daniel **Music** Alice Cooper,
ZZ Top, Ted Nugent, War, Lynyrd Skynyrd, Deep Purple **Cast** Jason London, Rory
Cochrane, Wiley Wiggins, Sasha Jenson, Michelle Burke, Adam Goldberg, Ben Affleck

Set in the American bicentennial year of 1976, Richard Linklater's
Dazed and Confused (1993) pivots upon the coming of age crux
about whether to ditch tradition. The worry is over the
continuing importance of emulating one's parents or
mimicking, and therefore fitting in with, peers.

This means the film is thematically concerned with clashing
values between an aging, masculine prerogative toward
discipline and control (i.e., those with memories of both a Great
Depression and World War Two) and the laxity of a new, post-
1960s ethic comprised of individual fulfillment and fair play (i.e.,
boomers with their factions of Civil Rights agitators, flower
children, Vietnam vets, women's libbers, and the usual corporate
drones). In other words, *Dazed and Confused* pits the jocks
versus the nerds, beauties versus beasts, prigs versus rowdies,
and the dazed versus the confused, infusing the whole piece
with rock of ages and retro chic 1970s detail.

The soundtrack alone suggests that Linklater worships at
the altar of the Fender Custom Shop. There's "Sweet Emotion"
by Aerosmith, "School's Out" by Alice Cooper, "Low Rider" by
War, "Rock & Roll All Nite" by Kiss, the ballad "Summer Breeze,"

◄

American Graffiti
for the 1990s
generation and a
film that cements
its virtue as a
nostalgic
masterwork
combining deft
characterization
and affection for
the moment.

and "Free Ride" by The Edgar Winter Group. On-screen we see aged denim worn tight, novelty T-shirts, tie-dye, fringe, headbands, tube socks, sideburns, straight hair, and a whole lot of drinking and doping. The fact is that *Dazed and Confused* nails the period details, not so much with 100 percent fidelity to the moment, but more from the way Linklater makes 1976 feel so emotionally correct and right for the times.

"NOW ME AND MY LOSER FRIENDS ARE GONNA HEAD OUT TO BUY AEROSMITH TICKETS. TOP PRIORITY." *"PINK"*

The film's ensemble cast stretches out across several story lines but the main thread centers on football star "Pink" Floyd (Jason London), who is expected to lead his fellow athletes and conform to the standards of his coach, which includes paddling frosh boys and avoiding substance abuse in preparation for his senior football season. To one side of Pink's divided self is the crazed male element embodied by Fred O'Bannion (Ben Affleck), a boy-man content to repeat a year of high school so that he might vent his humiliation on weaker and younger kids. But Pink is also sympathetic to freshman-to-be Mitch Kramer (Wiley Wiggins), with whom Pink asserts a paternal role that sees their two seemingly unrelated high school lives overlap through a single night of meandering, keg partying, and reconciliation with the potential responsibilities of coming adulthood. **GC-Q**

▶
The cast included rising stars like Rory Cochrane, Adam Goldberg, Matthew McConaughey, Cole Hauser, Milla Jovovich, Joey Lauren Adams, Parker Posey, and Renée Zellweger.

TERENCE STAMP   HUGO WEAVING   GUY PEARCE

DRAG IS THE DRUG!

PRIX DU PUBLIC
CANNES 94

PRISCILLA
QUEEN OF THE DESERT

POLYGRAM FILMED ENTERTAINMENT EN ASSOCIATION AVEC THE AUSTRALIAN FILM FINANCE CORPORATION

PRÉSENTE UNE PRODUCTION LATENT IMAGE/SPECIFIC FILMS

TERENCE STAMP HUGO WEAVING GUY PEARCE ET BILL HUNTER "PRISCILLA FOLLE DU DESERT" (THE ADVENTURES OF PRISCILLA QUEEN OF THE DESERT)

DÉCORS OWEN PATERSON MONTAGE SUE BLAINEY DIRECTEUR DE LA PHOTOGRAPHIE BRIAN J BREHENY MUSIQUE GUY GROSS PRODUCTION EXÉCUTIVE REBEL PENFOLD-RUSSELL

PRODUIT PAR AL CLARK ET MICHAEL HAMLYN ÉCRIT ET RÉALISÉ PAR STEPHAN ELLIOTT

Bande originale du film disponible sur compact disque et cassette. Distribution Polygram

THE ADVENTURES OF PRISCILLA, QUEEN OF THE DESERT 1994 (AUSTRALIA)

Director Stephan Elliot **Producer** Al Clark, Michael Hamlyn **Screenplay** Stephan Elliot **Cinematography** Brian J. Breheney **Music** Guy Gross **Cast** Terence Stamp, Hugo Weaving, Guy Pearce, Bill Hunter, Sarah Chadwick, Rebel Penfold-Russell, John Casey, June Marie Bennett, Murray Davies, Frank Cornelius

During a journey across the Australian outback from Sydney to Alice Springs by three drag queens, "Priscilla" is transformed from a decommissioned school bus into a drag mobile, lilac-painted and filled with chic fabrics, a sewing machine, and a hidden sunbed. As with every good road movie, the characters are transformed, too, making an inner journey along with the physical one: one learns to be a father, one grows out of his own self-obsessed meanness, and one takes a chance on love.

The comedy lies in the taut, witty dialogue and in the contrast between the artificiality of the drag queens and the harsh reality of the outback and its down-to-earth people. These contrasts are not just played for laughs; they're also menacing and poignant. The outback is a physically perilous environment and full of homophobia, ranging from stunned disbelief to open violence. The three main characters are obvious outsiders, a fact made clear each time they perform their peculiar act, dressed in outrageous clothing singing along to the cheesiest songs, leaving Aussie audiences baffled, bemused, bored, or hostile.

◀

Terence Stamp as Bernadette conveys femininity and toughness: she is mistress of the bitchy one-liner, which can ease a tense situation, and she can hold her own in a fight without breaking a single French-manicured nail.

The Oscar-winning costumes are a sight to behold—the fearsome blue lizard costumes, reflecting the bizarre creatures encountered in the desert, for example—creating startling contrasts with the dusty, red desert scenery: Bernadette walking alone in a huge desert landscape in white linen; the three of them atop Uluru in sequins, feathers, and climbing boots; and craziest of all, the bus speeding along the dusty

"HERE'S HOPING THE DESERT'S BIG ENOUGH FOR THE BOTH OF US."

BERNADETTE

road with Felicia (Guy Pearce) perched on the roof on top of a giant stiletto, lip-synching to opera and with a swathe of silver fabric sweeping out behind him.

British actor Terence Stamp lifts the movie above its exaggerated silliness. His character, Bernadette, is a transsexual woman. Unlike the other drag queens, when out of the feathered and sequinned show outfits, Bernadette sticks to her elegant, middle-aged woman attire, all floaty scarves and flowing linen. Stamp gives every gesture a studied femininity. His expressive face makes Bernadette's boredom with the drag scene and her desperate longing for a loving relationship evident. There's no cheesiness in her developing relationship with the mechanic Bob (Bill Hunter), just the hesitant first steps of a couple of middle-aged people who have been disappointed by love in the past. **GC-Q**

▶ In one memorable scene, Mitzi (Hugo Weaving) wears a dress made entirely from flip-flops as he/she flounces down the main street of an outback town, the crinolines arranged to look like the Sydney Opera House.

Just because they serve you doesn't mean they Like you.

CLeRKS

A very funny look at the over-the-counter culture.

Miramax Films presents a View Askew Production "Clerks" Brian O'Halloran Jeff Anderson
/ Marilyn Ghigliotti Jason Mewes Lisa Spoonauer director of photography, David Klein
produced by Scott Mosier & Kevin Smith written & directed by Kevin Smith

featuring music by
SOUL ASYLUM, ALICE IN CHAINS, SEAWEED, THE JESUS LIZARD and BAD RELIGION

OPeN FOR BUSINESS SOON

CLERKS 1994 (U.S.)

Director Kevin Smith **Producer** Scott Mosier, Kevin Smith **Screenplay** Kevin Smith **Cinematography** David Klein **Music** Alice In Chains, Soul Asylum, Bad Religion, Supernova **Cast** Brian O'Halloran, Jeff Anderson, Marilyn Ghigliotti, Lisa Spoonhauer, Jason Mewes, Kevin Smith, Scott Mosier, Scott Schiaffo

When it comes to cinema, the term "independent" can seem little more than a parochial catchall for any film that doesn't emanate from a major Hollywood player. But every now and again, the genuine article—a movie where a lack of funds is more than compensated by enthusiasm and ingenuity—appears from nowhere to reach a wide audience. *Clerks* was a surprise box office hit and a launchpad for one of the most interesting film careers of the past twenty years.

Kevin Smith was a twenty-four-year-old film school dropout working in a New Jersey convenience store when he wrote and directed his debut. Shot in black and white film, the total outlay for *Clerks* was $27,575, funded by selling a chunk of Smith's extensive comic book collection, maxing out credit cards, and using the funds intended to complete his college education. And location was not a problem: it was shot in twenty-one days during closing hours at the Quick Stop store where he worked!

The premise behind *Clerks* (it can hardly be described as a plot) is a day in the life of Dante (Brian O'Halloran), a slacker in his early twenties employed at a convenience store. Preparing for his day off, the morning begins with an unexpected and

◄

"Just because they serve you doesn't mean they like you" ran one tagline for this movie. It was shot in the same store director Smith was working in at the time (in case the low-budget film flopped).

unwanted phone call ordering him to work. At the store, Dante spends much of his day whining to coworker/best friend Randal (Jeff Anderson) about his life—his issues with girlfriend, Veronica, the engagement of his ex, Caitlin . . . not to mention what becomes the movie's catchphrase: "I'm not even supposed to be here today!" Randal, meanwhile, does his best to annoy the customers, and ponders the slenderest aspects of popular

> "IN MY WORLD, EVERYONE HAS REALLY LONG CONVERSATIONS OR JUST PICKS APART POP CULTURE TO DEATH." *KEVIN SMITH*

culture, such as the relative merits of *The Empire Strikes Back* and *Return of the Jedi*, discussed with the same detail that a pair of philosophy majors might debate Wittgenstein and Spinoza.

It may all seem pretty unassuming stuff, but the movie very cleverly captures that early 1990s slacker *Generation X* vibe. It's a fabulously entertaining debut, even if as a piece of filmmaking there's little to suggest that Smith would go on to create such quality output as the touching *Chasing Amy* (1997), the controversial *Dogma* (1999), or the outrageously funny *Zack and Miri Make a Porno* (2008). But it's the genuine interaction between the characters, doubtless aided by a cast featuring many of the auteur's friends (notably Jason Mewes, with whom Smith makes a memorable cameo appearance as the now-legendary Jay and Silent Bob), which makes *Clerks* both a joy and one of the funniest movies of the 1990s. **TB**

▶
Dante (O'Halloran) is the very definition of the "MacJobber"—a smart young man with little focus and even less ambition, working in a menial occupation until he can think of something better to do.

"PULP FICTION FANS TAKE NOTE.
HAVE I GOT A PICTURE FOR YOU!"
—NEW YORK NEWSDAY

SHALLOW GRAVE

What's a little murder among friends?

FIGMENT FILM KERRY FOX CHRISTOPHER ECCLESTON EWAN McGREGOR "SHALLOW GRAVE"

R RESTRICTED

PolyGram Video

SHALLOW GRAVE 1995 (U.K.)

Director Danny Boyle **Producer** Andrew Macdonald, Allan Scott **Screenplay** John Hodge **Cinematography** Brian Tufano **Music** Simon Boswell **Cast** Ewan McGregor, Christopher Eccleston, Kerry Fox, Colin McCredie, Ken Stott, Jean Marie Coffey, Peter Mullan, Gary Lewis

Danny Boyle's 1995 directorial debut is a black comedy-thriller featuring Christopher Eccleston, best known at the time for his role in the TV series *Cracker*, and the relatively unknown Ewan McGregor and Kerry Fox as a trio of insufferably self-opinionated Edinburgh yuppies. Alex (McGregor) is a journalist, Juliet (Fox) is a hospital doctor, and David (Eccleston) is an accountant.

The three find themselves with a dilemma when they discover their new roommate lying dead from a drug overdose in his room with a suitcase full of cash stuffed under his bed. Rather than inform the police, Alex, Juliet, and David decide to keep the cash and dismember and bury the body so no one will ask any questions. The actual disposal of the body turns out to be much more complicated and gruesome than the three anticipated, but they've left it too late to back out now.

As tension grows, Alex and Juliet go on a spending spree to make themselves feel better. Their pointless waste of money and their disregard for the possibility of discovery drive the already flaky David over the edge, so he takes the suitcase and moves up into the attic to protect the money. Of course, suitcases full of cash usually involve ill-gotten gains, so pretty

◄

"Pulp Fiction fans, have I got a movie for you," ran one publicity review for this black-humored, edge-of-your-seat thriller.

soon the three find themselves faced with the dead man's terrifying, brutal accomplices. The only way out seems to be murder.

As holding on to the money becomes each character's central focus, the trust and friendship between them, so clearly visible in the hilarious opening scenes when they are choosing a roommate, disintegrates. McGregor, Eccleston, and Fox all

"I SUPPOSE SHALLOW GRAVE IS A CRUEL FILM, BUT THEN LIFE CAN BE CRUEL AND COLD." DANNY BOYLE

display the consummate skill they are justly celebrated for, as their characters gradually fall into terror and madness. As the police close in on them, they seem cut off together, far from the rest of the world in their lofty Edinburgh apartment (an amazing set that perfectly captures the high ceilings and huge cold rooms peculiar to that city's apartments). Glimpses of their lives outside the apartment intensify their alienation from the rest of the world and their dependence on each other. As each former friend threatens and is threatened by each of the others, the black comedy of the beginning of the movie gives way to nerve-racking thriller. The plot proceeds toward its inevitable violent climax at breakneck pace, not so fast as to make you get lost, but fast enough that logical flaws only occur to you once it's all over. The movie's black comic heart is restored at the end of the movie in a final witty twist. **GC-Q**

►
Christopher Eccleston is superbly tense and edgy as David, character traits he took with him for the groundbreaking TV series *Our Friends in the North* (1996).

LUMIERE, LE STUDIO CANAL +, FRANCE 3 CINEMA présentent une production CLAUDIE OSSARD

La Cité
des Enfants Perdus

Un film de JEUNET & CARO

avec RON PERLMAN · Daniel EMILFORK · Judith VITTET · Dominique PINON · Jean-Claude DREYFUS · Geneviève BRUNET · Odile MALLET · Mireille MOSSE · Serge MERLIN
François HADJI-LAZARO · RUFUS · Ticky HOLGADO · et la participation de Jean-Louis TRINTIGNANT
Scénario de Gilles ADRIEN, Jean-Pierre JEUNET, Marc CARO · Dialogues de Gilles ADRIEN · Directeur de la photographie Darius KHONDJI (AFC) · Décor Jean RABASSE
Costumes Jean-Paul GAULTIER · Son Pierre EXCOFFIER · Montage Hervé SCHNEID · Montage son Gérard HARDY · Musique Vincent ARKARDI et Thierry LEBON · Effets spéciaux numériques PITOF · Images et effets visuels Pierre BUFFIN
Directeur de production Daniel SZUSTER · Produit par Claudie OSSARD · Une coproduction CONSTELLATION, LUMIERE, LE STUDIO CANAL, FRANCE 3 CINEMA
Avec la participation du Centre National de la Cinématographie · Cofinancé par Cofinergie 4, Cofinergie 5, Studio Image Canal · et le soutien de la Procirep · Coproducteurs étrangers Elias Querejeta (Espagne), Tele München (Allemagne)
Avec le soutien du Fonds Eurimages du Conseil de l'Europe · et la collaboration du Club d'Investissement Média (Programme Média de l'Union Européenne)

Bande originale du film disponible sur CD et K7 · EAST WEST

THE CITY OF LOST CHILDREN

1995 (FRANCE • GERMANY • SPAIN)

Director Marc Caro, Jean-Pierre Jeunet **Producer** Félicie Dutertre, María Victoria Hebrero, José Luis Lopez **Screenplay** Gilles Adrien, Marc Caro, Jean-Pierre Jeunet **Cinematography** Darius Khondij **Music** Angelo Badalamenti **Cast** Ron Perlman, Daniel Emilfork, Judith Vittet, Dominique Pinon, Mireille Mossé

The generation of French filmmakers born after the close of World War Two, but before 1970, includes a number of technical artists that rival—image per image and explosion per explosion—Hollywood's high-concept storytelling machine. In particular, one thinks of Luc Besson, a crossover talent with feet firmly planted in his native country but who equally stretches out to international markets where his stylistic panache began paying dividends once *La Femme Nikita* (1990) introduced him to suburban teens in America's heartland.

Jean-Pierre Jeunet and Marc Caro are similar talents. Their journey began in the early 1970s when they became art school friends, Jeunet the budding filmmaker and Caro the slightly younger graphic artist. Together they produced animated shorts and eventually earned the privilege of making live-action features, debuting with the gross-out black comedy *Delicatessen* in 1991. Their follow-up film, *The City of Lost Children* (*La Cité des Enfants Perdus*), collects a number of tendencies that had been percolating in their earlier works and then ratcheted up the scope to an even more sweeping scale. Part of what

◀

Prepare for the way-out weird: cloned adult children arguing over primacy; a sentient octopus; and a pint-sized heroine with a mountain of a man sidekick who might once have played a TV beast.

becomes clear in this sophomore film is a reliance on set design that warps reality in favor of expressionistic emotional states. Jeunet and Caro also use a reliable group of collaborators, including actor Dominique Pinon, cinematographer Darius Khondji, and editor Hervé Schneid, each of whom adds continuity to a fantastic universe of extraordinary ugliness and perversity, often used to privilege largely symbolic characters

"WHEN YOU'RE BORN IN THE GUTTER, YOU END UP IN THE PORT."

MIETTE

caught up in protecting innocence in the midst of terrible, even fascistic, oppression. In *Lost Children*, children are kidnapped by Krank (Daniel Emilfork), a scientist who steals their dreams in an effort to reverse his own natural aging process. His cronies kidnap Denree (Joseph Lucien), younger brother of a former whale hunter called One (Ron Perlman).

▶ With his unusual facial features, Daniel Emilfork makes a mesmerizing villain in this compelling visual dystopia in the tradition of movies such as *Metropolis* (1927) and (1985).

To find his brother, One enlists the help of a street girl, Miette (Judith Vittet). They eventually reach the hideaway Krank lives in with his cloned dwarf wife, Mademoiselle Bismuth (Mireille Mossé), and his cloned sons (Pinon). They confront a talking brain in a fish tank, Siamese twins, and a friendly octopus, and finally rescue the kidnapped children. It's all done in earnest; there are no sideways glances in the film, and this earnest sentiment may be exactly what keeps these fantastical elements from wandering into the ridiculous. **GC-Q**

LA HAINE

jusqu'ici tout va bien...

lazennec présente
vincent cassel, hubert koundé, saïd taghmaoui dans un film de **mathieu kassovitz**

LA HAINE 1995 (FRANCE)

Director Mathieu Kassovitz **Producer** Christophe Rossignon **Screenplay** Mathieu Kassovitz **Cinematography** Pierre Aïm **Music** Assassin **Cast** Vincent Cassel, Hubert Koundé, Saïd Taghmaoui, Abdel Ahmed Ghili, Solo, Joseph Momo, Héloïse Rauth, Rywka Wajsbrot, Olga Abrego

In hindsight, there was a quaint brattiness to the way director Mathieu Kassovitz delivered *La Haine* on the international stage. Its Cannes premiere was complemented by casual dress, red carpet walks, and press conferences that broke down quite deliberately: Kassovitz had always aimed to disrupt, and though many bristled at the posturing, the strategy was no less effective. It was a kind of communications manifestation of the attitude of his protagonists and proclaimed that much more ardently the film's purpose: to show the France that was the France that is.

Three friends—one Jewish, one Arab, one black—bide their time in a run-down suburban Parisian housing project. They have no work as, for them, there is no work. They are consumed with the spirit of gangster life, but there's no real gangster life around for them to lead. They idle at parties where they're not particularly welcome. Then they find a gun and their gangster fantasy takes on a dangerous new dimension.

A good deal has been made of the company's pre-production preparation: shooting in an actual "cité," or housing project, it was important that their intentions were transparent.

◄

Bridging the gap between the "cinema du look" of the 1980s and some unknown future, *La Haine* (the "hate") created a "new French extremity," in cinephile James Quandt's sticking phrase.

At a time when few in proud, socially codified France were aware of the severity of the disconnect on their own doorsteps, Kassovitz was clear in achieving the tacit acceptance of the residents of the community he filmed by living there with his cast. During their stay, they were not only exposed to the mannerisms and way of life of the people they were depicting, but also to an alienation of their own as privileged artists

"WOW, WHAT A SPEECH! HALF MOSES, HALF MICKEY MOUSE." SAÏD

working in a hostile environment. The results are electric and one feels, no matter how much style is played with in telling the story, that we are getting extremely close to "the truth."

La Haine is particularly revered for its complexity; indeed, it has something almost for everyone: a buddy thriller art film, fast-paced, with daring camera movements, direct address, and contemporary music (few beyond les banlieues had likely heard this new crop of urgent French hip-hop at the time of *La Haine*'s initial release). This was, after all, a very early take on the tense situation in France's suburbs (*La Haine* is fifteen years old!), which have since exploded and where burned-out cars are a regular sight, if you ever make it out that far.

La Haine is a profoundly satisfying film: lively, fresh, and in your face, fusing cultural components customarily expunged from any record of French life while charting a new course. **GS**

► Kassovitz pulls no punches as he focuses on the searing cultural contradictions of contemporary French life. As one of the young men says: "In school we learned that hate breeds hate."

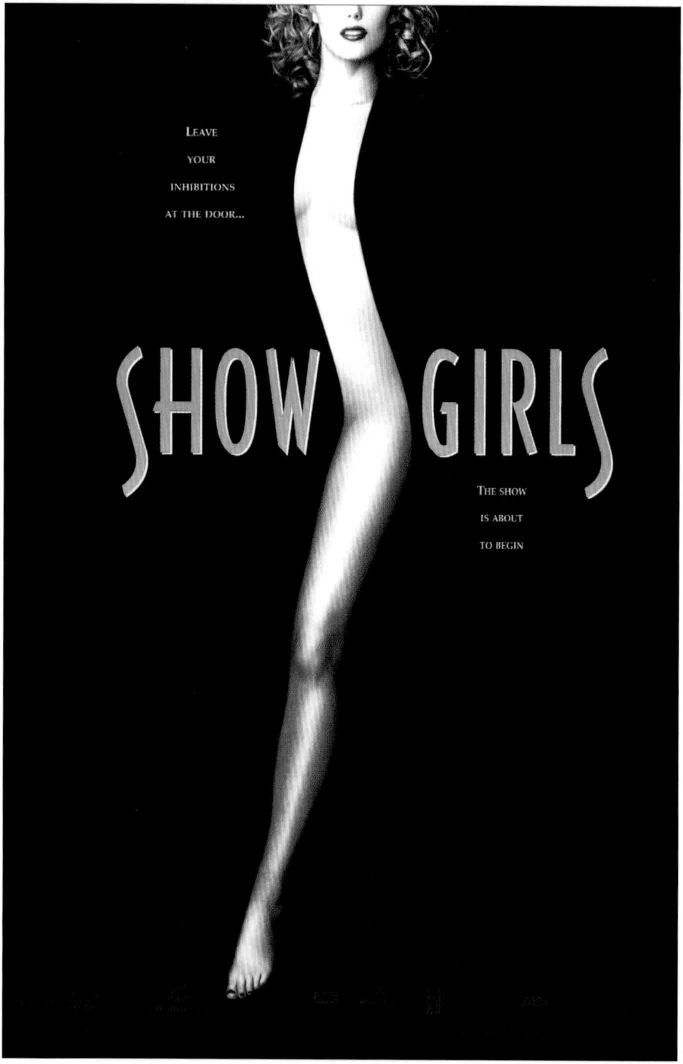

LEAVE
YOUR
INHIBITIONS
AT THE DOOR...
SHOW GIRLS
THE SHOW
IS ABOUT
TO BEGIN

SHOWGIRLS 1995 (U.S.)

Director Paul Verhoeven **Producer** Charles Evans, Alan Marshall **Screenplay** Joe Eszterhas **Cinematography** Jost Vacano **Music** David A. Stewart **Cast** Elizabeth Berkley, Kyle MacLachlan, Gina Gershon, Robert Davi, Alan Rachins, Gina Ravera, Glenn Plummer, Lin Tucci

This may be the defining moment for Joe Eszterhas, scribe of such exhaustingly dumb box office hits as *Flashdance* (1983) and *Basic Instinct* (1992). This is also the point of a film that refuses to die, despite a critical drubbing that's both well deserved and missing the point. Dress up any bad movie with nudity, and what you're left with is the puerile fantasy of a Czech-American screenwriter writ large through the eyes of a Dutch director slumming in Hollywood.

You could also see *Showgirls* as Eszterhas's $2 million theft of good taste. It truly is so bad that it forms a stratum of genius. But for all the spilled ink and invective that's been heaped upon it over the years, audiences have a soft spot for Elizabeth Berkley, that saccharine sweet vixen who responds to Gina Gershon's sexual come-on, which is also a moment for Gershon's character to pontificate on the value of sexual commerce, courtesy of champagne and the thrill of seeing breasts.

Nomi Malone (Berkley) is a good-looking dancer with ambitions of making it big as a Las Vegas showgirl. She hitchhikes to Sin City, loses her belongings, ends up being employed as a stripper, and is weirdly forced into the orbit of

◀

Another "so bad it's good" cult movie. A lot of talent and a big budget managed to create no more than high-gloss "tit-illation." It picked up the Worst Picture of the Decade and seven other Razzies.

the queen-bitch showgirl, Cristal Connors (Gershon). Her roommate, Molly Abrams (Gina Ravera), a seamstress, helps support Nomi as she navigates the chop around Cristal's wake. Pimps, competitors, and lap dances follow until Nomi is gradually drawn further into Cristal's web spun around the principle of "keep your friends close but your enemies closer," meaning: Cristal is actually quite fond of Nomi, as evidenced by

"IT'S AMAZING WHAT PAINT AND A SURGEON CAN DO."

CRISTAL CONNORS

a predatory lesbian pathology that's so stereotypically rendered that Gershon was certainly overlooked by AMPAS for an Oscar.

Suffice it to say but Nomi achieves the apex of Vegas stagecraft. Once there, she's filled with disgust. Then Molly is raped and beaten unconscious by scoundrels drawn from Nomi's circle. Culpable for her friend's condition, Nomi goes Rambo on Molly's rapist, smashing testes with high-heel bludgeons. A hospital confession concludes things, proving that Ms. Berkley is, especially in light of her TV roots, an empty vessel overfilled with dumb male fantasy that enshrines her, not in the floorshow of the Stardust Casino, but instead under the smoke and spotlights of the strip joint out of which she's conquered her sliver of Vegas. In the supporting cast look for Kyle MacLachlan, Glenn Plummer, Robert Davi, William Shockley, and even *Dancing with the Stars'* Carrie Ann Inaba. **GC-Q**

► Is she a stripper or is she a dancer? Just one of the questions that Nomi Malone (Elzabeth Berkley) must figure out.

james spader   holly hunter   elias koteas   deborah kara unger and rosanna arquette

in a film by david cronenberg

crash

1996 cannes winner

special jury prize for
originality, daring and audacity

ROBERT LANTOS and JEREMY THOMAS present in association with FINE LINE FEATURES in ALLIANCE COMMUNICATIONS PRODUCTION a DAVID CRONENBERG FILM JAMES SPADER
HOLLY HUNTER ELIAS KOTEAS CRASH DEBORAH KARA UNGER and ROSANNA ARQUETTE music HOWARD SHORE editor DENISE CRONENBERG sound RONALD SANDERS director of photography PETER SUSCHITZKY
producers ANDRAS HAMORI and CHRIS AUTY executive STEPHANE REICHEL and MARILYN STONEHOUSE produced by JEREMY THOMAS and ROBERT LANTOS directed by DAVID CRONENBERG based on J.G. BALLARD

NC-17 ●●● DOLBY SR   TMN   F

Visit the Fine Line Features Web Site at http://www.flf.com

CRASH 1996 (CANADA)

Director David Cronenberg **Producer** David Cronenberg **Screenplay** David Cronenberg (based on a novel by J. G. Ballard) **Cinematography** Peter Suschitzky **Music** Howard Shore **Cast** James Spader, Holly Hunter, Elias Koteas, Deborah Kara Unger, Rosanna Arquette, Peter MacNeill

In the 1990s it seemed impossible to shock viewers desensitized by floods of exploitation movies on video and specialist cable TV. But *Crash*, an adaptation of the eponymous J. G. Ballard book by former Baron of Blood David Cronenberg, managed to upset a lot of cinema audiences. Cronenberg already had a track record: his previous films had courted adversity worldwide for their grotesque, sexualized mutilations of the human body and awkward fusions of man and industrial technology.

Crash moves the novel's plot from the 1970s to the 1990s, and from London to Toronto (Cronenberg's hometown). James (James Spader) and Catherine (Deborah Kara Unger) are seemingly bored with their relationship, and they look for new thrills (the film starts with three sex scenes: Catherine cheating on James, James cheating on Catherine, and the two having sex while sharing their infidelities). After a near-fatal car crash, James becomes infatuated with Vaughn (Elias Koteas), a self-declared prophet who wants to "reshape the human body by modern technology," by fusing cars and people. Vaughn entertains his idea by reenacting famous car crashes (James Dean, Jayne Mansfield), but he also wants to put the concept

◄

In the United States, the owner of distributor Fine Line Features, Ted Turner, objected personally to the film and withheld its release for months. When it finally went on wide release, *Crash* did not become a box office success.

into practice, on the road. A vicious circle of wrecks, bodily scars, and unlimited sex ensues. Eventually, James and Catherine force Vaughn off a bridge into death. The film ends with them chasing each other in cars, looking for the "next one," the ultimate kick.

When *Crash* premiered at the Cannes festival in May 1996, opinions were starkly divided. The film eventually picked up a

"YOU COULDN'T WAIT FOR ME? YOU DID THE JAYNE MANSFIELD CRASH WITHOUT ME?" VAUGHN

special jury prize for "audacity," a category invented on the spot by the jury in order to mask its disagreements. This sharp split between reactions that found *Crash* the ultimate "cool" film (a term most supporters used), or a "depraved" film (the term adopted by most opponents), explains why, over time, it developed a cult reputation. In Europe, *Crash* was widely lauded. In the U.K., however, it fell foul to a tabloid press campaign that delayed its release by nearly a year and caused several counties to ban it outright (it still remains banned from some London cinemas). In time it managed to strike a chord with audiences looking, like James and Catherine, for a utopia usually absent from theaters. As a meditation on the search for pure love and passion in a world oversaturated by technological gadgets, cynicism, and a thirst for thrills, *Crash* offers such viewers not desperation, but hope. **EM**

► Rosanna Arquette as Gabriella seemingly enjoys her handicap and uses it to explore her sexuality.

FROM
ACCLAIMED
DIRECTOR
GUY MADDIN

One man's search for
amorous requital in a land
where the sun never sets.

PASCALE   SHELLEY   FRANK   ALICE   R.H.
BUSSIÈRES   DUVALL   GORSHIN   KRIGE   THOMSON

TWILIGHT OF THE ICE NYMPHS

TWILIGHT OF THE ICE NYMPHS

1997 (CANADA)

Director Guy Maddin **Producer** Ritchard Findlay **Screenplay** George Toles
Cinematography Michael Marshall **Music** John McCulloch **Cast** R. H. Thomson,
Pascale Bussières, Shelley Duvall, Frank Gorshin, Alice Krige, Ross McMillan, Frank
Kowalski, Breanne Dowhan

Guy Maddin has made his career crafting films of exquisite madness. He revels in the languages of low art and early cinema, making highly idiosyncratic and amusing pieces. Praise for his work is common, though few beyond Canada's borders really "get" all of its nuances: Maddin's is the vocabulary of a man who "stayed" in a country in which it is expected of the creative classes to congregate in the national cultural capitals.

Maddin has made his career in Winnipeg, and his isolation from the preening and backstabbing of his contemporaries has made his work more insular, honing a vision entirely his own. Aiding his claim as Canada's leading auteur is that, while describing the "Canadian Experience," he does not contend self-consciously with questions of a national nature, thus freeing him to explore his land of endless winter, living closer to those touchstones of the landscape that seem to animate the Canadian anima.

Maddin's films are dark, sinister, and fun. They're constructed almost experimentally: he plays with montage aggressively, and in order to achieve his vintage effect—replete with the sense of the film print having suffered damage from overuse—he

◀

Guy Maddin's films are a cinephile's paradise, but the critics were by no means generous; their initial incomprehension and expectation that the outlandish style would alienate led them to indict its surreality and broad humor.

recreates the flicker of the projector's lamp in his lighting. His style is still forming in *Twilight of the Ice Nymphs*, and is challenged along its progress by the relentlessly sunny clime he has created. His fetish for dark corners frustrated, he is forced, like his characters, to work these energies otherwise, to brilliant effect.

The story is dense: in the land of Mandragora, where a kind of love-madness pervades, the characters, frustrated by

"WHAT I WONDER IS: WILL THE ANGELS PUT US ALL BACK TOGETHER AGAIN?"

AMELIA GLAHN

ceaseless sunlight, obscure their desires. A released political prisoner (Nigel Whitney) falls madly in love with a spectral woman, and he returns to the family ostrich farm and his sister, Amelia (Shelley Duvall). The film looks like Baroque opera, and the themes concur; Mandragora is Winnipeg via the Mediterranean and Maddin creates an odd, apt composite in which Dr. Solti (R. H. Thomson) is infatuated with a statue of Venus, which seems to nurse an affinity for the character of Zephyr (Alice Krige). *Twilight of the Ice Nymphs* marked a major step forward in Maddin's work. Earlier films evinced an inward-looking view, as though Maddin did not expect that anyone outside his editing suite would ever see them. Today it is looked back upon with awe; acolytes come to him and are met with the breathless insistence: "But you *must* see *Twilight of the Ice Nymphs* . . ." **GS**

► A peerless synthesist with a restless imagination, Maddin's film language is notably old as this scene shows.

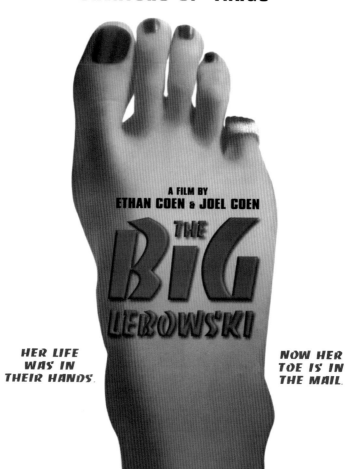

THE BIG LEBOWSKI 1998 (U.S.)

Director Joel Coen **Producer** Ethan Coen **Screenplay** Joel Coen, Ethan Coen
Cinematography Roger Deakins **Music** Carter Burwell **Cast** Jeff Bridges, John
Goodman, Julianne Moore, Steve Buscemi, David Huddleston, Philip Seymour
Hoffman, Tara Reid, John Turturro, Sam Elliott

A film that could only have been made at the hands of the
Coen brothers, *The Big Lebowski* is delightfully absurd, revolving
around an unemployed, White Russian-swigging stoner who
calls himself "the Dude" (effortlessly played by Jeff Bridges), and
a series of bizarre and unique characters he encounters after
falling victim to a case of mistaken identity.

Loosely based on the narrative structure of the Raymond
Chandler novel, *The Big Sleep*, the Coens opt to ignore a standard
linear plot in favor of slicing together a collection of wildly
madcap episodes all featuring Jeff "the Dude" Lebowski and
built around witty dialogue reducing plot to secondary status.
Such is the strength of the script and the actors involved, it's a
resounding success, with the viewer consumed more by what is
taking place on-screen than by any strong desire to witness a
resolution to the story. "The Dude" likes to spend his days in a
bowling alley with his friends, the Vietnam vet Walter (John
Goodman), an unhinged bundle of pent-up aggression, willing
to pull a gun on a fellow bowler who refuses to admit to an
illegal throw—"this is not Nam; this is bowling, there are rules"—
and Donny (Steve Buscemi), a gentle man eternally lagging a

◄
**The film itself has
developed a life of
its own, with fans
regularly staging
Lebowski Fest, a
convention where
participants bowl,
dress like their
favorite character,
and drink White
Russians, just like
"the Dude"
(Bridges).**

few seconds behind every conversation. The Dude's carefree existence is brought to a crashing halt when two inept heavies break into his apartment and urinate on the rug after mistaking him for a wheelchair-bound millionaire who also happens to go by the name Jeffrey Lebowski (David Huddleston).

Following Walter's advice, the Dude attempts to get redress for a rug that "tied the room together" and heads to the home

"BY THE WAY, DO YOU THINK THAT YOU COULD GIVE ME THAT $20,000 IN CASH?" THE DUDE

of Jeffrey Lebowski. This sets in motion a series of hilarious vignettes across L.A. with obvious nods to the conventions of film noir—taking the Dude through a bungled bag drop that contained a million-dollar ransom for the kidnappers of Lebowski's wife, and encounters with various characters, including an erotic artist (Julianne Moore) who likes to paint naked suspended from a harness, German nihilists, trophy wives, porn barons, Malibu cops, moronic teenage car thieves, and a marmot.

Among all this comedy caper is a fantastically over-the-top performance from John Turturro as Jesus, a cheesy, purple-clad bowling fanatic. *The Big Lebowski* sparkles with inventiveness, showcasing the Coen brothers' ability to meld a stylistic, entertaining story, littered with ironies and nuances, around the most unconventional themes and characters. **SG**

► **This dream sequence, called "Gutterball," is modeled on a Busby Berkeley musical with elements of Fritz Lang's *Metropolis* (1927).**

BUFFALO '66 1998 (U.S.)

Director Vincent Gallo **Producer** Chris Hanley, Deborah Brock, Gerry Gersham, Jordan Gertner **Screenplay** Vincent Gallo, Alison Bagnell **Cinematography** Lance Acord **Music** Vincent Gallo **Cast** Vincent Gallo, Christina Ricci, Ben Gazzara, Mickey Rourke, Anjelica Huston, Jan-Michael Vincent

Vincent Gallo is a man of many talents: a model (most famously for Calvin Klein), a musician, a songwriter, and a painter. However, it is for his work as an independent filmmaker that he is best known, especially in light of the deluge of histrionic responses by numerous film critics to his 2003 feature, *The Brown Bunny*, with its copious long takes, carefully lensed sequences of unabashed tenderness, and, of course, its infamous fellatio scene. It would be interesting to learn exactly how many of those reviewers lauded his debut film, *Buffalo '66*, which, although lacking a depiction of un-simulated oral sex, revealed a similar aesthetic rigor and penchant for sentiment.

Buffalo '66 tells the story of Billy Brown, who, as the film opens, is being released from prison after serving five years for the crimes of a bookie to whom he owed a substantial sum following the Buffalo Bills' loss in the Super Bowl—a defeat that resulted from a botched field goal by place kicker Scott Woods (a thinly veiled reference to former Bills Super Bowl goat, Scott Norwood). Despondent to the point of suicide, the newly freed Billy sets two objectives for himself. His first goal is to visit his parents, from whom he has been long estranged, and to whom

◀

Love, murder, and redemption: Is Layla's (Christina Ricci) love enough to stop Billy from going through with his ill-conceived plan to murder the former Bills kicker?

he feels that he must prove that he has made something of himself. His second goal is to kill Scott Woods, whom he blames for ruining his life. Stranded in the urban wasteland of downtown Buffalo with a painfully full bladder, Billy sneaks into a ballet studio to relieve himself. There he meets Layla (Christina Ricci), whom he quickly kidnaps, forcing her to accompany him to his parent's house and pose as his wife. Billy's mother, never

"THERE WAS NOBODY THAT I LIKED BECAUSE GIRLS STINK. THEY'RE EVIL. AND THEY'RE ALL BAD." BILLY BROWN

having forgiven her son for making her miss seeing the Bills play in a championship game when she went into labor, barely recalls even the smallest details of her son's life. Similarly, Billy's father is distant and melancholic, surfacing periodically to flirt openly with Layla, at one point burying his face in her cleavage. Set primarily around a dinner table, this scene of extreme suburban dysfunction plays out like a sequence from a Yasujiro Ozu film, if the acclaimed Japanese director were to have traded his classic "tatami shots" for a camera angle more akin to the height of a TV dinner tray.

▶

Billy Brown (Vincent Gallo) just out of prison in a grim and grimy Buffalo contemplates missed chances in life.

Attracted to Billy from the moment she sees him sneaking through the ballet studio, Layla falls deeper in love with the tortured ex-con, meeting his verbal abuse with warmth and sympathy in an attempt to provide him with the comfort she feels he deserves. **JMcR**

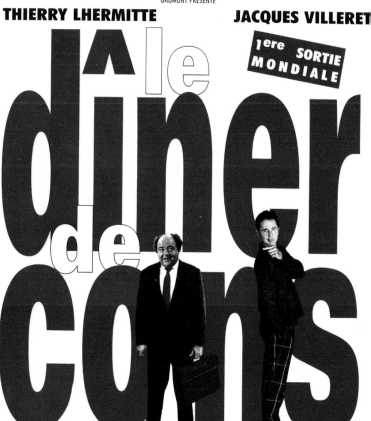

GAUMONT PRÉSENTE

THIERRY LHERMITTE   JACQUES VILLERET

le dîner de cons

1ère SORTIE MONDIALE

UN FILM ÉCRIT ET RÉALISÉ PAR **FRANCIS VEBER**

FRANCIS HUSTER - **DANIEL PREVOST** - **ALEXANDRA VANDERNOOT**

et **CATHERINE FROT** - Musique **VLADIMIR COSMA** Producteur délégué **ALAIN POIRÉ**

Image LUCIANO TOVOLI (AIC) - (ASC) - Montage GEORGES KLOTZ - Decors HUGUES TISSANDIER - Costumes JACQUELINE BOUCHARD - Direction de la production PHILIPPE DESMOULINS - HENRI BRICHETTI
Une coproduction GAUMONT - EFVE - TF1 FILMS PRODUCTION

LE DÎNER DES CONS 1998 (FRANCE)

Director Francis Veber **Producer** Alain Poiré **Screenplay** Francis Veber **Cinematography** Luciano Tovoli **Music** Vladimir Cosma **Cast** Thierry Lhermitte, Jacques Villeret, Francis Huster, Daniel Prévost, Alexandra Vandermoot, Catherine Frot, Benoît Bellal, Jacques Bleu

The "comédie de boulevard" is a grand, bourgeois French tradition, and every now and then one really, actually gets the pulse of its time and reaches forward to something larger. For a generation, *Le Dîner des Cons* has been that film. While the world at large is unfairly treated to almost every mistake Hollywood makes, much of world cinema goes unnoticed beyond its own linguistic borders, and unless one considers the kind of dreck that plays for months at French multiplexes, its uniqueness is unlikely to impress.

Pierre Brochant (Theirry Lhermitte) and his well-heeled, high-placed friends organize a weekly dinner, a "dîner de cons." The concept: each man procures a man whom he believes to be exceedingly "con"—dull, stupid, an idiot—and endeavors to make them speak as much as possible. Then, after the guests leave, they assess their fools and elect the most stupid of the lot. For the current get-together, Pierre, a publisher, has come up short and relies upon a referral from a country club friend, a sort-of "scout": a civil servant at the Ministry of Finance named François Pignon (Jacques Villeret). The overture is made, and Pignon arrives at the elegant apartment of Pierre to find his

◀

Directly translated, "the dinner of the idiots" is an astute farce that has no moral ax to grind, instead suggesting we're all jerks, people are funny, and we are all fools.

patron laid up with a back complaint, earned earlier that day on the links. Pierre's early efforts to send his guest off fail, and they are both drawn into farcical intrigue involving an old friend, a mistress, a discontented wife, and an auditor.

The farce is rendered visually and the boulevard aspect is referenced swiftly in the credit sequence, which resembles nothing more than the placards that decorate the theaters of les

"YOU HAVE CHANGED MY LIFE, MONSIEUR BROCHANT."

FRANÇOIS PIGNON

Grands Boulevards (a stage adaptation has played for some time to audiences at one of these venues). Farces do well with single sets, and Pierre's apartment is pidgin Chabrol with a twist. His view of the Eiffel Tower is so close as to appear an actual threat (the proximity a pronounced inside joke). No one has so perfect a view, except Pierre Brochant: he has everything and is no one.

Beyond farce, *Le Dîner des Cons* is also a kind of odd couple buddy film; it is also, not unlike *Ridicule* (1996), a film that tackles the particular French custom of social mockery as sport. *Le Dîner des Cons* turns the rule on its head: the "dinner game" is actually named for the idiots who host it, who promote themselves in their elevated positions as greater, wiser men. The thing is, after all this, François remains the butt of our jokes. Not only are the men who have determined to toy with him boors, but François himself is, authentically, a bore. **GS**

► In this classic French farce, Pignon (Jacques Villeret) may end up saving the day in spite of his unsophisticated bungling.

RUN LOLA RUN 1998 (GERMANY)

Director Tom Tykwer **Producer** Stefan Arndt **Screenplay** Tom Tykwer
Cinematography Frank Griebe **Music** Tom Tykwer, Johnny Klimek, Reinhold
Heil **Cast** Franka Potente, Moritz Bleibtreu, Herbert Knaup, Nina Petri, Armin Rohde,
Monica Bleibtreu, Ludger Pistor, Heino Ferch

It is almost always a criticism when a film is described as "style over substance," but in the case of Tom Tykwer's breakthrough film *Run Lola Run* (*Lola rennt*), it stands as the ultimate compliment. A smash in its native Germany before becoming a surprise hit in the United States after the 1999 Sundance Film Festival, *Run Lola Run* is essentially a video game in the form of a film, with heroine Lola (a perfectly cast Franka Potente) going through three twenty-minute, virtually real-time scenarios to obtain 100,000 Deutschemarks to save her boyfriend, Manni (Moritz Bleibtreu), from ruthless crime lord, Ronnie (Heino Ferch).

Low-level flunky Manni was charged with getting a bag of money to Ronnie, but he absent mindedly left the bag behind on a train. With twenty minutes remaining before he is due to meet Ronnie, he phones Lola, who tells him to wait for her and she'll find a solution. She runs and runs and runs, and Tykwer replays this scenario three times.

Events and people's lives, both major and minor, apparently change with each run. And with those alterations, the entire scenario changes. In the first or second run, she may bump into a woman pushing a stroller, and she won't bump into her

◄

A rare but welcome example of a European foreign language action picture with techno soundbeat and frantic-paced direction that gives Hollywood's dominance a good run for its money.

in the third run. And the ever-gimmicky Tykwer briefly pauses to show us the future of these extraneous characters in the form of a series of quick-cut photographs. No real reason. Just style over substance. Two quotes from legendary German football player/manager Sepp Herberger open the film, one being "After the game is before the game." The game is played. Whatever happens happens. Lola runs. Then runs again.

"THE BALL IS ROUND. THE GAME LASTS 90 MINUTES. THAT'S A FACT. EVERYTHING ELSE IS PURE THEORY." *HERR SCHUSTER*

With its brief eighty-minute running time, *Run Lola Run* doesn't have a chance to overstay its welcome. It's a stunt of a film—from Potente's shockingly red hair to the pulsating techno score (composed in part by Tykwer) to the sense of constant movement and frenetic pace, either by Potente or by Tykwer's camera work— but an incredibly stylish one.

Tykwer is a unique voice in filmmaking who has had sporadic acclaim in the subsequent years after this movie's outing, with films running the gamut from highbrow (*Heaven* in 2002, originally planned for the late Krysztof Kieslowski), commercial (*The International* in 2009), to the completely insane (his adaptation of Patrick Suskind's novel *Perfume: The Story of a Murderer* in 2006, a not-always-successful film that's too ambitious to simply dismiss). However, the dirrector has yet to again receive the accolades he received with *Run Lola Run*. **MT**

► **Scarlet-haired Lola (Franka Potente) in a rare moment of dialogue rather than running.**

RUSHMORE 1998 (U.S.)

Director Wes Anderson **Producer** Barry Mendel, Paul Schiff
Screenplay Wes Anderson, Owen Wilson **Cinematography** Robert
Yeoman **Music** Mark Mothersbaugh **Cast** Jason Schwartzman, Bill Murray,
Olivia Williams, Seymour Cassel, Brian Cox, Mason Gamble, Sara Tanaka

Both visually and thematically, Wes Anderson's sophomore
film, *Rushmore* (1998), is a perfect link between his first movie,
Bottle Rocket (1996) and his third, *The Royal Tenenbaums* (2001).

All three films are cowritten by Anderson and writer–actor
Owen Wilson. All three films explore the theme of eccentric
males—both youths and adults—who strive to make
meaningful connections with others while searching for their
niche in an inconsistent world. All three films utilize visual
trademarks that both pay homage to other directors and help
to define Anderson's own filmmaking style. Lastly, all three
films enjoyed significant and merited critical accolades.
Rushmore, however, has come to enjoy a well-deserved cult
standing. Indeed, repeated screenings of the film allow viewers
to understand that beyond its quirky charm, *Rushmore* provides
a thoughtful, funny, beautiful, and original American take on
love and friendship.

The film focuses on the tumultuous friendship and romantic
rivalry between a precocious teenager, Max Fischer (Jason
Schwartzman), and a cynical millionaire, Herman Blume (Bill
Murray). Max seems to thrive at his private school, Rushmore,

◄

***Rushmore* occupies
a unique place in
the landscape of
U.S. cult cinema,
even among
Anderson's oeuvre.**

where he finds identity as the center of virtually every campus activity. As his unrequited crush on new Rushmore teacher Rosemary Cross begins to intensify, Max is expelled from his beloved school and must negotiate in his new surroundings. Herman, in contrast, is a world-weary soul, a man who jumps into his own beautiful inground pool and wonders whether to even bother resurfacing. Estranged from his wife and twin sons,

"YOU KNOW, YOU AND HERMAN DESERVE EACH OTHER. YOU'RE BOTH LITTLE CHILDREN." ROSEMARY CROSS [TO MAX]

Herman is introduced to Max, whose enthusiasm he admires. Just as the two disconnected males begin to find that they can rely on each other, their shared admiration for Miss Cross drives a wedge between them that eventually leads to an all-out war. *Rushmore*'s treatment of how Max and Herman struggle against each other, and within themselves, is comical and touching.

Rushmore is a remarkable film, and not just for its gorgeous visual accomplishments that have become a trademark for Anderson. The film's unique characters and brilliant casting bring Anderson and Wilson's innovative script to life. Schwartzman is iconic as the eager but adrift Max, and Murray's performance as Herman helped to reinvent him as an actor. Murray would again work with Anderson in several of his movies, including *The Life Aquatic with Steve Zissou* (2004), in which he plays the title character and *Fantastic Mr. Fox* (2009). **AK**

► Jason Schwartzman perfectly cast as the private school achiever who finds himself displaced.

OFFICE SPACE 1999 (U.S.)

Director Mike Judge **Producer** Daniel Rappaport, Michael Rotenberg, Mike Judge **Screenplay** Mike Judge **Cinematography** Tim Surhstedt **Music** John Frizzell **Cast** Ron Livingston, Jennifer Aniston, Stephen Root, David Herman, Ajay Naidu, John C. McGinley

Originating from his ideas worked up in a series of animated shorts called *Milton*, director Mike Judge's *Office Space* brilliantly spoofs the daily grind and pettiness of office work. His live-action movie lampoons both management-speak and procedure-obsessed managers.

Peter Gibbons (Ron Livingston) works as a computer programmer for Initech, a company where he complains that every day is worse than the one before (and hence every day is the worst of his life). His life is made even harder by his over-officious passive-aggressive boss, Bill Lumbergh (a wonderfully obtuse Gary Cole), who is obsessed with report writing and who makes Peter work weekends. To relieve the stress of this everyday drudgery, his girlfriend convinces him to see a hypnotherapist, who quickly convinces Peter not to take things quite so seriously. Unfortunately, the hypnotherapist suffers a heart attack before he can bring him out of hypnosis. As a result, Peter is left in a permanent state of relaxation, with a newfound carefree attitude toward his work. He sleeps in, turns up late for work, takes down the partition in his office cubicle, and generally acts as if he doesn't have a care in the world. In one

◄

Despite being a box office and critical flop upon initial release, *Office Space* has garnered a strong cult following among IT workers but has also proved to be a breakout hit on DVD.

memorable scene, after Peter is called in to talk to the "two Bobs," a pair of management consultants who are interviewing employees with a goal of laying off expendable staff, he gives them an honest rundown of his day: coming in fifteen minutes late, entering by the side door to avoid detection, staring at his screen for an hour to look like he's working, doing that again after lunch, and being motivated to work purely so that he

"BOB, IT'S NOT THAT I'M LAZY, IT'S THAT I JUST DON'T CARE . . . WHERE'S THE MOTIVATION?" *PETER GIBBONS*

doesn't get yelled at by his eight different bosses. Peter concludes the interview by telling the Bobs that he probably only does about fifteen minutes of real work a week. They immediately recommend him for promotion. Eventually Peter, along with fellow Initech employees Samir and Michael, concocts a plan to steal money from Initech using a scheme they take from *Superman III*. Naturally, all goes horribly wrong.

► **Two coworkers (Ajay Naidu and David Herman) can't believe the laid-back audacity of their fellow worker (Ron Livingston).**

Ron Livingston is a wonderfully serene presence as a man imprisoned by his office cubicle, worn down by the daily grind and inanity of endless report writing. But the film is stolen by Stephen Root as the socially challenged Milton (recognizable in any office environment and described by the Bobs as the "squirrely looking guy, mumbles a lot"), whose obsession with keeping his red stapler and quibbles over his desk space are at the root of the film's riff on office politics. **RH**

神様、冗談だったら、やめてください

深作欣二監督作品
バトル・ロワイアル
SPECIAL 特別篇 VERSION

BR
BATTLE ROYALE

R-15
祝 中学卒業
中学3年生だったばかりに、この映画を見られなかった皆様へ。

第13回東京国際映画祭特別招待作品　第30回ロッテルダム国際映画祭招待作品
第24回日本アカデミー賞9部門受賞　優秀作品賞　優秀監督賞　優秀脚本賞　優秀主演男優賞　優秀音楽賞　優秀録音賞　優秀編集賞　新人俳優賞　話題賞
第43回ブルーリボン賞受賞　作品賞　新人賞(藤原竜也)

原作:高見広春(太田出版 刊)

R-15　藤原竜也　前田亜季　山本太郎　栗山千明　柴咲コウ　安藤政信／ビートたけし

www.battle-royale.com

BATTLE ROYALE 2000 (JAPAN)

Director Kinji Fukasaku **Producer** Kinji Fukasaku, Kenta Fukasaku **Screenplay** Kenta Fukasaku **Cinematography** Katsumi Yanagijima **Music** Masamichi Amano **Cast** Takeshi Kitano, Tatsuya Fujiwara, Aki Maeda, Chiaki Kuriyama, Sosuke Takaoka, Takashi Tsukamoto, Tarô Yamamoto, Yukihiro Kotani

Based upon the best-selling novel by Koushun Takami, *Battle Royale* is set in a dystopic future at which time parliament has passed the Millennium Educational Reform Act, or B.R., as a mechanism to deal with economic collapse and juvenile delinquency. Under the Act, a class of high school students are chosen at random by lottery and are taken to a deserted island where they are forced to kill each other until there is only one left. Break the rules of the competition, and an armed collar placed around the neck of the contestant explodes.

The forty-two students in Shiroiwa Class 3-B are the "lucky" winners of the lottery, and armed with a variety of weapons (including a machine gun, a tracking device, and poison) have to fight to survive until the end of three days—the time limit for the game. The students are faced with a moral dilemma: what is more important, survival or friendship?

While some of the students, including Chigusa (Chiaki Kuriyama) and one of the two "transfer" students, Kiriyama (Masanobu Ando), embrace the rules of the game, killing indiscriminately, others including Shuya Nanahara (Tatsuya Fujiwara), Noriko Nakagawa (Aki Maeda), and the second

◀

The success of *Battle Royale* led to the inevitable sequel. In 2002, Fukasaku began work on *Battle Royale II,* despite the fact he was dying of bone cancer. He died during production, and his son, Kenta, completed the film.

transfer student, Kawada (Tarô Yamamoto), work as a team and try to escape the Island. Others, torn between impossible choices, commit suicide. Orchestrating the game behind the scenes is an old teacher of Shiroiwa Class 3-B, Mr. Kitano, played by the famous Beat (Kitano) Takeshi, a star of the yakuza genre.

Battle Royale contrasts high-octane action with more meditative scenes interspersed with flashbacks in which the

> ## "LIFE IS A GAME. SO FIGHT FOR SURVIVAL AND SEE IF YOU'RE WORTH IT. NOTHING'S AGAINST THE RULES." MR. KITANO

characters develop more fully: in one flashback we see Chigusa's mother selling her to a pedophile, and in another we learn of Shuya's father's suicide. As such, the film places blame for juvenile "delinquency" squarely on the breakdown of the family. Although this is a common theme in contemporary Japanese film, here resistance to authority is viewed as a positive rather than negative attribute: a necessary part of the rite of passage from teenager to adult.

► **The school kids have every weapon imaginable at their disposal from Uzi submachine gun to traditional swords to cyanide.**

Battle Royale is an exceptional film that deals with themes specific to Japan, such as the conflict between the individual and the group, the universality of adolescence, and intergenerational conflict. Despite its violence, *Battle Royale*'s moral message shines through, emphasizing the need for understanding between generations and the importance of friendship in an increasingly alienated consumer society. **CB**

MEMENTO 2000 (U.S.)

Director Christopher Nolan **Producer** Suzanne Todd, Jennifer Todd
Screenplay Christopher Nolan **Cinematography** Wally Pfister **Music** David Julyan
Cast Guy Pearce, Carrie-Anne Moss, Joe Pantoliano, Mark Boone, Jr., Russ Fega, Jorja
Fox, Stephen Tobolowsky, Kimberly Campbell, Larry Holden

In the opening credit sequence of *Memento*, a Polaroid photo
of a dead man slowly develops, and we travel backwards in
time to see the murder being committed. The movie then
chronicles the lead-up to the murder in a fractured series of
episodes that run forward but in reverse chronological order.
The end of each new episode overlaps slightly with the
beginning of the previous one, anchoring them together.

These episodes are linked by black and white scenes running
in chronological order, featuring Leonard Shelby (Guy Pearce)
talking on the telephone in his motel room, although for most
of the movie we do not know how these scenes fit into the
narrative. Leonard was hit on the head on the night his wife was
raped and murdered, and since then he cannot form any new
memories. Nothing stays in his mind for more than a few
minutes, no matter how vital or dramatic. "If you talk for too
long I won't know how we started," he says into the phone. The
comment, like many moments in the movie, seems incidental at
the time, but its significance becomes chillingly clear later on.

The effect of the fragmented and backwards structure
makes the audience share Leonard's condition and presents us

◄
Director
Christopher Nolan
has used an
intriguing and
intricate structure
to fashion a tense
and atmospheric
thriller from
insubstantial
material.

with the confusion he experiences because, like him, we are unaware of the events that have led up to the present ones. Each short episode represents the little loop of present Leonard is forced to live in. As the narrative progresses, the meaning of events we have already seen changes, as people's motives for their actions are revealed. Pearce's Leonard is utterly convincing: detached from the present by his condition but haunted by his

> # "JUST BECAUSE I DON'T REMEMBER DOESN'T MAKE MY ACTIONS MEANINGLESS." LEONARD SHELBY

past. He is alienated and confused, but the movie exploits the comic potential of it, too, as a sheepish motel clerk admits to renting him two rooms, and Leonard takes a shower when he's supposed to be waiting for someone in a bathroom. To enable himself to function and pursue his life's work—finding his wife's murderer—Leonard writes himself notes, takes Polaroid photos, and tattoos key pieces of evidence on his body. "Facts," he says, "not memories. That's how you investigate." But as we move back through time, discovering the context of his actions, it becomes clear that facts are not enough.

► **Leonard (Guy Pearce) and the seductive Natalie (Carrie-Ann Moss) trying to piece together mementos and memories.**

If the narrative of *Memento* had run forward, it would be sorely lacking in the deception and twists and turns of plot that create an effective thriller. As each new scene unfolds, we learn more, and at the same time facts that seemed concrete are undermined, until the finale blows out everything. **CW**

DONNIE DARKO 2001 (U.S.)

Director Richard Kelly **Producer** Adam Fields, Nancy Juvonen, Sean McKittrick
Screenplay Richard Kelly **Cinematography** Steven Poster **Music** Michael Andrews
Cast Jake Gyllenhaal, Holmes Osborne, Maggie Gyllenhaal, Daveigh Chase, Mary
McDonnell, James Duval, Arthur Taxier, Patrick Swayze, Drew Barrymore

Donnie Darko perfectly captures America's start to the twenty-
first century. The film paints a picture of middle-America as a
confused, desperate, and paranoid society tearing at the seams,
a snapshot of the spectacle and confusion in the United States
right before and after 9/11.

Donald "Donnie" Darko (Jake Gyllenhaal) is a troubled
teenager—a chronic sleepwalker in deep therapy and under
heavy medication. Donnie's life is shaken up when in the week
preceding the presidential elections (of 1988, the year of the
story), a jet engine falls through the roof of the family home
into his room. Luckily, Donnie is out sleepwalking—a trip during
which a giant, creepy rabbit (called Frank) warns Donnie the
world will come to an end in twenty-eight days, six hours, forty-
two minutes, and twelve seconds. As Donnie struggles to find
the meaning of this message, he becomes embroiled in a small
school uprising (supporting his liberal teacher—Drew
Barrymore), exposes a pedophilia racket run by a motivational
speaker (Patrick Swayze), and chats to his friends about the sex
lives of the Smurfs. On top of this comes enigmatic encounters
with Grandma Death and the mysterious Frank. In the end,

◄

**The release of a
2004 "director's
cut" that tried to
explain some of the
original's mysteries
almost destroyed
the burgeoning
cult. But fans kept
preferring the
original, now
regarded as one
of the best ever
independent films.**

Donnie realizes Grandma Death and Frank are instructing him to go back in time and sacrifice himself in order to save the life of his girlfriend, Gretchen (Jena Malone), who has been run over by a car. A jet engine falls again through the family roof, and this time Donnie lies in his bed, laughing maniacally.

Upon release, *Donnie Darko* was what one critic called "an impressive failure." Obviously, viewers did not want to see a

"28 DAYS, 6 HOURS, 42 MINUTES, 12 SECONDS. THAT IS WHEN THE WORLD WILL END." FRANK

story about jet parts falling from the sky, the world's end, or even undoing one's wrongs, so soon after the attacks on the World Trade Center in September 2001, not even at Halloween (the film's opening weekend slot). Nor did they care much for the many references to high school shootings such as Columbine. But after the film's initial run, it became a surprise success during midnight showings in New York.

The movie also found appreciative audiences on DVD, especially in the U.K., where the 1980s retro soundtrack became a huge hit and the Tears For Fears single "Mad World" performed by Gary Jules became No. 1. Against the prevailing gung ho mores of the time, *Donnie Darko* puts a menacing, pensive, reflective, and ironic tone, a relief from blockbuster warmongering. Before long, *Donnie Darko* had obtained a firm countercultural following. **EM**

► **Jake Gyllenhaal excelled as the supremely dark, sheepish, laid-back "doom generation" pinup as the world went crazy around him.**

HEDWIG
AND THE ANGRY INCH

NEW LINE CINEMA PRESENTS A KILLER FILMS PRODUCTION HEDWIG AND THE ANGRY INCH STARRING JOHN CAMERON MITCHELL

CASTING SUSAN SHOPMAKER PRODUCER COLIN BRUNTON DIRECTOR OF PHOTOGRAPHY ALEX STEYERMARK ANIMATION BY EMILY HUBLEY

ART DIRECTOR MIKE POTTER COSTUME DESIGNER ARIANNE PHILLIPS PRODUCTION DESIGNER THERESE DEPREZ EDITOR ANDREW MARCUS EXECUTIVE PRODUCER FRANK G. DEMARCO MUSIC AND LYRICS BY STEPHEN TRASK

EXECUTIVE PRODUCERS MICHAEL DE LUCA AMY HENKELS MARK TUSK PRODUCED BY CHRISTINE VACHON KATIE ROUMEL PAMELA KOFFLER WRITTEN FOR THE SCREEN AND DIRECTED BY JOHN CAMERON MITCHELL

www.get-hed.com

HEDWIG AND THE ANGRY INCH
2001 (U.S.)

Director John Cameron Mitchell **Producer** Christine Vachon **Screenplay** John Cameron Mitchell, Stephen Trask **Cinematography** Frank G. DeMarco **Music** Stephen Trask **Cast** John Cameron Mitchell, Miriam Shor, Michael Pitt, Andrea Martin, Stephen Trask, Rob Campbell, Thedore Liscinski, Michael Aronov, Maurice Dean Witt

Those of us who adored John Cameron Mitchell's cult off-off-Broadway rock opera could not have dreamed that its auteur would have proved so full-blooded a cineast. Anyone who witnessed the unapologetic stadium-rock-cabaret of Hedwig's stage incarnation would have scoffed at the prospect of a screen adaptation. But, as with most successful adaptations of off-kilter stage musicals, the tactic to leave the stage itself well behind—with the spirit of the stage (its chaos, its noise, its human energy) brought very much to the fore—paid off electrically.

Hansel (later Hedwig, played by John Cameron Mitchell), a glam rock-obsessed adolescent in communist East Berlin, determines to escape to the West by undergoing a sex change operation, assuming his mother's identity and marrying American G.I. Luther (Maurice Dean Witt). The procedure, however, is "botched" and Hansel (now Hedwig) is left with the "angry inch" of the film's title: a one-inch piece of sex stuck stubbornly to her pelvic region. Once relocated to America, Hedwig, drunk on vermouth and bitter at her lot, takes her sullen Christian neighbor under her rock wing and fashions

◄

Despite its rock cladding—a transplanted stage musical—*Hedwig* is in fact a very sensitive romance, fraught with sadness, disappointment, and hope.

from him a veritable rock god, rebranded Tommy Gnosis (Michael Pitt). For Hedwig, the relationship is far from platonic, complicating matters considerably, and as Tommy gains international notoriety, Hedwig's rage consumes itself and multiplies. Now on tour with her own band, The Angry Inch, Hedwig crosses America playing seafood chain restaurants in Tommy's shadow, daring their inevitable encounter.

"I HAD TRIED SINGING ONCE BACK IN BERLIN. THEY THREW TOMATOES. AFTER THE SHOW, I HAD A NICE SALAD." HEDWIG

One of the great coups afforded by the film adaptation is the locating of Hedwig's gigs in the fictional Bridgewater seafood chain (obviously modeled on Red Lobster), and the distressed looks on the faces of the patrons who certainly did not tuck in their bibs to be assaulted by a six-foot transvestite fronting an alt-rock band. In the role of Hedwig, Cameron Mitchell lets loose in hitherto unseen ways. This is a performance of astonishing freedom and nuance. As he tears off his wig near the finale, we are actually stunned. The tactic is stagey and not, in itself, new, but his delivery of it is so terrifyingly exposed that we feel, finally, the anguish of a human being stripped bare. Cameron Mitchell's silky, unemphatic unfolding of Hedwig's ongoing monologue is pitch-perfect, in no way hinting at the film's stage origins. **GS**

► Hedwig (Cameron Mitchell) does his David Bowie-Lou Reed-Iggy Pop tribute. The music in *Hedwig* is rock musical music that resembles actual rock music. This alone would secure a cult following.

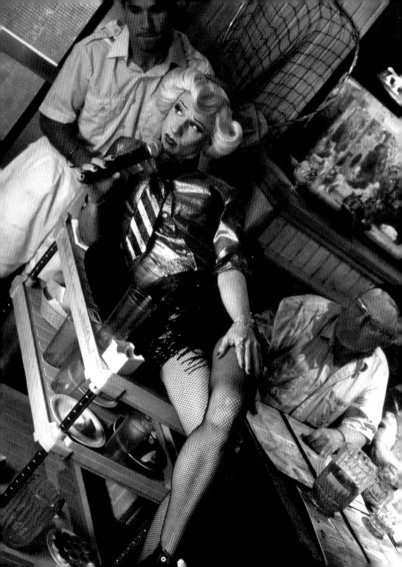

愛は、かなりイタイ。

殺し屋1

浅野忠信×三池崇史×山本英夫

www.koroshiya-1.com

KOROSHIYA ICHI

ICHI THE KILLER

2001 (JAPAN • HONG KONG • SOUTH KOREA)

Director Takashi Miike **Producer** Akira Funatsu, Dai Miyazaki **Screenplay** Sakichi Satô **Cinematography** Hideo Yamamoto **Music** Karera Musication **Cast** Tadanobu Asano, Nao Omori, Shinya Tsukamoto, Shun Sugata, Toru Tezuka, Yoshiki Arizono, Paulyn Sun (Alien Sun), Susumu Terajima (Sabu), Hiroshi Kobayashi

In recent years, he's mellowed out and his output has relatively slowed down, but there was a period in the early 2000s when Japan's Takashi Miike was arguably the premier cinema outlaw. From 1996 to 2004, Miike made a staggering number of films at a pace that made the mid-to-late 1970s Rainer Werner Fassbinder look like Terrence Malick. A good number of these films were controversial, outrageously transgressive works that, like them or not, provoked a reaction. Films like the horrific *Audition* (1999), reality TV indictment *Visitor Q* (2001), *The Happiness of the Katakuris* (2001), and almost David Lynch-esque *Gozu* (2003) are some standout Miike essentials. There's certainly an argument for putting *Audition* top of the pole, but Miike's defining statement is arguably his gloriously over-the-top yakuza thriller, *Ichi the Killer*.

Based on Hideo Yamamoto's (not to be confused with the film's cinematographer) manga, *Ichi* doesn't really center on the title character, a childlike hit man (Nao Omori) prone to crying fits and under the extreme psychological manipulation of Jijii (Shinya Tsukamoto), who's trying to start an all-out yakuza war.

◄

Ichi the Killer is a film filled with an almost cartoonish level of violence and gore, and is guaranteed to have something that will offend everyone.

Ichi and Jijii are important characters, but the film's focus—and iconic figure—is sadomasochistic, pain-obsessed gangster Kakihara (Tadanobu Asano). With his bleached-blond hair and his "Glasgow grin," held together by an earring in each cheek, Kakihara is a movie villain like no other, and could be seen as a major influence on Heath Ledger's Joker in *The Dark Knight* (2008). Kakihara is the kind of guy who hangs a rival yakuza

"JUST CONCENTRATE ON HOW GOOD IT FEELS TO BE CAUSING SOMEONE PAIN." KAKIHARA

naked, with hooks through his flesh, while piercing the guy's face with kabob skewers and pouring hot tempura oil all over him in order to extract information. And when the guy turns out to be innocent, Kakihara makes amends by cutting off his own tongue. And liking it.

As with his other films of the period, Miike's intention is precisely to get any kind of reaction out of the viewer. *Ichi the Killer* has something outrageous happen every few minutes—it could be tongue-ripping, nipple-slicing, cheek-tearing, artery-spraying, body-splitting, finger-breaking, or grease-burning. Or maybe just a simple, old-fashioned decapitation. But, even with all that aside, it's a good thriller filled with liberal doses of very dark humor, and as nasty as Kakihara is, there's no denying that he's quite funny, and *Ichi the Killer* is an essential journey into the world of Takashi Miike. **MT**

▶
"Giving pain is a serious business," says Kakihara (Asano), as he launches on a sadomasochistic revenge mission.

THE ROOM

CHLOE PRODUCTIONS/TPW FILMS PRESENTS A WISEAU-FILMS PRODUCTION TOMMY WISEAU "THE ROOM" JULIETTE DANIELLE
GREG SESTERO PHILIP HALDIMAN AND CARLOS MINNOTT MUSIC BY MLADEN MILICEVIC EDITED BY TOMMY WISEAU EDITOR SAFOWA BRIGHT
EDITED BY ERIC VALKUT CHASE PRODUCTION DESIGN MERCE DESIGNS ASSOCIATE PRODUCER TODD BARRON PRODUCERS CHLOE LIETZKE DREW CAFFREY TOMMY WISEAU
PRODUCED BY GREG SESTERO WRITTEN BY TOMMY WISEAU DIRECTED BY TOMMY WISEAU

www.TheRoomMovie.com

WISEAU FILMS

Only In Theaters

THE ROOM 2003 (U.S.)

Director Tommy Wiseau **Producer** Tommy Wiseau, Greg Sestero **Screenplay** Tommy Wiseau **Cinematography** Todd Baron **Music** Mladen Milicevic **Cast** Tommy Wiseau, Juliette Danielle, Greg Sestero, Philip Haldiman, Carolyn Minnott, Robyn Paris, Mike Holmes, Kyle Vogt, Greg Ellery, Dan Janjigian, Daron Jennings

The shout "You're tearing me apart, Lisa!" has fast become one of the characteristic features of the midnight cult phenomenon that is The Room, the Citizen Kane of bad movies. At heart, The Room is the story of the downfall of Johnny (Tommy Wiseau), a well-meaning man, betrayed by his fiancée, Lisa (Juliette Danielle) and his best friend, Mark (Greg Sestero). Upon discovering the affair, wronged Johnny kills himself, after a dramatic rant in which he screams in agony that this act of martyrdom will show 'em all. After his death, everyone breaks down in remorse—Johnny indeed showed them all.

The Room takes itself so seriously yet contains so many inconsistencies that it becomes a send-up of melodramas and soaps. Completed independently by Wiseau for $7 million (a budget about which he remains secretive) in spite of a lot of the crew quitting during production, The Room stands out because it is unbelievably single-minded. The opening credits reveal "a Wiseau film," with Wiseau as director, producer, screenwriter, and star. A bad sign, because Wiseau insists on setting the film almost entirely in (guess what?) a room, with red walls and pictures of spoons, in which each scene begins

◄

This is a movie you can throw spoons at—and scores of cult fans at special word-of-mouth screenings do just that.

with a nearly identical shot of a door through which new characters (some of whom are never properly introduced) enter and announce themselves ("Oh hi Lisa, Oh hi Johnny"). Within the room, characters chat about nagging problems ("I love him, I don't love him"), confront demons (cancer, drugs, crime, alcoholism, jealousy), and have sex—a lot of sex, with prominent nudity not just of Lisa but also of Johnny, who we

"AS FAR AS I'M CONCERNED, YOU CAN DROP OFF THE EARTH. THAT'S A PROMISE" MARK

repeatedly see humping her amidst clichéd set ups of candles, roses, silk curtains, and slow-motioned tracking shots. Wiseau's performance and mannerisms are so over the top that even what should be casual scenes of bonding (men dressed in tuxedos throwing footballs) or comfort (his relation to his younger protégé) become hyperinflated with innuendo.

▶
Whether comedy, sex-thriller, melodrama, or ego trip, *The Room* defies description and is, for its growing number of fans, "a life-changing experience."

After a brief unsuccessful run in Los Angeles, *The Room* found an unexpected audience at late-night screenings in art house and college campus theaters, where viewers began celebrating it as an ironic masterpiece: an antithesis of professionalism and craftsmanship. During screenings, people shouted at the screen (yelling "Alcatraz!" at stock shots of San Francisco), and threw spoons and footballs around. Wiseau wisely embraced the newfound following and now claims *The Room* was always intended to be a pitch-black comedy. **EM**

下妻物語
しもつまものがたり

わたし根性ねじまがってまーす♡

友達いないだろ。

shimotsuma-movie.jp
携帯はこちら stm.tv

深田恭子　土屋アンナ
宮迫博之　篠原涼子　樹木希林
阿野サダヲ　岡田義徳　小池栄子　矢久乃　庄薫拓久　荒川良々　本田博太郎

オリジナル・テーマソング◆Tommy heavenly⁶

KAMIKAZE GIRLS 2004 (JAPAN)

Director Tetsuya Nakashima **Producer** Takashi Hirano **Screenplay** Tetsuya Nakashima **Cinematography** Masakazu Ato **Music** Yoko Kanno **Cast** Kyôko Fukada, Anna Tsuchiya, Hiroyuki Miyasako, Sadao Abe, Eiko Koike, Shin Yazawa, Hirotarô Honda, Kirin Kiki, Haruo Mizuno, Ryôko Shinohara

A sugary sweet confectionary mix of Japanese pop culture, *Kamikaze Girls* is a vibrant kaleidoscope of fashion and femininity tied up in a pink parcel with ruffles galore. Told mainly through flashbacks, punctured with anime fantasy sequences, *Kamikaze Girls* focuses on the growing friendship between a young "Lolita," Momoko Ryugasaki (Kyôko Fukada), and a "Yanki," Ichigo Shirauri (Anna Tsuchiya)—representatives of two (incompatible) subcultural trends in contemporary Japan.

The seventeen-year-old Momoko lives with her father and grandmother in Shimotsuma in Ibaraki Prefecture. Her only escape from the tedium of small-town life is her Rococo fantasies of eighteenth-century France (known as the Lolita subculture in Japan) and her frilly doll-like dresses that she buys from Baby, The Stars Shine Bright, a Lolita fashion shop in Tokyo. While Momoko is the very epitome of sweet Lolita and all things flouncy and feminine, Ichiko is the opposite, a member of the Ponytails biker gang (known as *bosozoku*), all masculine attitude and Yanki aggression. A common interest in fashion as the ultimate signifier of identity brings the two teenage girls together, when Momoko advertises her

◄

Shimotsuma Monogatari (its original title) is a sensory overload of vibrant colors and textures, teenage angst, and shojo (girl's) culture, almost too kawaii (cute) for words.

father's cheap Versace knockoffs on the Internet and Ichigo, looking for a jacket to wear to a wedding, answers the ad.

This fantasy submersion into contemporary Japanese pop culture is backed by a J-pop soundtrack and a succession of cartoonish caricatures, including a flamboyant fashion owner (Yoshinori Okada), the improbably phallic-haired Unicorn Ryuuji (Sadao Abe), and Momoko's one-eyed, ex-pugilist grandmother

> # "HUMANS ARE COWARDS IN THE FACE OF HAPPINESS. IT TAKES COURAGE TO HOLD ON TO HAPPINESS." *MOMOKO RYUGASAKI*

(Kirin Kiki). As the friendship grows, the film takes a darker tone, culminating in the confrontation between the biker gang and Momoko, who rescues Ichigo from the battling gang members. The two ride off in a fanstasy scene on Ichigo's motorbike.

Despite its sumptuous and saccharine surfaces, *Kamikaze Girls* is a film that mediates on the prevalence of alienation among contemporary Japanese youth—there is something sour festering under all the surface sweetness. *Kamikaze Girls* has a stylistic sensibility that distinguishes it from many contemporary Japanese films and is a welcome contrast to the more extreme violent visions of Japanese youth culture in films such as *Battle Royale* (2000) and *Suicide Circle* (2001). While it shares a sense of a generation in crisis, misunderstood by adults, *Kamikaze Girls* prefers to offer an affirmation of life, living, fantasy, and most of all fashion. **CB**

► **Japanese youth culture is celebrated rather than relegated to the margins of society in this life-affirming movie.**

NAPOLEON DYNAMITE 2004 (U.S.)

Director Jared Hess **Producer** Jeremy Coon, Sean Covel, Chris Wyatt
Screenplay Jared Hess, Jerusha Hess **Cinematography** Munn Powell
Music John Swihart **Cast** Jon Heder, Jon Gries, Efren Ramirez, Tina Majorino,
Aaron Ruell, Diedrich Bader

One of the most curious film successes of the past decade,
Napoleon Dynamite began life as an assignment for Jared Hess
while completing his film degree at Brigham Young University.
Peluca is a black and white short that for nine minutes follows
Seth (Jon Heder) as he skips school with two of his friends to
buy a wig. Shown at the 2003 Slamdance Film Festival, Hess
procured finances to turn it into a full-length feature, changed
the lead character's name, and thus was born *Napoleon
Dynamite*. A huge hit at the Sundance Festival in 2004, it was
picked and distributed as a part of Fox's Searchlight program
and went on to gross almost $50 million worldwide—one
hundred times its original budget.

Napoleon Dynamite is a bespectacled, gape-mouthed,
gawky high school student from Preston, Idaho, who lives
with his grandmother, older brother Kip, and a llama called
Tina. Generally, life sucks for Napoleon as he daydreams his
way through school, doodling make-believe creatures and
being avoided by girls and bullied by other boys. He has only
two friends, Pedro, the school's only Latino, who has a cool
bike and a mustache, and the painfully shy Deb. The story

◀
**The lo-fi film
proved so popular
it even spawned
a mini offshoot
industry: "Vote
For Pedro" T-shirts,
board games,
and books of
quotations; you
can even get
a complete
*Napoleon
Dynamite*
makeover—
wig and all.**

revolves around Pedro running for class president against the popular dumb-blonde cheerleader, Summer. With Napoleon as his running mate, Pedro's campaign goes well until he is about to deliver his final speech and discovers that all the candidates are expected to perform a party piece. With nothing prepared, a despondent Pedro mumbles his speech, but with uncharacteristic quick wit, Napoleon steps in to

"IT WAS ME BEING ABLE TO LOOK BACK ON HOW AWKWARD I WAS IN SCHOOL AND LAUGH ABOUT IT." *JARED HESS*

perform a bizarre disco dance routine, winning a standing ovation from the school audience and the election for Pedro.

Napoleon Dynamite was shot down by critics, excepting the odd grudging admission that for a director just out of school it was an impressively assured piece of work. The film's staggering performance would make it one of the most talked about word-of-mouth box office hits ever. But why did it get to be so popular? Did audiences genuinely empathize with Napoleon and his friends? After all, films about teenage alienation have been raking them in since James Dean screamed, "I don't know what to do anymore, except maybe die," back in 1955. But there's *nothing* in the way of existential angst in Napoleon's world; would modern teenagers relate to him in this way? In the end, perhaps it's simply that—unless you're Roger Ebert—you come away from the film on such a high that you want to evangelize about it. **TB**

► Napoleon's jaw-dropping disco dance is the film's defining scene, a moment as delicious as it is unexpected. Here, the hopeless geek (Jon Heder) has his prom dance with Deb (Tina Majorino).

LAURA

"Hard luck in
a red kimono."

BRICK

A detective movie by Rian Johnson

brickmovie.net

WINNER | SPECIAL JURY PRIZE | ORIGINALITY OF VISION | SUNDANCE 2005

BRICK 2005 (U.S.)

Director Rian Johnson **Producer** Ram Bergman, Mark G. Mathis
Screenplay Rian Johnson **Cinematography** Steve Yedlin **Music** Nathan Johnson
Cast Joseph Gordon-Levitt, Nora Zehetner, Lukas Haas, Noah Fleiss, Matt O'Leary,
Noah Segan, Emilie de Ravin

Brimming with style and substance, *Brick* marks the dynamic film debut for director Rian Johnson. Part *The Maltese Falcon*, part *The Breakfast Club*, the film takes the gritty world of hard-boiled detective novels and the film noir genre out of the back alleys of the big city and drops it neatly into the abandoned hallways of high school.

Following the mysterious death of his ex-girlfriend, Emily (Emilie de Ravin), high school student Brendan Frye (Joseph Gordon-Levitt, a.k.a. Tommy Solomon in the TV show *3rd Rock from the Sun*) takes it upon himself to uncover the circumstances behind her demise. The investigation finds him traversing the cliques in high school, from the jocks to the geeks to the stoners. The more he digs, the more Brendan discovers that Emily had fallen in with a bad crowd all seemingly connected to the town's drug kingpin nicknamed The Pin (Lukas Haas).

At the center of *Brick* might just be one of the most complex scripts to grace the high school setting. Yet it works beautifully, as the mystery is genuinely engaging. Johnson loads the film with rich character detail as he deftly transfers high school stereotypes into the detective world of rats, thugs, and dames.

◄
The smoky bars, dim lights, and gangster patois transplanted to a modern Californian suburb and high school as "detective" Levitt goes in search of "brick" (a block of heroin).

While embracing the tough gumshoes and femme fatale trappings of the detective genre, Johnson also fashions an innovative and surreal vision of suburbia—a shadowy world of half-truths existing in dimly lit basements and mostly devoid of adults. He also films the proceedings with a sense of rhythm that matches the snappish speaking styles. All of this is echoed with a haunting score by his cousin, Nathan Johnson.

"THERE'S A THESAURUS IN THE LIBRARY. YEAH IS UNDER "Y." GO AHEAD, I'LL WAIT." BRENDAN FRYE

Equally important to the execution is a willing cast able to handle the hard-edged, incredibly stylized dialogue ("He's a pot-skulled reef worm with more hop in his head than blood."). The pulpy origins are obvious, but the end result is surprisingly fresh when delivered by the young cast. Moments of dark humor involving high school hierarchy and adults also add to the script. Interestingly, Johnson secured two former child actors—Gordon-Levitt and Haas—to play the hero and villain. Gordon-Levitt is pitch-perfect as the subtly flippant Brendan, unafraid to take a beating in order to get information. Haas, known for his child turn in *Witness* (1985), is suitably creepy as the drug lord, whose stylized look evokes the vampire Nosferatu. The film met with great acclaim at the Sundance Film Festival in 2005. It was nominated for Grand Jury Prize and won a Special Jury Prize for Originality of Vision. **WW**

▶
Brendan (Gordon-Levitt) on the trail of his vanished ex-girlfriend.

INDEX

CONTRIBUTORS

(AK) Dr Amy Kushner is an English lecturer at the University of Wisconsin-Parkside, U.S. She has contributed to all of the books in the 101 series and is the co-author of *But They Didn't Read Me My Rights: Myths, Lies, and Oddities about our Legal System*.

(CB) Colette Balmain is an independent scholar and author of *Introduction to Japanese Horror Film*. She is currently writing her second book on Korean horror and is the editor for *World Cinema Directory: Korea*.

(CK) Carol King is a freelance writer based in London and Sicily. She writes about cinema, art and travel. She is the author of a biography of British actor and director Peter Glenville.

(CW) Claire Watts is a freelance writer and editor based in southern Scotland.

(EM) Ernest Mathijs teaches at the University of British Columbia, Canada. He is the co-editor of *The Cult Film Reader*.

(GC) Guy Crucianelli is a writer whose work has appeared at *Senses of Cinema*, *Bright Lights Film Journal* and *Popmatters*.

(GC-Q) Garrett Chaffin-Quiray lives in San Diego County where he teaches media history. He is also a working writer and has been published in various newspapers, journals, and books, including *Senses of Cinema*, *Kinoeye*, *Film Quarterly*, and *The San Francisco Chronicle*.

(GS) Glen Sheppard has been involved in the operation of several prominent film festivals the world over, notably the Toronto International Film Festival, where he worked for five years. He has written on film for some years as well as freelancing for various publications.

(IC) Dr Ian Conrich is the author or editor of twelve books including *The Cinema of John Carpenter: The Technique of Terror* (2005), *Film's Musical Moments* (2006), *Contemporary New Zealand Cinema: From New Wave to Blockbuster* (2008), and *Horror Zone: The Cultural Experience of Contemporary Horror Cinema* (2009).

(JM) Jay McRoy is Associate Professor of English and Cinema Studies at the University of Wisconsin-Parkside, U.S., and author of *Nightmare Japan*.

(MH) Mike Hobbs is a screenwriter, novelist, consultant to the LSE, ghostwriter, and business writer. He has had 15 books published to date.

(MT) Mark Tinta is a freelance film writer based in Ohio, and dives into Criterion box sets and Uwe Boll film fests with equal enthusiasm.

(RH) Russ Hunter writes on film and is currently co-editing (with Alexia Kannas) *The Cinema of Dario Argento*.

(SG) Simon Gray has been a freelance writer for over 10 years. His specialist fields are music, film, travel and food and drink.

(TB) Terry Burrows has written over 60 books and contributed to numerous periodicals on a diverse range of subjects, including cinema, television, music, business and technology. He is also a widely recorded musician who has taught at universities.

(WW) William Sean Wilson is a film writer currently residing in Williamsburg, Virginia. He graduated from The College of William & Mary with a degree in Literary and Cultural Studies with an emphasis in film.

PICTURE CREDITS

Many of the images in this book are from the archives of The Kobal Collection, which owes its existence to the vision, courage, talent and energy of the men and women who created the movie industry and whose legacies live on through the films they made, the studios they built, and the publicity photographs they took. Kobal collects, preserves, organizes, and makes these photographs available. Quintessence wishes to thank all the film distribution and production companies and apologizes in advance for any omissions or neglect, and will be pleased to make any necessary changes in future editions.

The following images are from The Kobal Collection:

2 Criswell & Wingnut Films **8** Buñuel-Dalí **11** Buñuel-Dalí **12** G&H Productions **16** Paramount **19** Paramount **20** ПKO **23** RKO **24** Paramount **27** Paramount/G. E. Richardson **28** United Artists **31** United Artists **36** Allied Pictures **39** Allied Pictures **40** Criswell **43** Criswell **44** Raven Films **48** Associated British **51** Associated British **55** Allied Artists **56** Anouchka/Orsay **60** Goosedown/Vulcan **63** Puck Film Productions **64** Eve Production Inc **67** Eve Production Inc **75** Factory Films **80** Paramount **83** Paramount **88** Columbia **91** Columbia **92** 20Th Century Fox **95** 20th Century Fox **99** Prods Panic **100** Films La Boetie/Euro International **108** Warner/Goodtimes **111** Warner/Goodtimes **112** Paramount **115** Paramount **116** Universal/GTO **120** CCC Telecine **123** CCC Telecine **124** 20th Century Fox **127** 20TH Century Fox **128** Greenwich **131** Greenwich **132** International Films/New World **135** International Films/New World **136** Dreamland Productions **139** Dreamland Productions **140** Warner Bros. **143** Warner Bros. **144** AIP **148** United Artists **151** United Artists **152** Tango Film **155** Tango Film **156** Italonegglio/Lotar Film **159** Italonegglio/Lotar Film **164** Portrait Films **168** 20th Century Fox **171** 20th Century Fox **172** Sippy Films **176** RBT Stigwood Prods/Hemdale **179** RBT Stigwood Prods/Hemdale **180** Ayer/MC Elroy/South Australian Film Corp. **183** Ayer/MC ELROY/South Australian Film Corp **184** Kobal **188** Cinemagic Pictures **192** Universal **195** Universal **196** Hammer **199** Hammer **200** AIP-Filmways **203** Mad Max **204** Monty Python Films **207** Monty Python Films **208** Paramount **211** Paramount **212** Universal **215** Universal **219** NAVARON Films **220** Handmade Films **224** Basket Case Productions **227** Basket Case Productions **228** HERZOG/FilmVerlad Der Autoren/ZDF **231** Herzog/FilmVerlag Der Autoren/ZDF **235** Wild Style **239** Sherwood Prods Inc **240** SPINAL TAP Production **243** Spinal Tap Production **244** Troma **247** Troma **248** De Laurentiis **251** De Laurentis **252** Silver Screen/HBO/TRI STAR **255** Silver Screen/HBO/Tri-Star **260** Handmade Films **263** Handmade Films **264** Universal **267** Universal **268** Cannon **271** Cannon/Andrew Cooper **272** 20th Century Fox **275** 20th Century Fox **276** Road Movies/Argos Films/WDR **279** Road Movies/Argos Films/WDR **280** IRS Media **283** IRS Media **284** New Line **287** New Line **291** Condor Films **292** El Deseo S.A. **295** El Desea-Lauren **296** Cinemarque-New World **299** Cinemarque-New World **300** MTI/Orion **303** MTI/Orion **304** Shapirp Glickenhaus **308** Circle Films **311** Circle Films **312** Julie Corman/Concorde **315** Wingnut Films **316** Universal/Gramercy **319** Universal/Gramercy **320** Polygram/Austarlian Film Finance **324** View Askew **327** View Askew **331** Channel 4 Films/Glasgow Film Fund **332** Claudie Ossard/Constellation **340** MGM/UA **343** MGM/UA/Murray Close **344** Columbia Tri-Star **347** Columbia Tri-Star/Michael Gibson **348** Zeitgeist Films **351** Zeitgeist Films **352** Polygram/Working Title **355** Polygram/Working Title **356** Cinepix Film **359** Cinepix Film **364** Arte/Bavaria/WDR **368** Touchstone **371** Touchstone **372** 20Th Century Fox **375** 20Th Century Fox/Van Redin **376** TOEI **383** Summit Entertainment **384** Flower Films/Gaylord/Adam Fields Prod. **387** Flower Films/Gaylord/Adam Fields Prod./Dale Robinette **388** New Line **400** Amuse Pictures **404** Access Films/MTV Films/Napoleon Pictures Ltd **408** Focus Features **411** Focus Features/Steve Yedlin

Other images:

15 RA/Lebrecht Music & Arts **32** Everett Collection/Rex Features **35** Everett Collection/Rex Features **47** Everett Collection/Rex Features **59** RA/Lebrecht Music & Arts **68** Everett Collection/Rex Features **71** RA/Lebrecht Music & Arts **72** Everett Collection/Rex Features **79** Everett Collection/Rex Features **103** RA/Lebrecht Music & Arts **107** Everett Collection/Rex Features **119** Allstar/Cinetext/Universal Pictures **147** Allstar/Cinetext/Warner Bros.. **160** 20th Century Fox/Everett/Rex Features **163** 20th Century Fox/Everett/Rex Features **187** Allstar/Cinetext/Columbia Pictures **191** Everett Collection/Rex Features **223** Allstar/Cinetext/Handmade Films **256** Allstar/Warner Bros.. **259** Allstar/Cinetext/Warner Bros.. **288** Terryho Ponožky **307** SNAP/Rex Features **323** Allstar/Polygram **335** Allstar/Cinetext/Canal+ **336** RA/Lebrecht Music & Arts **339** RA/Lebrecht Music & Arts **363** RA/Lebrecht Music & Arts **367** Allstar/Cinetext/Columbia Pictures **379** Allstar/Tartan Video **380** Allstar/Newmarket **391** Allstar/New Line **403** Viz Media/Everett/Rex Features **407** FoxSearch/Everett/Rex Features

ACKNOWLEDGMENTS

Quintessence would like to thank the following people for their help in the preparation of this book: Dave Kent and Phil Moad at the Kobal Collection, Stephen Atkinson at Rex Features, Paul McFegan at Allstar Picture Library, Elbie Lebrecht at Lebrecht Music and Arts and Jiří Kofroň at terry-posters.com .

General Editor Steven Jay Schneider would like to thank all of the contributors, along with everyone at Quintessence.